Merriam-Webster's Rules of Order

Merriam-Webster's Rules of Order

Laurie Rozakis

Merriam-Webster, Incorporated
Springfield, Massachusetts

A GENUINE MERRIAM-WEBSTER

The name *Webster* alone is no guarantee of excellence. It is used by a number of publishers and may serve mainly to mislead an unwary buyer.

Memam-Webster™ is the name you should look for when you consider the purchase of dictionaries and other fine reference books. It carries the reputation of a company that has been publishing since 1831 and is your assurance of quality and authority.

Library of Congress Cataloging-in-Publication Data

Rozakis, Laurie.
Merriam-Webster's rules of order / Laurie Rozakis.
p. cm.
Includes index.
ISBN 0-87779-615-7
1. Parliamentary practice. I. Merriam-Webster, Inc.
II. Title.
JF515.R79 1994
060.4'2—dc20 94-16769
CIP

Printed and bound in the United States of America

123456QP/M00999897

Contents

Acknowledgments

Like many other Merriam-Webster general reference books, this book benefited from the combined efforts of its many editors. The manuscript was edited and prepared by Jocelyn White Franklin, associate editor, with the guidance of John M. Morse, executive editor, and Mark A. Stevens, senior editor. The index was prepared by Eileen M. Haraty, assistant editor. Electronic text files were prepared for the typesetter by Brett P. Palmer, assistant editor. Proofreading was provided by Susan L. Brady, Jennifer N. Cislo, Peter D. Haraty, Brett P. Palmer, and Katherine C. Sietsema, assistant editors; and Rebecca R. Bryer and Jill J. Cooney, editorial assistants, under the direction of Madeline L. Novak, senior editor. Data entry for the index was done by Florence A. Fowler. Dr. Rozakis was assisted in her preparation of the manuscript by Ellen Lichtenstein. The publisher especially appreciates the many helpful suggestions of parliamentarian Jane M. Klausman.

Foreword

This book is Merriam-Webster's entry into the field of parliamentary law and procedure, through the text of Dr. Laurie Rozakis, author and experienced officer of numerous boards of local and national organizations.

For anyone interested in the fundamentals of parliamentary procedure and its application in today's meeting arena, the book is an excellent all-around, easy-to-follow educational tool. The author's stated objective, "to make parliamentary procedure understandable," is achieved through a concise, step-by-step coverage of the principles of parliamentary law. Dr. Rozakis transforms these democratic principles from theory to everyday application by the use of charts, examples, and "user-friendly" business language.

Although *Merriam-Webster's Rules of Order* is based on *Robert's Rules of Order,* it does not attempt to be a comprehensive treatment of all aspects of parliamentary law. Instead, its main purpose is to prepare the interested reader for participation as a leader or member at any type of business meeting. *Merriam-Webster's Rules of Order* does occasionally diverge from "Robert," especially in its effort, which many parliamentarians support, to update the latter authority's somewhat archaic language for the making of motions.

The information presented here extends beyond parliamentary law to educate the reader on the planning and arranging of a meeting. For instance the book outlines the importance of the meeting site and the many other elements so easily overlooked in setting up a productive meeting. Chapter 8, "How to Run a Meeting," is a thorough guide with detailed explanations on meeting agendas, procedures, and actions.

Interested in establishing a new organization? The author addresses the complexities of the entire process, including the initial and second organizational meetings, the voting procedure for establishing the temporary organization and officers, and the steps required to evolve to a permanent arrangement. Sample bylaws are also provided as a model to follow.

Throughout the book the author expands on all types of meetings, but the depth of the coverage provided for school boards and other public meetings is particularly notable. The sample meeting script in Chapter 7 is an explanation in itself, illustrating the important do's and don'ts of meeting action vital to the successful conduct of the public business session.

Of particular help for the meeting participant are the examples throughout the book of what to say and how to say it in the various parliamentary situations. Scripts provided on each type of meeting are an outstanding feature. The role-playing that this permits is the answer to the "what to say" obstacle that often challenges even the experienced meeting leader.

Once the meeting framework has been established, the meeting itself is brought to life through the activity of officers, board, and members, including their various reports.

Are you reluctant to chair a committee because of a lack of experience? Chapter 4 guides you from A to Z with information on conducting a committee meeting, composing minutes, establishing an agenda, devising committee rules, presenting reports, and handling issues of privacy.

Chapters 5 and 6 are the "workhorse" chapters, discussing the all-important types of motions: main, subsidiary, privileged, and incidental. Each motion is covered in detail as to definition, characteristics, guidelines, and voting requirements, with examples of when the motion may be used and the appropriate language for the processing of the motion. A valuable aspect of Chapter 6 is the detailed treatment of procedural strategies to effect the adoption or defeat of a motion.

Merriam-Webster's Rules of Order further addresses such other topics as:

- *Voting,* a frequent matter of concern to both officer and member. The need for a quorum is addressed, along with its relationship to the voting members. The why, when, and where of voting are addressed in depth, along with the parliamentary language to be used with each process. In one of the book's many illustrative charts, the type of vote required on each motion is described.
- *Discipline,* another area of anxiety in today's meetings. The chapter on how to maintain decorum supplies ideas to aid both the presiding officer and the member in disciplinary situations involving members and nonmembers.
- *Role of the presiding officer,* including the officer's responsibilities, rights, and limitations. A very useful feature of the book is the wording supplied for the chair to use throughout the meeting, enabling the inexperienced officer to function

> smoothly, secure and confident in the knowledge of his or her responsibilities.

In summary, *Merriam-Webster's Rules of Order* is an aid to leadership development. It is an excellent introduction to the parliamentary field, supplying the basic details of parliamentary procedure in a format the reader can readily understand and put to immediate use in the next meeting he or she attends. The book is not intended to address every minute point necessary to complete understanding of parliamentary law in all its applications, however. The interested participant may have to delve further into editions of the complex reference books of General Henry M. Robert to supplement his or her research on specific problems.

Finally, the real importance of *Merriam-Webster's Rules of Order* is in its immediate usability by today's leaders involved daily in the thousands of meetings held throughout the world in business, education, public service, community service, and other professional and social areas. As the author says, "Parliamentary law can be used whenever people have an equal voice in the business of an organization." This book provides the means to understand and apply it properly.

Jane M. Klausman, CPP, PRP
1993–94 President, American Institute of Parliamentarians
April 1994

Introduction

Merriam-Webster's Rules of Order applies the classic rules of parliamentary procedure used in all levels of our government to any organizational meeting where a standard parliamentary procedure handbook is required. Parliamentary law can be used to help people run meetings for an astonishingly wide variety of organizations. Here is just a sampling:

Professional associations	Labor unions
Civic associations	Condominium shareholders
Historical societies	Scientific groups
Charitable organizations	University senates
Sales representatives	Senior-citizen groups
Garden clubs	Advertising representatives
Service groups	Youth groups
Parent-teacher organizations	School boards
Library boards	Corporation shareholders
Academic departments	Regional or national organizations

Traditionally, parliamentary law was used to run meetings of nonprofit groups, community organizations, and governmental agencies. It is commonplace in school and library boards, parent-teacher associations, and shareholders meetings. Increasingly, however, officers in for-profit companies are applying parliamentary law to their meetings, since it provides a way for people in industry to conduct their business quickly, efficiently, and fairly. Parliamentary law can help transform interminable, unproductive meetings to useful gatherings where work is accomplished briskly and fairly. Parliamentary law can be used in any deliberative assembly—whenever people have an equal voice in the business of the organization. While businesses may not follow the letter of parliamentary law, many of them do apply specific principles of parliamentary law to their gatherings, and the practice is on the rise.

Under general parliamentary law, any deliberative assembly can tailor the rules of parliamentary law to suit the needs of its organization. The members of the group need only adopt their own written rules, in the form of bylaws. Increasingly, more and more businesses are doing just that. *Merriam-Webster's Rules of Order* will help you learn parliamentary law and adapt it to the needs of your own organization. It can also be used in any organizational meeting where a standard parliamentary-procedures handbook is required. Further, this book avoids the stilted academic prose that makes some other guides to parliamentary procedure sound like dry-as-toast legal briefs. Rather, *Merriam-Webster's Rules of Order* uses everyday business language to explain how to ensure that meetings are productive for everyone. Special features include the following:

- A clear discussion of the actions required of different meeting participants
- Language and format accessible to busy chairpersons, officers, executives, support personnel, and meeting participants
- Abundant examples of all motions and resolutions
- Handy, easy-to-read tables at the beginning of every chapter
- A sample meeting script

With a little practice, you will find that using parliamentary procedures enables meetings to run more smoothly, quickly, and fairly. Applying the guidelines shown in this book will also help preserve the underlying principles of parliamentary law: to express the will of the majority and protect the rights of the minority.

Merriam-Webster's Rules of Order

Chapter 1

Why Parliamentary Law Is Necessary

> Know all about parliamentary law, but do not try to show off your knowledge. Never be technical, or more strict than is absolutely necessary for the good of the meeting. Use your judgment; the assembly may be of such a nature through its ignorance of parliamentary usages and [its] peaceable disposition, that a strict enforcement of the rules, instead of assisting, would greatly hinder business; but in large assemblies, where there is much work to be done, and especially where there is liability to trouble, the only safe course is to require a strict observance of the rules.
>
> *Robert's Rules of Order Revised,* 1915

THE CHAPTER AT A GLANCE

What Is Parliamentary Law?

Definition

Parliamentary law is a series of rules that were formulated to facilitate the transaction of business and to promote harmony and cooperation within an assembly. Also generally called "Robert's Rules of

Order" after the most famous American book of parliamentary rules, Henry Martyn Robert's 1876 *Robert's Rules of Order,* parliamentary law is intended to help organizations conduct their business and carry out their intentions. It has but one purpose: to help get business accomplished in a timely, fair manner.

Contrary to what you may have heard, parliamentary law was not created to confuse people or to stand in the way of the will of the majority. It was instead devised as a logical method for dealing with many orders of business and different personalities.

Principles of Parliamentary Law

The overall principles of parliamentary procedure are often more important than the trivia of the rules. In fact, insisting on an overly technical observance of every small point of parliamentary law is a misuse and misunderstanding of the procedure. The technicalities of parliamentary law are not to be used merely for their own sake—although some people may attempt to do so. You will be at many meetings that require the strict application of the technical rules of parliamentary law if business is to be accomplished fairly. In other instances, however, the rules can be relaxed and the meeting can proceed informally without any loss of equality. The presiding officer is the best judge of these situations. An effective officer knows when to apply the rules strictly and when to take a more relaxed approach. Below is an overview of the basic guidelines of parliamentary law.

Majority-vote decisions Decision making by majority vote is an underlying principle of parliamentary law. No group can survive if controlled by a minority. As Thomas Jefferson wrote in 1817: "To consider the will of the society enounced by the majority of a single vote, as sacred as if unanimous, is the first of all lessons in importance, yet the last which is thoroughly learnt. This law once disregarded, no other remains but that of force, which ends necessarily in military despotism."

Equal rights and privileges Every member possesses the same rights as every other member. This means that each member has the right to propose motions, to debate them, and to oppose them, to try to persuade others to their point of view, to nominate others for office and to be nominated themselves, and to vote on all issues.

A member has the right to do anything that other members of the organization can do. But even more than this, every member is obligated to insist on the protection of his or her rights and the rights of all other members.

Rights of members Parliamentary law protects the right of members to be dealt with fairly and equitably. This encourages everyone's cooperation and the efficient order of business. The following member rights are guaranteed under parliamentary law—the right to:

- Receive notices of meetings.
- Attend meetings.
- Make motions.
- Second motions (when they need a second).
- Debate motions (when they can be debated).
- Vote on motions (except those on which the person has a conflict of interest).
- Nominate people for office.
- Be nominated for office.
- Elect people to office in the organization.
- Be elected to office in the organization.
- Know the meaning of the question people are debating.
- Object when rules are being violated.
- Appeal the decision of the chair.
- Be protected from personal abuse and attack.
- Have access to minutes of meetings.
- Receive the treasurer's report.
- Get a copy of the organization's bylaws.

Equal obligations Since all members have equal rights, it follows that all members have equal duties and obligations to the organization. For example, it is the duty of the presiding officer to see that equality of rights, obligations, and duties be maintained among all members.

Obligations of members Along with rights come responsibilities. For a meeting to function smoothly under parliamentary law, members must have specific obligations as well as guaranteed rights. When everyone understands his or her duties as part of a team, business will be accomplished with much greater ease. Under parliamentary law members have the following responsibilities:

- Attend meetings.
- Be on time.

- Stay until the end of the meeting.
- Be ready to talk knowledgeably and intelligently on a topic.
- Be attentive.
- Be open-minded.
- Participate actively in the meetings.
- Work with others in a cooperative fashion.
- Treat everyone with courtesy.
- Speak openly, but also let others have their turn to speak.
- Follow the rules of debate.
- Make points concisely.
- Attack issues, not people.
- Abide by the final decision of the majority.
- Respect the chair's opinions and rulings.
- Insist on law and order at meetings.
- Work to maintain dignity and decorum.
- Be familiar with the basic rules of parliamentary law.
- Obey the rules of the organization.
- Be familiar with the organization's bylaws.
- Pay all dues and assessments.
- Bring in or recommend new members, if appropriate.
- Select well-qualified officers.
- Participate in committees.
- Vary committee work.
- Promote the organization's growth and influence.
- Enhance the organization's reputation.

Protection of minority rights Democratic organizations, those governed by parliamentary law, protect certain basic minority rights, which can never be infringed upon. These include the following rights:

The right to be heard
The right to protest
The right to seek to convince
The right to understand fully the questions under discussion

Keep in mind that the composition of the "majority" and "minority" is constantly changing, depending on the issue under discussion in the assembly. Those who are members of the minority during one debate might be members of the majority on the next issue. As a result, protection of minority rights is of vital importance to every member of an organization. Members of the majority who ignore the rights of the minority can expect to find the same methods used against them when they are members of the minority.

Full and free discussion Another fundamental right of parliamentary law is the full and free discussion of every proposition presented for decision by the assembly. This is the right of free speech, the right to hear and to be heard. Each member is guaranteed the right to discuss a question fully and freely without interruption, subject only to the rules applicable to all other members.

Simple and direct procedure Believe it or not, parliamentary law is intended to guarantee that the simplest and most direct procedure will be used to accomplish a purpose. As Thomas Jefferson stressed, the use of confusing technicalities or devious approaches to accomplish an aim should be ruled out of order by the presiding officer when "the same result may be had more simply."

Order of motions The introduction and disposition of all motions is governed by a definite, logical order. Because there are many motions made during the course of the average meeting, each motion must be arranged by order of importance. The more important motions have a priority or precedence that governs the way they are proposed and acted upon. This hierarchy of motions prevents motions from piling up on one another in confusion. Each motion has its own specific rank. If this ranking is followed, the business of the assembly will be accomplished in a timely manner.

Consideration of one question at a time To expedite business and prevent the meeting from disintegrating into chaos, only one question can be considered by the assembly at a time. If each motion is considered on its own and in its proper order, confusion is prevented and business accomplished more quickly.

Voting Before members vote, they have the right to know the question before the assembly. It is the responsibility of the presiding officer to keep the pending motion clearly before the assembly at all times. If any member is unclear about the content of the motion under discussion, what it means, or what its effect will be, that member has the right to request that the presiding officer clarify the matter. Only a fully informed member will be able to rise to a parliamentary inquiry, or to ask a question of the presiding officer, or to otherwise participate meaningfully.

It is the obligation of each member to use his or her best judgment when voting on an issue or a candidate. But in order to do so, every member is entitled to have a reasonable knowledge of the facts of the issue. Under parliamentary rules, all members have the right to request an explanation of any pending question that they do not understand in order to enable them to make a more informed voting decision.

Delegating duties Keep in mind that every member of an organization cannot be involved with every single project sponsored by the group. To expedite business, the organization may delegate certain specific responsibilities and duties to various members—but the organization must retain the right of final decision.

In democratic organizations, especially governments, many important duties are delegated to officers and to committees. Since these bodies act as representatives of all members, they must be given both the authority and the power to carry out decisions. Nonetheless, when an officer or a committee submits a report to the organization as a whole, the group has the final authority to accept or to reject the individual recommendations. The members of the organization retain the right to withdraw any authority they have delegated, as well as the right to make the final decision in any matter.

Maintaining impartiality The rules of parliamentary law must be administered impartially. Presiding officers serve their organization most effectively when they remain strictly neutral. To help maintain impartiality, officers presiding over large meetings should not take part in the debate. This rule is relaxed for officers in charge of smaller groups, such as committees and boards. In large organizations the presiding officer most often votes only to break a tie.

Presiding officers should not show favoritism toward their friends by giving them more than their share of opportunities for advancement within the organization. Neither should a presiding officer take revenge on opponents by denying them their rights or privileges.

Among the greatest strengths of any presiding officer are the ability to maintain impartiality, to deal with disagreements among members, and to treat everyone with the same evenhanded justice.

This is the surest way for presiding officers to win the trust and confidence of their membership. Clearly, impartiality is not confined to presiding officers; it is much desired among all officers and members of an organization.

Parliamentary Law—Summary

In essence, parliamentary law protects the rights of the individual and those of the group. The following rights are guarded:

- The rights of the individual
- The rights of the minority
- The rights of the majority
- The rights of members absent from the meeting

A deliberative assembly is free to act as it wishes—as long as it considers the rights of all members.

What Is a Parliamentarian?

A parliamentarian is an individual skilled in parliamentary law, able to locate references in an authoritative volume of parliamentary rules of order within a reasonable length of time. Generally, parliamentarians are consultants who advise the presiding officer, officers, and committees on matters of parliamentary procedure. As advisers, parliamentarians must be:

- Familiar with the organization's rules.
- Objective in offering advice.
- Tactful and diplomatic in dealing with all members.
- Impartial, fair, and ethical.
- Conscientious and professional in keeping secrets.
- Able to see a problem unfolding and to head it off with a few quiet words to the presiding officer.
- Reliable in keeping commitments and carrying out responsibilities.
- Familiar with past policies and problems of the organization.
- Well-acquainted with the leaders of an organization.

Assigned a seat next to the chair, parliamentarians act as advisers during a meeting, offering advice to the presiding officer to use at his or her discretion. In addition, they may be:

- Consulted before the meeting and during recesses to help make the meeting run smoothly.
- Called upon to speak to the assembly to explain the most complex aspects of parliamentary law.
- Asked to help others learn parliamentary law by teaching classes.
- Consulted by the bylaws committee or the person who actually drafts the bylaws.
- Asked to hold office hours during conventions and seminars to teach and advise people.

You may have first turned to parliamentary law as a way of learning how to more effectively chair or participate in a meeting. But don't be surprised if you find that you are soon on your way to becoming a skilled parliamentarian!

How Did Parliamentary Law Originate?

The roots of parliamentary law run surprisingly deep in history. Below is a time line of the important landmarks in the history of parliamentary law.

DATE	EVENT
c. 1300 B.C.	The Hebraic council marks the first popular election among the tribes of Israel.
c. 750 B.C.	The Greek agora is the center of assembly, from which develops a bicameral form of government, the ballot, the quorum, and the idea of eloquence in debate.
c. 450 B.C.	The Roman forum institutes the first legal code, the practice of majority vote, and the use of shorthand for taking notes or minutes.
930 A.D.	In Iceland the Vikings create the *Althing*, the first parliament.
1215	King John signs the Magna Carta, which gives the nobles their first civil rights and regularizes the judicial system, thereby forming the basis of English constitutional liberties. "No freeman shall be taken or imprisoned, or exiled,

	or in any way destroyed, nor will we go upon him, nor will we send upon him, except by the lawful judgment of his peers or by the law of the land."
1275	The powers of the presiding officer are defined for the first time in England.
1321	The first book on parliamentary law is issued in England.
1340	The English parliament separates into two houses of government.
1377	The first Speaker of the House of Commons is installed.
1580	Minutes of a meeting are accorded legal status.
1581	The concept of "one subject at a time" is introduced.
1592	Proponents of both sides of an issue are formally given equal opportunity to speak. The word *chairman* is used for the first time.
1604	Taking a negative vote is required.
1610	Discussion is ordered to pertain to the issue on the floor.
1619	The first legislative assembly in America is established in Jamestown, Virginia.
1640	Questions may be divided if each part can be treated independently.
1774	The first use of the term *deliberative assembly* occurs in England and America.
1801	Thomas Jefferson publishes his manual of parliamentary law.
1876	General Henry M. Robert publishes his rules of parliamentary law.

How Did Parliamentary Rules of Order Develop in America?

At first, parliamentary rules of order referred to the customs and rules of conducting business in the English Parliament. The rules provided for the following:

- Maintaining decorum in discussion
- Treating one subject at a time
- Making the chair always tally votes for both sides of the issue
- Confining debate to the merits of the question under discussion
- Alternating between opposite points of view in discussion

The rules applied to what is called a *deliberative assembly,* a group of people meeting to decide on a common action. Realizing the effectiveness of these guidelines, American politicians adopted these rules to govern the House of Burgesses, as the representative governing body of the early colony of Virginia was known.

Thomas Jefferson's manual Thomas Jefferson was instrumental in spreading parliamentary law throughout America. In 1801, during his presidency, Jefferson published the first American book on parliamentary law, *Manual of Parliamentary Practice*. "The proceedings of Parliament in ancient times, and for a long while, were crude, multiform, and embarrassing," he wrote to explain his decision. Jefferson's manual was the main source for American parliamentary law until 1845.

Cushing's manual In 1845 Luther Cushing published his *Manual of Parliamentary Practice: Rules of Proceeding and Debate in Deliberative Assemblies*. As clerk of the Massachusetts House of Representatives, Cushing was well-versed in the workings of the government. The book, which came to be known simply as "Cushing's Manual," answered many of the important questions about running a governmental deliberative assembly. As a result, it was soon standard fare on many levels of government, from federal to state to local.

Robert's rules of order Army engineer Henry Martyn Robert took on the task of creating a system of parliamentary law that could apply to all deliberative assemblies at all times. It took him more than 30 years, but by 1876 he had published his first version of *Robert's Rules of Order*. General Robert had originally designed a folio of about 16 pages; by the time he finished the book, it had nearly 200 pages. The first print run sold out in four months; by 1915 more than half a million copies were in circulation. The book became the standard parliamentary law guidebook for organizations, schools, and clubs. Its users were enthusiastic about Robert's codified rules, for they greatly helped them run efficient, fair meetings. Now there was a way to control dictatorial chairpersons and overbearing members, destructive filibusters and disruptive behavior, and to guarantee that the will of the majority would prevail but that the rights of the minority would be protected.

Parliamentary rules of order today Today parliamentary law is used at all levels of government—federal, state, municipal, and town. The usefulness of parliamentary law in government and community affairs is unquestioned; what is becoming increasingly plain is that parliamentary law also provides a way for people in corporate life to conduct their business efficiently, helping transform interminable, unproductive meetings into useful gatherings where work is accomplished briskly and fairly.

The Deliberative Assembly

Parliamentary law applies to a *deliberative assembly,* a number of people gathered to discuss an issue of importance to the entire group. The group operates on its own to reach a consensus. Every member has the right to speak and to reach his or her own decision on the issues. To make sure that the decision reached is acceptable to the majority of members, each member's vote has the same importance as every other member's.

The underlying principle of the deliberative assembly is the concept of *majority vote*: more than half the people in attendance must agree on an issue. In certain instances, more than a majority vote is required to pass a measure. Regardless of the exact number of votes needed to pass an issue, there is no "punishment" for holding a minority opinion; members who do not agree with the outcome still belong to the assembly. (Absent members do not vote.)

A specific number of people have to be in attendance for the assembly to be considered a valid meeting; this specific number is called a *quorum*. Requiring a quorum to conduct business helps guarantee that the will of the majority of the members prevails and that the rights of the minority are protected.

Those who take part in the assembly are called *members*. This means that they are fully empowered to participate in the business of the assembly. As such, they are accorded the right to *make motions, vote,* and *debate issues*.

Types of Assemblies

A deliberative assembly can take five main forms:

1. Organized society
2. Legislative body
3. Board
4. Convention
5. Mass meeting

Organized society The most familiar of all groups, an organized society is a gathering of people who belong to an organization that meets on a regular basis. The members of an organized society may undertake civic, charitable, or political projects, for example. A service organization such as Rotary, a charitable group such as Overland Park Volunteers, and a political association such as the Republican Party are all organized societies. So are the Parent-Teacher Association, the Veterans of Foreign Wars, and the local historical society. To qualify as an organized society, the association must have a regular meeting schedule and official membership requirements.

Legislative body A legislative body is a group of people elected for a specific term of office to make laws. Congress and a state legislature are examples of legislative bodies. While all legislative bodies follow parliamentary law, each also has its own bylaws.

Board A board is a body of people elected or appointed to administer, manage, or adjudicate. Boards are like deliberative assemblies except that they have no minimum size and their function is determined by the powers delegated to them by the organization. As a result, boards are usually much smaller than deliberative assemblies. The bylaws of the organization should specify the board's composition, duties, and meeting schedule. (See also page 59.)

Convention A convention is an assembly of delegates selected specifically to represent a larger group of people during one session. In most cases, a local organization will select delegates to attend a national or international meeting of the group. Conventions can be large or small, brief or extended, educational or business-oriented. Only those delegates who have the proper credentials are allowed to vote at a convention, and at the end of the convention the assembly is disbanded. (See also page 84.)

Mass meeting A mass meeting is a gathering of an unorganized group that has been called to address a particular problem and is open to anyone who has an interest in the issues being discussed. Despite its name, a mass meeting does not have to be a large gathering; on the contrary, there may be relatively few people in attendance. A mass meeting might be held to gather support for setting aside a tract of land for a nature preserve or to protest a planned tax increase, for example. Although attendance may be limited to those people who have a legitimate stake in the proceedings, those admitted to the meeting have a right to participate fully. It is understood that those calling the meeting have the right to restrict the meeting to the subject at hand, but those in attendance have the right to decide what action will be taken on the issue. (See also page 81.)

Assembly Rules

In general, an assembly can establish any rules that it wishes. In actual practice, people have discovered that assemblies operate more fairly and smoothly if certain rules are always included and if some rules are easier to set aside than others. The four main types of rules are *corporate charter, bylaws* and/or *constitution, rules of order,* and *standing rules*. Each is discussed below.

Corporate charter A corporate charter is a legal document that includes the information necessary to incorporate the organization under state or federal law. Depending on the individual state laws, this document is necessary if the organization will be involved in such legal matters as drafting contracts, hiring employees, and holding real estate, for instance. Organizations that do not engage in such legal matters usually do not require a corporate charter, but this is a matter for an attorney to determine. According to the law, a corporate charter supersedes all other assembly rules.

Bylaws and/or constitution An organization's bylaws and/or constitution describe the rules that apply to that particular organization, not the rules of parliamentary procedure. The terms *bylaws* and *constitution* are often used interchangeably and generally mean the same thing, although the term *bylaws* is used more commonly. Those organizations that have both a constitution and bylaws usually include fixed laws in the constitution and rules that can be amended in the bylaws.

The bylaws should contain the following provisions:

- Organization's name
- Definition and purpose of the organization
- When the organization meets
- Qualifications for membership
- How officers are selected and their duties
- Definition of the executive board
- How committees are created
- Procedure for amending bylaws and/or constitution
- Title of adopted parliamentary guide
- All further rules necessary for smooth functioning of the organization

Nearly all organizations recognize the necessity of having a set of bylaws. If you are preparing the bylaws for your organization, consider getting copies of those from similar organizations. Use these as templates for your own bylaws, selecting those passages that suit your organization's needs and rejecting those that do not. (See also page 36.)

Rules of order The rules of order are the parliamentary rules an organization follows. The bylaws, in contrast, refer to the specific functions of an organization. The rules of order can pertain to nearly all organizations; the bylaws are specific to one. Most organizations adopt rules of order by specifying which book of parliamentary law they will follow when disputes arise. When such an authority is adopted, its rules are considered binding except where they conflict with the organization's bylaws. Many organizations include the following provision in their bylaws concerning their rules of order:

▶ "The rules contained in [name of parliamentary guide] shall govern the society in all cases in which they apply and in which they are not inconsistent with the bylaws of this organization."

Standing rules Standing rules are additional rules adopted by an organization to cover its day-to-day workings. They are subject to the will of the majority at any meeting. For example, a standing rule might state the time a meeting convenes or whether refreshments are to be served at meetings. Standing rules are generally passed when the need arises, not all at once as with the bylaws. Once standing rules have been passed, they can be changed at the same meeting only by a motion to reconsider (see page 166). However, at any future meeting they can be suspended, modified, or rescinded by a majority vote. A standing rule cannot be passed unless it is in accordance with the bylaws.

Chapter 2

Planning Meetings

The Chapter at a Glance

Preplanning

Parliamentary law is one of the most important elements in a productive meeting, but it cannot compensate for insufficient planning. Effective meetings are largely the result of thorough planning with close attention to detail.

Successful meetings are marked by several common qualities. First, members of the group clearly understand the meeting's purpose and deal with items on the agenda fairly and honestly. They set high but realistic goals and work smoothly and thoughtfully to accomplish these ends. Second, participants focus on issues rather than personalities and communicate freely with each other to achieve the meeting's goals. Everyone in the group shares responsibility for the outcome of the meeting by facing problems openly and dealing with them before they become major issues, balancing the needs of individual members with the needs of the entire organization. Lastly, members realize that the process used to reach a meeting's goal can be as important as the goal itself.

Complete planning, coupled with a firm understanding of parliamentary law, is the best way to ensure successful and effective business meetings that share the qualities described above. Consider the following points when planning a meeting:

Focus on the Purpose for Meeting

Start by focusing on the reason the assembly should be convened. List the objectives of the meeting. For instance, the meeting might be necessary to organize a fund-raising event, plan a major purchase, exchange information, learn new skills, or settle matters of personnel or policy. But before the planning continues, decide if the meeting is really necessary or if the organization is instead meeting out of habit. It is important to realize that members involved in a useless meeting may question the motives of the person who called the meeting and wonder if it was called to exercise power rather than to accomplish business. Purposeless meetings can cause resentment within an organization, making members unwilling to meet even when the purpose for the meeting is unquestioned.

Acknowledge Unstated Objectives

The apparent purpose for meeting may not match the unstated purposes of the participants. All participants come to meetings with their own goals, which are rarely stated outright and may sometimes not even be recognized by the individuals themselves. For instance, a historical society may have a biweekly meeting to discuss ways to publicize the history of its community. Some members may be sincerely concerned with elevating the historical reputation of their region; others may be far more interested in building up their own reputation in the community as scholars or persons with a distinguished lineage. Effective meetings acknowledge and deal with these unstated objectives so that participants can get on with the stated purpose of the meeting and accomplish the business on the agenda.

Organize the Details

The most effective meetings are the result of good organization and close attention to detail. The amount of organization and planning needed depends on a number of factors. The first of these is the number of members who are expected to attend: the larger a meeting, the more planning will be required. The purpose of the meeting is a second important aspect of planning. The anticipated mood of the participants is a crucial third factor, as adversarial or hostile meetings take far more planning than cooperative ones. The final factor is location, as it is easier to plan an on-site than an off-site meeting.

One of the most effective ways to organize meeting details is through a list. Jot down all the elements necessary to ensure a productive meeting. Lists will vary depending on the needs of each organization and the stated purpose of the meeting. A sample list could include the following items:

Mailings	Clerical staff
Program committee	Facilities
Meeting coordinator	Meeting chair
Agenda	Meeting site
Registration staff	Troubleshooters
Guest speakers	Refreshment committee
Exhibits	Publicity
Audiovisual equipment	Meals
Entertainment	Finance committee

Draft a Meeting Plan

Compare lists and isolate the items necessary for the specific meeting. Gather suggestions from fellow members. Consider the purpose of the meeting, what support will be forthcoming, ways to set up and run the meeting, funding, and possible trouble spots. Draft a realistic timetable.

It is important to involve fellow members at the planning stage. When people are included in a meeting from its inception, they have a greater stake in its outcome. This added commitment can greatly contribute to a successful, productive meeting.

Keep Records

Take advantage of the latest computer technology to create spreadsheets, tables, and graphs to plan and project meeting goals. Be sure to make backup copies of disks, keep hard (paper) copies, and store all records in a safe place. For very large or important meetings, have a member store a copy of the records as well.

Financing a Meeting

Cost is usually a negligible consideration at small meetings, but it can become a prime consideration at major meetings. The following items should be considered when an organization is planning a large meeting:

Establish a Finance Committee

The chair should establish a committee to share the responsibilities. A mix of experienced and less-experienced members should be included. If the organization chair has not selected a finance committee chair, the committee should do so at its first meeting.

The committee should meet as soon as possible to consider its specific task and discuss how best to accomplish its goals. Members may wish to consult with other financial committees within the organization or in similar organizations to gather advice. Then the committee should plan a budget and establish lines of responsibility. It is also important to codify the proposed meeting schedule and ascertain the number of guests, speakers, rooms, meals, and so on. Increasingly, organizations are handling these matters on computer spreadsheets. The chair should assign specific tasks and make sure that members exchange telephone numbers and schedules.

The committee chair should speak with the presiding officer of the organization to find out if the meeting is expected to make a profit, break even, or actually lose money. Do not assume that every meeting must make a profit or break even; large meetings will often be held to strengthen the organization's image and attract new members and corporate sponsors for key programs. The chair of the finance committee and the presiding officer of the organization should work together to draft a budget for the meeting. The budget should be in writing so as to reduce the chance for disputes.

The committee chair should also meet with the organization's treasurer to find out who will allocate funds, approve expenditures, pay invoices, and handle the financial paperwork. The finance committee should read the organization's bylaws in order to clearly understand its fiscal guidelines.

Coordinate Committees

After the finance committee has a working budget, the chair should meet with the presiding officers of all the other meeting-related committees to compare budgets and plans. The chair of the finance committee should find out how much money each of the other committees needs and incorporate this information into the budget. If the resulting total falls within the guidelines of the resources allocated for the meeting, a final budget should be released. If not, the committees must meet to find ways to reduce expenses. Together the committees must forge a budget that everyone finds acceptable.

Record Expenses

The finance committee must next establish a method for tracking all incoming and outgoing money, contracts, and other related documents. If necessary, a committee member should be appointed to pay all invoices in a timely manner. In addition, all invoices and payments must be recorded. Computer spreadsheets are especially useful for these bookkeeping tasks.

Arranging a Meeting Site

Select a Meeting Site

Once the budget has been completed and approved, the committee can select a meeting site. The setting can have a great influence on the mood, tone, and ultimate outcome of a meeting. A well-appointed conference room, for instance, can help make the participants comfortable; a crowded hall with glaring light and uncomfortable plastic chairs, in contrast, can disorient and upset them. Meetings may be on- or off-site; there are advantages and disadvantages to each.

On-site meetings Gathering in the usual location tends to be convenient and inexpensive, since the location is often already available. But if the organization meets only rarely, it may have difficulty procuring its regular room for an extra meeting. In addition, there are many distractions to meeting on-site, including the press of everyday affairs.

Off-site meetings Meeting in a new location frees participants from the distractions of the usual meeting location, and the change of scene raises expectations for a pleasant meeting. When it is anticipated that a meeting between two different organizations may be fractious, an off-site location has great benefits. Meeting in a neutral setting eliminates the feeling of advantage one side may have over the other and helps reassure participants that the meeting will be conducted without bias. On the other hand, it can be expensive to transport and house members off-site. This additional cost may greatly outweigh any psychological advantages of meeting in a new location.

Consider the following points when selecting an off-site meeting location:

- Cost of rooms
- Cost of travel
- Ease of travel
- Site reputation (Is this a location that will attract people and boost registration?)
- Comfort
- Amenities (tennis courts, swimming pool, golf course, and so on)

Also be especially sensitive to any special needs that members may have. For example, organizations will wish to use meeting sites that are accessible to the handicapped; check for ramps, special parking, and wheelchair-accessible rest rooms. In addition, the organization may wish to include special equipment for the hearing- or visually impaired, and provide for special dietary requirements such as vegetarian, salt- and fat-free, and kosher meals.

Video- and Teleconferencing

One increasingly popular hybrid of the on-site and off-site meeting is video- and teleconferencing. This method allows all of an organization's widely scattered members the convenience of meeting on-site, since they can "attend" the meeting without ever leaving their own meeting halls or incurring the expense of transportation, room, and board. When setting up a video- or teleconference, consider the differences in time zones, especially when people in other countries are participating. The time must be mutually convenient for all members so as to ensure that no one is disenfranchised.

Arranging for Speakers

A large meeting will often be organized around a guest speaker. A service organization, for instance, may hire a professional fund-raiser to assist in efforts to generate income for its philanthropic projects; a school board may call in educational consultants before embarking on a new program. The larger a meeting, the more planning will go into hiring speakers.

Considering Speakers

Most organizations know what topic they wish a speaker to address, but they may not know of expert speakers in that field. Organizations should begin the task by establishing a committee to handle speaker arrangements. To find speakers, members of the speakers' committee can seek out people in allied fields to find out which people make the most successful speakers. They can also inquire about the speakers' fees.

Speakers' Bureaus

Many organizations sponsor a speakers' bureau, a clearinghouse of well-known and effective speakers who address certain types of meetings for free. For example, many large newspapers and community organizations have speakers' bureaus.

Selecting Speakers

In selecting speakers, members of the committee should consider the following factors:

1. What are the speaker's qualifications?
2. How will this speaker enhance the program?
3. What is the speaker's reputation?
4. Who recommended the speaker?
5. Will the speaker be available?
6. Is the speaker acceptable to the majority of the people attending the program?
7. What is the speaker's fee?

It is important to take the time to pick a speaker who addresses the purpose of the meeting as closely as possible. A dynamic speaker can set the tone for an entire meeting; an ineffective speaker, in contrast, can overshadow even the most careful preparations.

Keeping Records

Once the speaker has been selected, it is time to set up the paperwork. Many organizations have forms for this purpose; if not, committee members will have to create their own forms. Important forms include contracts, biographical data (for introductions and program notes), supply and equipment requirements, and travel forms.

Speakers' Packets

All speakers should be sent letters of information to help them prepare for their presentations, including four main mailings: an invitation, a confirmation, an information packet, and a thank-you letter. Each is described below.

Formal letter of invitation This letter should provide background on the organization and the title and purpose of the meeting. Any brochures from the organization should be included as well. The invitation should also outline all the arrangements that have been agreed to by both parties.

Confirmation letter After the speaker accepts, the committee should send a letter of confirmation restating all the important details (date, time, place, topic, duties, and fee), along with the contract and any other forms the speaker has to complete. As a courtesy, enclose a stamped self-addressed envelope. If the speaker declines the offer, send a formal letter of refusal; this will help prevent any misunderstandings later on.

Packet of information and welcome letter Giving speakers clear written guidelines can greatly help make the meeting go as smoothly as possible. About two weeks before the meeting, send the speaker a welcome letter with a packet of information that includes the following information:

- Title and purpose of the meeting
- Meeting date
- Location of the meeting, including a clear map
- Description of the audience size and composition
- Contract
- Organization policy on travel reimbursement
- Telephone or fax contact numbers

Thank-you letter After the meeting, send the speaker a letter of acknowledgment and thanks for helping to make the meeting a success.

Audiovisual Needs

The audiovisual needs of the speaker rarely depend on the size of a meeting. The amount and type of equipment required depend more on the purpose of the meeting, its topic, and its budgetary constraints. Possible audiovisual aids include:

Spotlights and special lighting
Microphones and public-address systems
Chalkboards, easels, pads and markers, and electronic boards
Slide projectors, overhead projectors, and filmstrips
Tape recorders
Music
Televisions and VHS recorders

Publicity

Publicity requirements differ between small and large meetings. For most small meetings, a simple written notice suffices. Large meetings require much more elaborate publicity. Publicity for each type of meeting is explained below.

Small-Meeting Publicity

Notify participants of a small meeting via telephone, fax, interoffice memo, or E-mail. In some organizations, it is commonplace for the secretary to post meeting notices on centrally located bulletin boards or insert the notice in the minutes. The latter is the recommended method for meeting notification. In fact the bylaws of many organizations specify that members must be notified of meetings in writing.

Below is a sample notice for a meeting of the membership committee for a community organization:

NOTICE

Members of the South Huntington Rotary Club membership committee are hereby notified that the next meeting of the Committee will be held in South Huntington, New York, at the Huntington Manor Fire House, on June 2, 1994, at 1:00 p.m. Please call the clerk, Mr. John Duffy, by May 15.

Large-Meeting Publicity

Begin by establishing a committee to handle the diverse publicity needs of a large meeting. The committee should include people with different talents, as well as individuals who have and have not worked on past publicity committees. Balance the committee by seeking a variety of members. For example, some members should be skilled in writing press releases, letters, and advertisements, while others will need to know how to keep well-organized records, obtain mailing lists, and work with outside promotional resources. It is also a good idea to see how similar organizations have publicized their large meetings and which methods have given them the best results.

Chapter 3

Setting Up a New Organization

THE CHAPTER AT A GLANCE

First Meeting

There are a number of steps necessary to establishing a new organization. Each of these is described below, arranged in the order they should be followed.

Call the Meeting

When a group of people decides to set up a permanent organization, they should begin by contacting anyone who is interested in the cause. Unlike a mass meeting, it is important that only those sincerely interested in the concerns of the new organization be notified. This will help prevent an unruly gathering as well as the possibility of attracting people who have no interest in the topic.

Two effective ways to contact prospective members are by speaking with them in person or by sending them letters. These methods have proven more effective than a general announcement or public posting. When a sufficient number of invited prospective members has responded, each individual should be informed of the time and place for the meeting and given a description of the purpose of the organization.

The first meeting is often a combination of business and fellowship; it may take place at a luncheon or dinner, for example. As a courtesy, the organizers usually wait a few minutes past the appointed time for starting the meeting to make sure that all interested parties have arrived. If the meeting has been set for 8:00 p.m., for example, the call to order could occur at 8:15 or 8:20. One of the organizers will then step forward and call the meeting to order, as the following example demonstrates:

▶ The organizer says, "At this time, the meeting will please come to order."

Elect Temporary Officers

When the meeting has quieted down, the speaker calls for the election of temporary officers. For the first meeting, only a chair pro tem and a secretary pro tem are required. It is a good idea to speak to several individuals before the meeting to see if they wish to be nominated for office. The speaker or someone from the floor can nominate these candidates. However, anyone can be nominated, even if he or she has not previously expressed an interest in running for office in the organization. The following example shows how to make a nomination.

▶ The organizer says, "The first order of business is the election of temporary officers. Nominations for chair are now open."

or

The organizer says, "I move that [name of person] act as chair."

Another person says, "I second the motion."

The speaker continues to call for nominations until everyone has had a chance to speak. Even though the nominations are open, in most cases only one person is nominated for the office, since the audience recognizes the interest and expertise of the individual who organized the meeting. In the case of a sole nominee, he or she can be elected by acclamation (see page 241). If there is more than one nominee, however, all nominations are voted on by voice. The speaker puts the question to a vote, as follows:

- ▶ The speaker says, "It has been moved and seconded that [name of person] act as chair pro tem. All those in favor of the motion please say aye [pause for response]. All those opposed please say no [pause for response]."

If the nominee has a majority, the motion is carried; if not, the process is repeated until a chair pro tem is elected. The chair pro tem then takes over, and a secretary pro tem is elected by the same process, as the following example shows:

- ▶ The chair pro tem says, "The first order of business is the election of the secretary pro tem. Nominations are open for that position."

If there is more than one nominee, the chair takes a vote on each in turn, until a candidate receives a majority. The secretary then takes a seat next to the chair.

Explain the Purpose of the Meeting

With officers in place, it is time to address the purpose of the proposed organization. The chair pro tem or the meeting organizer should briefly describe the reasons why the meeting was called and what the organizers wish to accomplish. Others in the audience can add their comments as well, and the chair might also wish to call on specific individuals to speak. The following dialogue illustrates this process.

- ▶ The chair says, "We are meeting here today to form a new society to [purpose of society]."
  A member says, "Mr./Madam Chair."
  The chair says, "Ms. Swanson."

Ms. Swanson says, "Will this organization also be concerned with [additional purpose/issues]?"

The chair should make sure that all interested parties have a chance to speak but that no one faction is allowed to monopolize the discussion. This informal talk affords everyone an opportunity to exchange views and clarify the purpose of the organization.

Informal Discussion—Summary

Since this is an informal discussion, no motions are made and there is no limit on speaking time. Instead, the chair guides the discussion to allow all participants equal access to the floor.

Offer Resolutions

When the conversation is completed, an individual should offer a resolution stating the purpose of the organization. In most cases, the person offering the resolution will be someone instrumental in having called the meeting. It is recommended that the meeting organizers prepare the resolutions ahead of time, enabling the assembly to take specific action on the issue in a speedy manner. An example of a resolution follows:

▶ "*Resolved,* That it is the sense of this meeting that an organization for [state the purpose of the group] should be formed at this time."

The resolution must be seconded and read aloud by the chair to be open for debate, as the following example shows.

▶ The chair says, "The question concerns the adoption of the resolution just read. The question is open for debate."

When the debate winds down, the chair calls the question for the vote.

▶ The chair says, "Is the group ready for the question? [pause]. Those in favor of adopting the resolution please say aye [pause to count votes]. Those opposed please say no [pause to count votes]."

The chair then announces the result of the vote:

▶ The chair says, "The ayes have it—the resolution is adopted."

or

The chair says, "The motion is carried—the resolution is adopted."

or

The chair says, "The motion is lost—the resolution is defeated."

It is important to realize that the resolution is a statement of intent; it does not create the organization. The organization can be formed only by ratifying bylaws and having members sign the roll. Nonetheless, the resolution must be voted on according to the process described above.

Draft Bylaws

One of the most important steps in establishing a new organization is drafting the bylaws, a set of rules by which it conducts business. The bylaws should contain all the important rules of an organization. These rules should be so central to its function that they cannot be changed without giving prior notice to all members. Once adopted, the bylaws cannot be suspended, but they can be amended. The word *bylaws* comes from the Danish laws set up for the *bye* or town.

It is recommended that the bylaws committee consult with other similar organizations and solicit copies of their bylaws to use as models. The committee can also consult a parliamentarian or an attorney, who is often called in to read through the final draft of the bylaws before they are presented to the assembly. Attorneys are helpful when the proposed organization will own a great deal of property or land.

A motion must be made that the chair appoint a committee to draft the bylaws, as shown below:

▶ A member says, "I move that the chair appoint a committee of [number of members] to draft bylaws for the assembly, and that the committee report at an adjourned meeting of this assembly."

Since no other business can be addressed until the bylaws have been written and adopted, the next motion should be to fix the date, time, and place of the next meeting. At that time the bylaws committee should be ready to make its report.

Fix the Time to Which to Adjourn—Summary

Don't confuse the motion to Fix the Time to Which to Adjourn with a motion to Adjourn. A motion to Fix the Time to Which to Adjourn does not affect the time at which the present meeting will adjourn; rather, it sets up the next meeting.

If the motion is made while a question is pending and no other meeting is scheduled, it is a privileged motion, taking precedence over all other motions and yielding to none. In these instances, it requires a second and a majority vote, and it can be reconsidered; but it cannot be debated.

If the motion is made while another matter is not pending, however, it is a main motion. It still requires a second but is now debatable. It also needs a majority vote, and can be reconsidered.

To make the motion in either case, a member says, "I move that when this meeting adjourns, it will adjourn to meet next Monday at 7:00 p.m."

Bylaws format The content of the bylaws is determined by the needs of the organization. Even though bylaws can be amended, most organizations try to anticipate future needs when drafting their bylaws, to reduce frequent bylaw amendments. Below is a list of items generally included in bylaws, arranged in a conventional format. Each article is usually designated by a roman numeral.

Article I: Name of Organization List the organization's full, legal name.

Article II: Purpose of the Organization In most instances, the purpose of the organization can be listed in one sentence. While there is no rule that the purpose must be that briefly stated, it is a good idea to be as concise as possible. This brevity helps make the document clear.

Article III: Membership Most organizations include some or all of the following items:

- Attendance requirements
- Fees and dues
- Qualifications for membership
- Classes of members, such as active and inactive

Article IV: Officers To make this section as clear as possible, include the following:

- Number of officers in the organization
- Officers' duties
- How officers are elected or appointed

Article V: Meetings State the time and place where the meetings will be held. Consider also including information on the annual meeting.

Article VI: Board of Directors To describe the composition of the board, the following information is usually included:

- Which officers and/or members will serve on the board
- Board's authority
- Rules that govern the board

Article VII: Committees Describe the creation of all committees that the organization is likely to require, including descriptions of both standing and special committees.

Article VIII: Parliamentary Authority State which book of parliamentary rules of order the organization will use as its standard reference guide. Be sure to include the copyright date as well. The following text illustrates the wording of this provision: "In all instances when they are applicable and not inconsistent with these bylaws and any other special rules the organization shall adopt, the rules contained in the current edition of [name of parliamentary guide] shall govern this organization."

Article IX: Amendment of Bylaws It is also important to include provision for amending the bylaws, as follows:

- Two-thirds vote needed
- Stipulation of prior notice
- Type of notice required, oral or written

Amending Bylaws at a Convention—Summary

At a national convention, newly proposed amendments may also be submitted in writing for consideration at least 24 hours before being brought for action. A two-thirds vote of the delegate body is required in order for the amendment to be considered. For the proposed change to become an amendment to the bylaws, it must be approved by 90 percent of the delegates present and voting.

Useful bylaw provisions In addition to the basic guidelines listed above, there are other useful provisions that organizations may wish to include in their bylaws. These provisions are important because carefully planned bylaws can head off potentially serious problems, especially in such areas as leadership, notification, elections, and voting. Effective bylaws can also help make the organization more efficient. Below are some especially useful bylaw provisions, arranged in alphabetical order.

Annual audit The financial records of the organization should be audited annually and at such other times as may be requested by the board. The larger the organization and the greater its assets, the more important an audit becomes to avoid financial irregularities—or the appearance of them. The auditing can be done by an internal committee or an external agency, depending on the organization's size and assets. All audit reports must be approved by the board of directors. Copies of the reports should also be made available to the members of the organization.

Bonding Most organizations require officers and agents of the board responsible for the receipts, custody, and disbursement of funds to furnish fidelity bonds for the faithful performance of their duties. The sums of these bonds should be fixed by the board of directors, and the cost of the bonds paid by the organization.

Conducting business by mail A standard bylaw provision for many organizations applies to conducting business by mail, since it provides a useful and relatively low-cost way to contact both officers and members. Mailing such documents as ballots, agendas, and minutes is especially useful for organizations with a large membership. Consider using fourth-class, book-rate mail for material that does not have to arrive quickly. When time is a crucial factor, use first-class mail, or, if documents must be delivered the following day, a courier service is recommended.

Most organizations include a mail provision for voting. In order to be counted, mail-in votes must be received from at least a majority of the board members within the time limitations specified in the announcement in the mail referendum. Action taken by mail should be verified and made part of the minutes of the next regular session of the board of directors. The following example illustrates how this provision can be worded:

- ▶ "The board of directors may submit proposals for consideration and approval by the membership in mail referendums. A [insert appropriate percentage] of members voting shall be necessary for approval of the proposals."

Conducting business by telephone It is commonplace for organizations, especially large groups, to include a provision in their bylaws that allows the board of directors to meet by telephone *conference call.* This can make it easier to assemble a quorum of officers on short notice and enable the group to deal with pressing business promptly and efficiently.

Board members must be given sufficient advance notice of the telephone conference call, and a majority of the board members must participate in the conference-call meeting. An organization can meet by conference call if every participant has a conference-call line and understands how to access it. No member can be disenfranchised. If members live in different states or countries, the chair should consider relevant time differences when planning the conference call. Below is an example of the wording used for this bylaw provision:

- ▶ "In case of emergency, action may be taken by the board by telephone (conference) call. There must be concurrence of a majority of the members and such action shall be noted in a special memorandum placed in the minutes book and signed by the person obtaining such concurrence and shall be reported in the minutes of the next meeting."

Conducting business by E-mail (electronic mail) This provision is especially useful when an organization is pressed for time and desires a verifiable written contact with members. Consider using this method also when a matter is highly charged or a document is too long to be read over the telephone.

As with telephone conference calls, all officers or members participating in an E-mail transmission must have access to E-mail and understand how to operate the system. A training session is a worthwhile investment of time and money. While it is not difficult to send or receive E-mail, participants must be comfortable with the technology so that no one can later claim that he or she did not participate in the vote. The following example shows how to word this bylaw provision:

▶ "In case of emergency, action may be taken by the board by E-mail. There must be concurrence of a majority of the members and such action shall be noted in a special memorandum placed in the minutes book and signed by the person obtaining such concurrence and shall be reported in the minutes of the next meeting."

Conducting business by fax (facsimile machine) As with E-mail, this is another fast and low-cost method for transmitting documents and conducting business. It is especially useful when emergency matters arise. Faxing a brief document is less expensive than using a courier service, for a fax costs the same as a telephone call. Unlike conference calls and E-mail, members can use a public fax service if they do not own a fax machine. To include this provision in the bylaws, follow the wording used for the E-mail transmission.

Dissolution of a nonprofit organization Since the assets of a nonprofit organization are tax exempt, they can only be disposed of by special provision. All of the property and assets remaining after all debts, obligations, and expenses have been paid can be distributed only to those organizations that are covered by Section 501(c) of the Internal Revenue Code. The board of directors should determine the final distribution of the organization's assets, in accordance with the law.

Indemnification Officers and employees of an organization should be indemnified for costs or liabilities in connection with any lawsuit involving them in their official capacity. No member or employee should be indemnified when negligent in the performance of duty.

Quorum Under regularly established parliamentary law, a meeting cannot be held unless there is a quorum. To cover specific and very select circumstances, an organization may wish to include a bylaw provision for holding valid meetings without a quorum. Since this can be illegal in certain instances, this provision should be considered carefully.

Sample bylaws Below is a sample set of completed bylaws for the board of trustees of a nonprofit organization. The model includes the common basic provisions as well as some of the relevant bylaw provisions discussed on page 33. These bylaws also provide the organization with a director, a paid position considered necessary to successfully running this specific society.

Notice the style of these sample bylaws. The members of the bylaws committee chose to capitalize such nouns as the names of officers (President, Vice President, Clerk), trustees, the board, and the annual meeting. They arranged the information according to articles and sections that apply specifically to establishing the board of trustees of an organization. The model presented here is a sample of one possible style. The style that your organization selects for its bylaws is largely a matter of individual choice, as long as the necessary provisions are included.

Sample Bylaws

Bylaws of the Board of Trustees of the ________ Historical Society

Article I: Membership

The Board of Trustees shall consist of five (5) members, one of whom shall be elected annually for a term of five (5) years, at the Annual Meeting. Trustees must be United States citizens and have been a member of the Society for at least ten (10) years. If the office of any Trustee becomes vacant for any cause other than the expiration of term, such vacancy shall be filled by appointment by the Board of Trustees as prescribed by law and the Board Charter. Resignation by a member of the Board of Trustees shall be in writing and delivered to the President of the Board at least five (5) days prior to any regular meeting. This provision may be waived by the Board of Trustees by a unanimous vote of the Board at any meeting.

Article II: Powers and Duties

Section 1:

The Board is the legal entity charged with the management and responsibility for the Society. The Board shall establish the objectives of the Society and determine the policy for the development of such objectives. The Board, in turn, shall delegate the Director in charge of the Society within the framework of the established policy. The Director shall be responsible for the care of buildings, equipment, and the employment and direction of the staff and for the operation of the Society under the financial conditions set forth in the annual budget.

a. Policies and regulations for the guidance of personnel not inconsistent with these bylaws shall be made by the Director from time to time with the approval of the Board.
b. Regulations respecting the use of discipline and other matters requiring regulation may be made and altered by the Director, subject to the Board's approval.

Section 2:
A prime obligation of the Board shall be to regulate the funds necessary to operate the Society within the objective and policy specified. Upon receiving recommendations from the Director, the Board shall prepare the annual budget and establish all procedures necessary to fully and properly discharge its responsibility for the sound financial management of the Society.

Article III: Audits

The Board shall have an audit of business records of the Society at the end of each fiscal year, and at other times when it deems necessary.

Article IV: Officers

Section 1:
Officers of the Board shall be chosen at the regular meeting in January and shall be chosen as follows: President, Vice President, and Secretary. The term of each officer shall be one year. No officer shall serve more than three consecutive terms, but each shall continue beyond that time if necessary until his or her successor is elected and qualified.

Section 2:
The President of the Board shall preside at all meetings, appoint all committees, authorize all calls for any special meetings, and generally perform the duties of the presiding officer.

Section 3:
The Vice President of the Board shall assume the duties of the President in the case of the absence or inability of the President. In the case of absence or disability of both the President and the Vice President, the remaining three Trustees may elect one of their number to perform temporarily all the duties of the President.

Section 4:
In case of vacancies in offices, the succession shall be as follows: The Vice President shall succeed the President, the Secretary shall succeed the Vice President, and a new Secretary shall be elected. If two offices are vacant, the remaining officer shall succeed to the highest vacant office, and the vacant office shall be filled by election.

Section 5:
The Secretary shall sign the minutes after the approval by the Board.

Section 6:
The Board may appoint a Clerk of the Board. The Clerk of the Board shall be responsible for keeping a true and accurate account of the proceedings of all public board meetings.

Section 7:
The Treasurer of the Society shall have charge of all the Society's funds and shall, in addition to the President's or Vice President's signatures or authorized signatures, sign checks on the account on the authorization of the Board, and shall report at each regular meeting the state of the funds. In the absence or incapacity of the Society's Treasurer, the Director will act as the Assistant Treasurer.

Section 8:
The Board shall appoint the Treasurer, Attorney, and Auditor annually at its January meeting.

Article V: Meetings

Section 1:
The regular meeting of the Society shall be held on the first Monday of each month. In the event of a lack of a quorum, the regular meeting will be postponed to the second Monday of the month.

Section 2:
The Annual Meeting shall be held at the same time as the regular meeting for the month of January. The newly elected officers will start their fiscal year at the January meeting.

Section 3:
The time and date of the regular monthly meeting may be changed by a majority vote of the members present at any meeting, providing announcement of such change was stated in the agenda given to all Board members prior to the meeting.

Section 4:
Special meetings may be called by the President or by the President upon request of any member of the Board for the transaction of only such business as stated in the call for the meeting.

Section 5:
In case of an emergency, action may be taken by the Board in telephone concurrence of a majority of the members, and such action shall be noted in a special memorandum placed in the minutes book and shall be reported in the minutes of the next meeting.

Section 6:

a. Notices of all public meetings shall be given to all members at least five (5) days before the meeting.
b. Public notice of the time and place of a meeting scheduled at least one week prior thereto shall be given to the public and the news media seventy-two (72) hours before such meeting.
c. Public notice of the time and place of every other meeting shall be given, to the extent practical, to the public and media at a reasonable time prior thereto.
d. The public notice provided for shall not be construed to require publication as a legal notice.

Section 7:
All meetings shall be open to the general public, except only in those circumstances where confidential discussion is of the utmost necessity, as provided by law.

Section 8:
If a member of the Board is unable for good reason to attend a scheduled meeting, the Director will be notified as soon as possible. If a quorum cannot be met, the Director shall notify the remaining members of the postponement or cancellation of the meeting as appropriate.

Section 9:
An executive session may be convened upon a majority vote of the total membership of the Board at an open meeting, after identifying the general area or areas of the subject or subjects to be considered. Only the subjects listed below may be cause to convene an executive session:

a. The proposed acquisition, sale, or lease of real property, but only when the publicity would substantially affect the value of the property;
b. The medical, financial, credit, or employment history of any person or corporation, or matters leading to the appointment, employment, promotion, discipline, suspension, dismissal, or removal of any person or corporation;
c. Collective negotiations pursuant to Article 14 of Civil Service Law;
d. Discussion regarding proposed, pending, or current litigation;
e. Information relating to current or future investigation of prosecution of a criminal offense which could imperil effective law enforcement if disclosed;
f. Any matter which might reveal the identity of a law enforcement agent;
g. Matters which imperil public safety if disclosed.

Section 10:
Minutes of all open meetings and all formal actions of executive sessions shall be kept.

a. Minutes of all regular meetings will be completed within ten (10) working days of the meeting and will be available in the Director's office for inspection by all Board members.
b. There is no requirement for minutes of sessions held for the purpose of discussion at which no formal action is taken.
c. Minutes of executive sessions must be available to the public within one week of such meeting, provided, however, that they shall not include any matter which

is not required to be made public by the Freedom of Information law.

Section 11:
The Director or Assistant Director shall attend all Board meetings.

Article VI: Committees

The following committees shall be appointed annually by the President:

Building and Grounds
Public Relations
Personnel
Finance and Budget

The President is an ex officio member of all committees.

Section 1:
Special committees for the study and investigation of special problems may be appointed by the President, such committees to serve until the completion of the work for which they were appointed.

Section 2:
All committees are to make reports to the Board and act only on the Board's recommendations.

Article VII: Quorum

A quorum for the transaction of business shall consist of a majority of the members of the Board.

Article VIII: Order of Business

Section 1:
The order of business at regular meetings shall be as follows:

1. Call to order
2. Salute the flag
3. First public participation
4. Approval of the minutes (either read or previously received)
5. Approval of the bills
6. Report of the Director
7. Report of committees
8. Unfinished business
9. New business
10. Second public participation

11. Executive session
12. Adjournment

Section 2:
An agenda of the matters to come before the Board shall be sent to each member of the Board in advance of the meeting. Any member of the Board may suggest items to be placed on the agenda, but the final arrangement of the agenda shall be left to the President of the Board and the Director, provided that it does not contradict the order of business listed in Section One (1). Board members desiring matters to appear on the agenda should submit them at least one week before the Board meeting. In the event of failure to do so, the Board member shall give a public explanation for the reason for such failure.

Section 3:
Parliamentary law shall be the final authority in the transaction of all Board business.

Article IX: Amendments
These bylaws may be amended by a majority vote of the Board of Trustees after the amendment has been considered for two (2) meetings, providing the amendment was stated in the call for the meeting.

Define a Code of Ethics

We live in an increasingly litigious society. Recognizing the realities of modern life, many organizations governed by parliamentary law are seeking to protect themselves by adopting a code of ethics as well as bylaws. A code of ethics defines appropriate behavior for board members, officers, or any other members of the organization for whom such guidelines might apply. It carefully delineates ways in which board members should conduct themselves to avoid actual impropriety or the appearance of it.

The following sample code of ethics describes each of the areas considered the most important to safeguarding an organization's reputation.

Sample Code

Code of Ethics
Board of Trustees of the __________ Historical Society

This Code shall be distributed to all Board members at the Annual Meeting in January.

As per Article 18, Section 806 of the ________ State General Municipal Law, the following Code of Ethics shall be in force for all members of the Board of Trustees of the ________ Historical Society.

Article I: Conduct

Trustees of the ________ Historical Society shall conduct themselves in such a manner so as not to give the impression that any person can influence them or unduly enjoy favor from them with regard to the performance of their official duties.

Article II: Potential Conflict of Interest

Section 1:

The Trustees of the ________ Historical Society shall not receive monetary or material benefit as a result of their dealings with the Society. This does not apply to those instances specifically excluded from law, such as contracts with voluntary nonprofit corporations or associations.

Section 2:

Trustees shall publicly disclose any of the following interests that they may have with a company doing business with, or proposing to do business with, the Society. For the purposes of this Code, an interest shall be considered any of the following:

a. Employment with said company;
b. A business relationship with said company;
c. A financial interest, other than the holding of common stock, in said company;
d. A family relationship with the principals or employees of said company.

Section 3:

Public disclosure shall be made to the Board of Trustees at a regularly scheduled public meeting within thirty (30) days of the time the Trustee acquires, or learns of, an interest as defined above. This public disclosure shall include the name of the company doing business with, or proposing to do business with, the Society and the interest in that company the Trustee has, as outlined in Section 2:a.–d. above. This disclosure shall be recorded in the official minutes of the Board of Trustees.

Section 4:

Members of the Board of Trustees, by official motion, may then ask that the disclosure be sent to the Board's attorney for his or her advice as to whether the disclosed interest constitutes a conflict of interest that is prohibited by the law or by this Code of Ethics. The reply of the attorney or any other authority he or she chooses to consult on this matter shall become part of the official minutes of the Board of Trustees.

Article III: Areas of Conflict

Trustees of the ________ Historical Society shall further refrain from engaging in any of the following activities:

a. Making personal investments in any enterprises that will create a conflict with their duties to the Society;
b. Using their position to obtain employment in the Society for members of their family or their friends;
c. Entering into arrangements with clients for compensation in matters that are before the Board of Trustees;
d. Disclosing confidential information acquired during the course of their official duties;
e. Using this information to further their personal interests;
f. Soliciting or accepting any gift under any circumstances in which it could be inferred that the gift was intended to influence or reward the Trustee for official action;
g. Engaging in negotiations with companies doing business with or proposing to do business with the Society without the knowledge and authorization of the Board of Trustees.

Article IV: Penalty for Misconduct

Section 1:

In addition to any penalty contained in any other provision of law, any Trustee who knowingly and intentionally violates any of the provisions of this Code may, by majority vote of the Board of Trustees, be suspended or removed from office pending legal resolution of the matter in question.

Section 2:

In the event of any misconduct, maladministration, or malfeasance in office, a Trustee may be removed from office.

Section 3:

This Code may be amended by a majority vote of the Board of Trustees after the amendment has been considered at two (2) meetings, providing the amendment was stated in the call for the meeting.

Second Meeting

The time and place of the second meeting was established at the first meeting by the motion to Fix the Time to Which to Adjourn. The chair pro tem and the secretary pro tem are still in office, and they remain so until permanent officers can be elected. There are five main items on the agenda of the second meeting:

1. Read and approve the minutes
2. Adopt the bylaws
3. Sign in members
4. Elect officers
5. Appoint committees

At the beginning of the meeting, the chair pro tem calls the meeting to order, as the following example shows:

▶ The chair pro tem says, "The meeting will now come to order."

Read and Approve the Minutes

When the meeting has come to order, the chair pro tem calls for the reading and approval of the minutes of the first meeting, as would happen near the opening of a regular meeting of an established organization. The following example demonstrates how this is done:

▶ The chair pro tem says, "The secretary will please read the minutes of the last meeting."

The minutes can be approved as read or corrected and then approved. The motion is made as follows:

▶ The chair pro tem says, "If there is no objection from the floor, the minutes will stand approved as read [or as corrected]."

Adopt the Bylaws

Next the bylaws committee presents its report to the organization. Some organizations may have also drafted a separate constitution or corporate charter; if so, these documents are presented for approval first. In most instances, the bylaws and the constitution are one document and would be presented together for approval. The motion to approve the bylaws is made as follows:

▶ The chair pro tem says, "The next order of business is adopting the bylaws. May I have the report of the bylaws committee, please."
The chair of the bylaws committee says, "Mr./Madam Chair, the bylaws committee has written the following draft of the bylaws to present. I have been directed to move for its adoption."

The committee chair would then read the entire document to the assembly. If members have already read copies of the proposed bylaws, this reading may be omitted. In that case, the bylaws chair can move for immediate approval of the bylaws, as follows:

▶ The bylaws chair says, "Mr./Madam Chair, I now move the adoption of the bylaws."

Motion to Approve the Bylaws—Summary

Motions to approve committee reports do not require a second, unless the committee has only one member. Therefore, there is no need to second a motion to approve the bylaws, since it is offered by a committee.

If members have not read the proposed bylaws, the committee chair must read the entire document to the assembly. Before the reading, the chair pro tem should explain the process to the assembly, stressing that everyone will have a chance to comment on the document before it is presented for approval. Bylaws are most often approved one section at a time to make it easier for members to craft the document as necessary. The chair of the bylaws committee should explain each section as he or she reads it, and members should have an opportunity to debate each section and offer amendments as needed. The following examples illustrate this process:

▶ The bylaws committee chair says, "Are there any amendments to this article?" [pause to discuss each article].
When the entire document has been read, the chair of the bylaws committee asks for further amendments, as follows:

"The entire document has been read. Are there any additional amendments to the bylaws at this time?"
When everyone who so desires has offered suggestions, the chair pro tem calls for a voice vote, as follows: "Those who are in favor of adopting the bylaws say aye [pause to count votes]. Those opposed say no [pause to count votes]."

A majority vote is needed for passage of the bylaws. The chair then announces the result of the vote. If the voice vote was inconclusive, the chair can hold a rising vote (see page 247). If the bylaws passed, they are immediately in effect. If they are not approved, they can be reconsidered.

Adopting Bylaws—Summary

A main motion is required to adopt bylaws when forming a new organization. It requires a second and can be debated, amended, and reconsidered. The motion is not in order when another motion has the floor, and it requires a majority vote for adoption. Only a negative vote on the bylaws can be reconsidered.

Sign in Members

Directly after the bylaws (and constitution and charter) are adopted, members are formally enrolled in the organization. Members do so by signing in and paying any necessary membership fee. The members can sign the constitution or a membership roll prepared ahead of time by the secretary pro tem. The people who sign in at this meeting are called *charter members*.

Elect Officers

After everyone has been enrolled, it is time to elect permanent officers. The chair pro tem sets the process in motion, as follows:

▶ The chair pro tem says, "The next order of business is the nomination and election of permanent officers."

The method of election should have been determined by the organization's bylaws. In the absence of specific rules, however, an organization can conduct elections by acclamation, ballot, cumulative vote, mail, proxy, rising vote, roll call, show of hands, unanimous consent, or voice vote. It is recommended that permanent officers be elected by the ballot method. Members can vote on all candidates at once, with one ballot, or nominations for each office can be completed and members can vote on each office in turn. Be sure to allow sufficient time to hold another election if no candidate receives enough votes to be elected.

The secretary pro tem can prepare ballots before the meeting or, if this has not been done, during the meeting. It is recommended that the secretary pro tem prepare the ballots. Avoid having members cut up their own pieces of paper to make ballots, for this makes it difficult to keep track of legal and illegal ballots. A sample ballot and a complete description of the ballot process appear on pages 241–45. Unless expressly forbidden in the bylaws, members can vote for any person who is eligible to hold office, whether or not the person has been nominated for office.

Elections—Summary

The chair pro tem must explain the election process to the members before the actual election. No member can be compelled to vote in any election. As a result, every member has the right to abstain or to pass in an election.

Appoint Committees

After the permanent officers are in place, the chair should appoint committees. Unless otherwise stated in the bylaws, the chair selects all committees and their chairs. If the membership is large or the chair is unfamiliar with many of the members, this step may be postponed until members have been consulted informally about their interests and abilities. Certain committees, however, have to be appointed immediately to enable the organization to set to work. The program, budget and finance, and membership committees are among those often appointed at the second meeting.

Before the meeting closes, the chair should attend to any pressing business. Once this has been resolved, a member should make a motion to adjourn. Subsequent meetings of the organization are conducted as regular or special meetings, depending on the business being considered. (Conducting a regular meeting is described on page 51, special meetings on page 53.)

Chapter 4

Types of Meetings

The Chapter at a Glance

Topic	Description	Page
Regular Meeting	Single official gathering of an organization to conduct business	51
Session	One of a series of inter-connected meetings, all on the same order of business	51
Executive Session	Meeting whose proceedings are secret	52
Special Meeting	Separate session of an organization held at a different time from the regular meeting	53
Adjourned Meeting	Meeting that continues the work of the preceding meeting	54
Annual Meeting	Meeting of an organization that holds only one membership meeting a year; or the yearly reorganization meeting of an organization	54
Occasional Meeting	Meeting of an unofficial organization	58
Board	Body of people elected or appointed to administer, manage, or adjudicate	59
Committee	Group of one or more persons, elected or	63

	appointed, to consider or to take action on a specific matter	
Mass Meeting	Meeting of an unorganized group which has been publicized	81
Convention	Assembly of delegates chosen especially for each session to represent a larger group of people	84

Definition of a Meeting

A *meeting* has traditionally been defined as a single official gathering of the members of an organization in one place to transact business. The meeting must be continuous, discounting a short break or recess. A meeting may last anywhere from a few minutes to several hours.

With modern technology such as video- and teleconferencing, the "one place" part of the definition takes on a whole new meaning. Increasingly, modern technology enables people separated by great distances from each other to meet in the same "place." While they can hold a meeting, they may in fact never even meet each other face-to-face.

Nevertheless, the customary image of a meeting is still defined as people gathered in one place, most often an office, conference room, or hall. The meeting may involve two directors discussing whether people in their departments should move to a flextime schedule, seven school-board members debating the introduction of a new reading curriculum, or a thousand people attending a seminar on the latest developments in their field.

It is important to identify the type of meeting you are holding or attending in order to know which rules will help you accomplish your goals. You probably have been in more meetings than you can even recall, and these meetings have been distinguished as much by their differences as their similarities. The one thing all meetings have in common, however, is that they gather people to accomplish business.

Let's take a look now at the types of meetings you are most likely to encounter—and ways that parliamentary law can help you organize and run each type to accomplish business fairly and smoothly.

Terms to Know

Before you read about the different kinds of meetings, there are some terms that you should know:

Recess A recess is a short break in a meeting to allow tellers to count votes, to enable members to step away from business for a few moments, to allow members to confer about the business on the floor, and so on. A recess does not disrupt the meeting, and business is resumed at the point where it had been left off. This term applies to all meetings.

Adjournment An adjournment is the act of ending a meeting or a group of meetings. This term applies to all meetings.

Adjournment sine die This term describes the act of closing several interconnected meetings. An adjournment sine die most often occurs at the end of a series of mass meetings or at the end of a convention. The term means adjournment *without day*, or indefinitely.

Regular Meeting

A *regular meeting*, also called a *stated meeting*, refers to the periodic business meetings of an established organization. The term is used most often to refer to a regular business session.

Purpose Some organizations meet often for social purposes and may conduct business at these meetings. Other organizations meet on a regular basis to conduct business, and their meetings may have social overtones.

Time Your organization may meet every Monday, the second Tuesday of the month, or four times a year—no matter what the schedule, it is regular. The time is determined by the rules of the organization's bylaws. When the meeting is over, the presiding officer declares that the meeting is adjourned. The organization would then meet again at the regularly scheduled time and place.

Session

A *session* is a series of interconnected meetings devoted to the same order of business. There may be any number of meetings in a session. In Congress, a session often contains hundreds of meetings scheduled over the span of a year. In an established organization with regularly scheduled meetings, each meeting completes a session, unless otherwise stated in the bylaws. To be considered a true session, all the meetings in a session must be on the same program or share the same agenda. The business is continued from meeting to meeting, often taking up at the point where it left off.

As a general rule, in each session the members are free to act as they choose with regard to each new motion, and members cannot restrict the actions of the majority of a later session. For example, a defeated motion cannot be brought up a second time during a session except by using the appropriate parliamentary motion that allows such an action. When a series of meetings are interconnected into a session, an adjournment at the end of each meeting does not end the session.

Purpose As with a regular meeting, the purpose of a session varies with the composition of the organization. The group may meet primarily to conduct business or mainly to socialize.

Time In an established organization whose bylaws provide for regular meetings, the length and the number of meetings in a session depend on the nature of the business to be conducted, its purpose, and the organization's bylaws. Most organizations try to avoid long sessions, for it can be difficult to maintain continuity over multiple meetings.

Adjournment is different for a session than it is for a regular meeting. When a meeting adjourns without ending a session, the time for the next meeting must be set. The ways to continue the meetings in a session are the following:

- By adopting a motion to fix the time at which to adjourn
- Through an agenda established before the meeting
- By specifying a time in the motion to adjourn
- At the chair's discretion (at the call of the chair)

Executive Session

An *executive session* is a meeting whose proceedings are secret. Originally the term was used for U.S. Senate meetings where presidential business was conducted, such as drawing up treaties or nominating cabinet officers. The key to an executive session is secrecy; this is so important that members who reveal what transpired at an executive session can be disciplined by the organization. The minutes from an executive session can only be read and approved at another executive session.

Purpose Organizations go into executive session when they want to discuss sensitive matters concerning issues that should not be shared with the general membership. Such issues most often include anything that might pose a security risk, such as discussion about installing a new alarm system, or issues that might cause embarrassment, such as discipline and personnel matters. In any organization, anything pertaining to discipline should be handled in executive session.

Members allowed to participate in an executive session are determined by the organization's bylaws. In most cases, only officers of the organization may attend an executive session; in other instances, members and guests whose input is necessary to the issue being resolved are also invited to attend.

Time An executive session can be called at any time during a meeting, but it is usually scheduled for the same time on the agenda of every meeting. Since a motion to go into executive session is a question of privilege, it is adopted by a majority vote (see also page 140).

Special Meeting

A *special meeting* is a separate session of an organization that is held at a different time from the regular meeting. The presiding officer can request a special meeting to deal with urgent matters of business that cannot wait until the next regular meeting. Each organization's bylaws should describe who can call a special meeting and how much notice is required. Special meetings are also known as *called meetings* because of the way they are convened.

Purpose The presiding officer calls a special meeting to consider one or more items of pressing importance to the organization. The meeting must adhere to its agenda; all business considered must pertain to the reason for meeting. Special meetings should be called only when there are matters of real importance to discuss; they should not be convened for trivial purposes.

Time A special meeting can be called at any time that is convenient for all those invited to attend. Members must be allowed ample time to respond to the notice of the time, place, and purpose of the meeting. Members are given at least three days' notice, but five days' notice is not unusual. Provisions for calling a special meeting are stated in the organization's bylaws.

Adjourned Meeting

An *adjourned meeting* is a meeting that continues the work of a meeting that came before it. Adjourned meetings take place most often when a regular or special meeting cannot complete its agenda during the allotted time. An adjourned meeting is not the same as the act of adjourning a meeting—the first continues a meeting; the second ends it.

Purpose The purpose of adjourned meetings is to continue unfinished business. As a result, think of an adjourned meeting as an adjournment of the regular or special meeting to a new time and place.

Time To schedule the adjourned meeting for a particular time and place, the organization's members must agree to *adjourn to* or *adjourn until* the next meeting. Adjourned meetings are often called for later the same day, so that members can easily recall the order of business.

Annual Meeting

The term *annual meeting* encompasses two different types of meetings. The first type describes an organization that holds only one membership meeting a year, such as a shareholders' meeting. During the rest of the year, the board of directors manages the affairs of the organization.

An organization can also call an annual meeting once a year to reorganize itself by electing officers, designating an official bank and newspaper, appointing committee chairs, and so on. During this second type of annual meeting, the minutes of the previous meeting are read and approved. The business of a regular meeting may be completed as well as the reorganization business. While business during this meeting can be conducted at any time during the year, reorganization matters are often included at this one yearly meeting. Below is a sample agenda for an annual meeting of this type, where the organization takes care of "housekeeping tasks."

Sample Agenda: Annual Meeting

Belvard Public Library
Memorandum for Consideration of the Board of Trustees
Reorganization Meeting of July 14, 1994

1. **Call to Order**
2. **Salute the Flag**

Reorganization

A. Oath of Office
To be administered to the newly elected trustee, ________, copy of said oath to be placed on file with the County Clerk: "I, ________, do solemnly swear (or affirm) that I will support the Constitution of the United States and the Constitution of the State of New York; and that I will faithfully discharge the duties of the office of member of the Board of Trustees of the Belvard Public Library, of the County of Suffolk, to the best of my ability."

B. Election of Officers
President
Vice President
Secretary

C. Treasurer
The Director recommends the appointment of ________ as the Belvard Public Library Treasurer for the fiscal year 1994–95, at a fee of $100 per month or $1,200 per annum, with proper bond.

D. Auditor
The Director recommends the firm of ________, CPA, to be appointed as auditors for the Belvard Public Library

for the fiscal year 1994–95, at an annual retainer of $4,200.

E. Attorney

The Director recommends the Board appoint the firm of ________, PC, as General Counsel to the Board for the fiscal year 1994–95, at an annual retainer of $2,000.

F. Clerk

The Director recommends the Board appoint ________ as Clerk of the Board for the fiscal year 1994–95, at the rate of $16.50 per hour.

G. Bank Depository

The Director recommends the designation of the Belvard office of the Archway Bank as depository for the funds of the Belvard Public Library during fiscal year 1994–95.

H. Newspaper

The Director recommends the Board designate the following newspapers: *Belvard Bugle, Patchogue Post,* and *Newsday.*

I. Positions/Rate of Pay

The Director recommends the Board appoint the following positions and rates of pay for all employees, effective July 1, 1994. Rates of pay for all titles except Director III, Assistant Director I, Library Aide, and Page are subject to agreement with the CSEA dated July 1, 1993–June 30, 1995.

Full-time Employees

Title	Number	Pay Rate
Director III	1	$50,000
Asst. Director I	1	$44,000
Librarian II	4	$31,000
Librarian I	2	$30,500
Principal Clerk	4	$28,500
Senior Clerk	5	$26,800
Accounts Clerk	1	$29,500
Bookmobile Driver	1	$19,400
Clerk Typist	6	$18,000
Clerk	8	$17,000
Custodian	2	$25,000

Part-time Employees

Title	Number	Hourly Rate
Librarian II	2	$21.50
Librarian I	4	$18.50
Library Trainee	4	$14.00
Senior Clerk	5	$14.25
Accounts Clerk	1	$12.00
Audiovisual Aide	4	$11.50
Page	20	$ 5.50

3. First Public Participation

4. Reading and approval of the Minutes of the June 9, 1994, meeting

5. Reading of the Treasurer's Report, subject to the Annual Audit

6. Reading and approval of the bills

7. Director's Report

8. Report of Committees

Buildings and Grounds
Personnel
Finance and Budget
School Board Liaison

9. Unfinished Business

10. Communications

11. New Business

A. As per Article VII of the Bylaws of the Board of Trustees, the Director recommends that the President appoint Chairs for the following committees for 1994–95:

Buildings and Grounds
Personnel
Finance and Budget
School Board Liaison

B. The Director recommends the following holiday schedule for fiscal year 1994–95:

November 25, 9 a.m. to 5 p.m.
December 24, 9 a.m. to 1 p.m.
December 31, 9 a.m. to 5 p.m.

12. **Second Public Participation**
13. **Executive Session**
14. **Adjournment**

Occasional Meeting

An *occasional meeting* is one held by members of an unofficial group; they are not affiliated with an organized society.

Purpose Occasional meetings are held to achieve a specific order of business. For instance, several people may get together a few times to authorize the establishment of a community plaque or to donate some equipment to the town park. Once their purpose is achieved, the group is disbanded; the members have never formed themselves into an organization.

Running an occasional meeting The first order of business is to select someone to run the meeting. It is recommended that the organizers get together before the meeting to decide who should chair the meeting; that person should be approached informally with the idea. Then anyone in the group can open the meeting by addressing those gathered, as follows:

▶ A person at the meeting says, "The meeting will please come to order. I move that [name of a person at the gathering] act as chair of the meeting."
A second person at the meeting says, "I second the motion."
The first person says, "It has been moved and seconded that [name of person nominated] act as chair of this meeting. Those in favor say aye [pause to tally votes]. Those opposed say no."
If the majority of people present vote for the candidate, the person who made the motion says, "The motion is carried. [Name of the person elected] will chair this meeting."
If the motion fails, the first person will announce this and ask that someone else be nominated for the position of chair.

In less formal meetings, a person may assume the chair by acclamation. Or, the person who opens the meeting may ask for nominations, as follows:

▶ A person at the meeting says, "The meeting will now come to order. May I please have a nomination for a chair?"

The new chair must then have a secretary elected. This follows the same procedure, as follows:

▶ The chair says, "May I please have a nomination for secretary?"
If only one person is nominated, the chair then says, "Those in favor of [name of the person nominated] acting as secretary of this meeting will say aye [pause to tally votes]. Those opposed will say no." The chair then announces the results.
If more than one person is nominated, the chair repeats each name and takes a vote on each candidate in turn.

Time Occasional meetings are convened as the need arises.

Board

A *board* is a body of people elected or appointed to administer, manage, or adjudicate. Boards are like deliberative assemblies except they have no minimum size and their function is determined by the powers delegated to them by the organization. Boards are usually much smaller than deliberative assemblies. In order for an executive board to function smoothly, the bylaws of the organization must specify its composition, duties, and meeting schedule.

Purpose In most cases, national, state, or local governments charge boards with a specific task. For instance, a library board of trustees is chartered by the state to manage the day-to-day functioning of the library; a co-op board may be empowered by the tenants' association to administer the rules of the building. Where the organization does not have a general voting membership, the board may govern the institution, as in a university board of trustees.

Time The body that governs the specific board generally establishes when and how often the board will meet. Also included in such provisions are procedures for calling special meetings.

Officers

Any board that is organized as a deliberative assembly requires officers. The minimum is a presiding officer and a clerk, but more officers can be elected as needed. In some instances, the board elects its own officers; in other cases, it is regular practice for the chair and clerk of the organization to function in the same capacity on the board, a common situation in most volunteer organizations and ordinary groups.

To ensure a continuity of leadership and a smooth transition among officers, many organizations stagger the terms of office. For example, some executive board members serve for one year, some for two, some for three, and so on. This must be specified in the bylaws.

Ex officio Members

In most instances, a board of directors is made up of the organization's officers, although other members may be included as well. Ex officio board members may also be included on the board because they hold office or chair a committee in the organization or in an affiliated group. Ex officio board members who are part of the organization have the same privileges as all other board members. Ex officio board members who do not have organization membership enjoy all the rights but none of the obligations of board membership; they can make motions and vote but are not obliged to participate and are not counted in the quorum.

Conducting Business

As with any deliberative assembly, a board is bound by the organization's bylaws, any special rules the organization has passed, and the rules of parliamentary procedure. Any board that is not part of a larger organization can establish its own rules, but these rules cannot be in conflict with the law or with any rules that created the board. The clerk should keep minutes of the proceedings of the board. Under most situations, only members of the board are allowed to read these minutes. To give the general organization membership access to these minutes requires either board approval or a two-thirds vote of the organization.

The rules for small and large boards differ, as described below.

Small boards In a small board meeting, with no more than about 12 members present, some of the formality necessary in a large assembly would stand in the way of accomplishing business quickly. As a result, the procedures governing these meetings differ from the rules that prevail in larger meetings in the following respects:

- Members are not required to obtain the floor (to rise and be recognized) before they speak and make motions.
- Motions do not have to be seconded.
- There is no limit to the number of times a member may speak on a question.
- Motions to limit or close debate generally are not entertained.
- Informal discussion of a subject is allowed if no motion is pending.
- When everyone understands a motion, a vote can be taken without a formal motion being introduced.
- The chair can speak in any discussion or debate without leaving the chair. This is an important distinction, for it can change the nature of the debate. The chair can also make motions and vote on all questions.
- Small-board minutes are accessible only to board members unless these board members grant permission to organization members to inspect them or unless the organization votes (by a two-thirds majority) to order the minutes to be produced and made available to all of the members.
- In small boards, there is no limit as to when or how often a motion to Reconsider can be made. Also, the motion may be moved by a member who did not vote on the losing side through abstention or absence. A two-thirds vote is needed unless everyone who voted on the prevailing side is present or has been notified of the intention to move to reconsider.

Executive board This type of board is one of the most commonly created small boards. Also called a *board of trustees, board of directors,* or *board of managers,* an executive board is established by organizations to help set policy for the group and to make other important decisions. In some cases the executive board makes decisions when a regular meeting is not scheduled or cannot be scheduled; in other cases the executive board has specific responsibilities apart from the rest of the organization.

While it is often easier and less unwieldy to have a small group come to a consensus for the larger organization, the amount of power granted to an executive board varies greatly from organization to organization. Executive boards of business corporations, for example, have total control to run the corporation; those of volunteer service organizations, in contrast, may have their power strictly limited by the group's bylaws. Volunteer organizations that meet infrequently usually delegate a great deal of authority to their executive boards, while organizations that meet often usually grant much less responsibility to these officers. Regardless of meeting schedule, the decisions of the executive board of a voluntary organization cannot conflict with any action the assembly as a whole has taken.

Large boards In large boards, where there are more than about 12 members present, the formality of a large assembly is maintained. The procedures governing such meetings are the same as those that prevail in other large meetings. Below are some sample guidelines for public participation in large board meetings.

- Before addressing the board, all speakers should state their name, address, and organizational affiliation.
- Questions and comments should be addressed to the entire board and not to individual board members, the president, or members of the audience.
- Speakers should hold comments and questions for the period set aside for public participation.
- When a specific topic is under consideration, questions and comments should be confined to the matter under discussion.
- A time limit is usually allotted to each speaker on any given item.
- A speaker who does not need the entire time allotted usually may not yield any unused portion of the time to another speaker.
- On controversial issues, speakers for and against a given topic may be recognized alternately by the chair.
- Speakers should use a centrally located microphone and lectern when available.
- Speakers are expected to observe the commonly accepted rules of courtesy, decorum, dignity, and good taste.
- Board members may interrupt speakers for the purposes of clarification and information.
- Written statements will usually be received by the board in addition to, or in lieu of, oral presentations.

Committee

Imagine this scenario: you are attending a regular meeting of a large organization to which you belong. Business is progressing at a brisk pace as the presiding officer moves items along the agenda with great skill and fairness. Thanks in part to the chair's knowledge of parliamentary law, there is little or no dissension and everyone is working together equitably. But part way through the agenda, it becomes clear to all members that even though the presiding officer is knowledgeable and the members are cooperative, the agenda will not be accomplished in the allotted time. The assembly is big and consequently unwieldy, and there is a great deal of business to accomplish.

This is a commonplace scenario among many organizations. Experienced parliamentarians recognize that most organizations are too big and their meetings too brief to do more than plan for work to be done. How can organizations get through all their work in a timely, equitable manner? For nearly all organizations, the answer lies in establishing committees.

Definition Parliamentary law defines a *committee* as a group of one or more persons, elected or appointed, to consider or take action on a specific matter. Unlike a board, a committee is not strictly defined as a form of assembly. Committees do not have regularly scheduled meetings, as do assemblies or boards of directors. In most instances committees cannot act independently from the larger organization. They are often empowered to investigate issues and offer reports, but if they are to take action they must obtain special permission from the organization, called *with power*. In some instances committees can function in nearly the same way as boards.

Although committees are often seen as small groups, in fact there is no size restriction; a committee can be either small or large, depending on the needs of the organization at that specific time. However, committees are usually far smaller than the general assembly (see pages 66–69 for exceptions).

Advantages of Committees

It is clear that dividing tasks and assigning them to separate committees is a great time-saver in large organizations, but the practice of forming committees is also helpful in smaller organizations such as boards. Committees have a number of other advantages, as described below.

Informal structure Small committees, those with about 12 people in attendance, are not bound by the formality that is often necessary to maintain order in a large assembly. The rules governing small committee meetings are different from those governing larger groups, in the following ways:

- Members are not required to obtain the floor before making motions and speaking; they do not have to rise and be recognized.
- A committee chair can participate in the debate without rising or leaving the chair.
- The chair of a committee is allowed to make motions and to vote on all questions, actions which are not allowed in a general assembly.
- Members can speak as long and as often as they wish.
- Motions to close or limit debate are not allowed.
- Motions do not have to be seconded.
- Questions can be raised while discussion is going on.
- Informal discussion is allowed if there is no motion pending on the floor.
- When all committee members understand a proposal, a vote may be taken without a formal motion being introduced.

Since committees are not restrained by some of the rules that govern general assemblies, they can often work more quickly and efficiently.

Size A small number of people can usually meet more often than a larger group. This is partly because it can be easier to convene a small committee meeting than a large one, especially through electronic means such as E-mail and fax. Further, a small group of people can often reach a decision more quickly than a larger group.

Expediency The judicious appointment of committees can help keep delicate, troublesome, and time-consuming debates out of the general meeting. If the committees are balanced and properly constituted with representatives of all interests, matters that could become rancorous in a large assembly can be handled quickly in a committee. As a result, committees can help members accomplish their work in a more expedient manner.

Outside consultants Since they are often smaller than general assemblies, committees can make better use of experts and consultants. Committees are more flexible about time and scheduling, which makes it easier to meet with specialists whose time is limited.

Privacy Committees are better equipped to handle delicate or potentially embarrassing questions, such as those having to do with finances and personnel. Therefore, committees are often used for such matters as salary raises, promotions, and discipline in business and for selection of officers and honors in honorary organizations.

Types of Committees

There are three main kinds of committees: standing committees, special committees, and committee of the whole; and two alternate forms of a committee of the whole: quasi committee of the whole, and informal consideration of a question.

Standing committees Standing committees have a continued existence, as they handle routine duties that need to be carried out on a regular basis. These may include attending to personnel matters, overseeing buildings and grounds, attracting new members, or awarding honors.

Formation Standing committees can be created in two ways: by a resolution passed by a two-thirds vote, and by any method included in the bylaws.

Term of office Since standing committees remain in existence for the duration of the organization, members serve extended terms. These terms are often the same as those served by officers in the organization. New members of standing committees are usually appointed when new officers are elected to head the organization.

Procedure Unless the bylaws state otherwise, standing committees report directly to the assembly and not to the board of directors.

Special (select or ad hoc) committees Special committees are established to accomplish a particular purpose and cease to exist once that purpose has been served. The presiding officer may appoint a special committee to revise the organization's bylaws or investigate the possibility of acquiring real estate, for example. Since each special committee is established to deal with a specific situation, one should not be established if its duties are covered by a standing committee.

Formation Special committees are created according to the guidelines in the organization's bylaws.

Term of office Special committees are disbanded when the particular task is completed. They may be recreated at a later date, however, if the same task or situation once again presents itself. An organization may create a special committee during a building project, for instance, and disband the committee when the building is completed. The committee may be recalled later if another building renovation is desired.

Procedure As with standing committees, special committees report to the assembly, unless stated otherwise in the organization's bylaws.

Committee of the whole A committee of the whole is a committee of the entire assembly and is suitable for organizations with large memberships of over 100 members. Recall that a committee can operate under less stringent rules than those that apply to an entire assembly. Forming the assembly into a committee of the whole allows the members to consider a specific issue with the freedom of a committee. Members can speak to an issue as often as they are able to obtain the floor, although not more than once until everyone has had a chance to speak to the issue. Further, when the assembly has become a committee of the whole or a variation, the presiding officer can then participate in the debate, make motions, and vote on all questions, actions which are not allowed in a general assembly. A committee of the whole can only make two motions: to amend and to adopt.

Formation An organization can create a committee of the whole when it wishes to debate a subject but not refer it to committee, or when the information on a specific subject is not yet fully clarified. To create a committee of the whole, a member should make a motion to commit, in the following form:

▶ A member says, "That the assembly does now resolve itself into a committee of the whole, to take under consideration [the specific resolution or subject]."

or

A member says, "I move to go into a committee of the whole to consider the pending question."

The motion needs a second. If the motion is carried, the presiding officer immediately calls another member to the chair and takes his or her place as a member of the committee. In large groups, the secretary also vacates his or her seat and the assistant clerk assumes it.

Term of office As with any special committee, a committee of the whole is disbanded when its specified task is completed. A committee of the whole may be re-formed at a later date, however, if the specific task once again presents itself.

Procedure As with other committees, a committee of the whole cannot change the motion it is debating. If there is no limit to debate, members can speak to an issue as long as they want. To close or limit debate in a committee of the whole, a member of the assembly has to make a motion. The following example illustrates the appropriate format:

▶ A member says, "I move that the committee rise and report."

Since the motion to rise and report is the same as a motion to adjourn, it cannot be debated. After the motion is made, members vote. If the motion passes, the presiding officer immediately resumes the chair and the committee chair returns to the floor. The chair of the committee then rises and reports as follows:

▶ The committee chair says, "I move that the committee rise."

or

The committee chair says, "As chair of the committee of the whole, I report that the committee has gone through the business referred to it, and I am ready to make a report when the assembly is ready to receive it."

The decisions are not considered final; rather, they have the rank of recommendations to be voted on by the assembly under their regular rules.

Quasi committee of the whole The difference between a committee of the whole and a quasi committee of the whole is one of size: a quasi committee of the whole is appropriate for medium-sized organizations, those of 50 to 100 members.

Formation A quasi committee of the whole is formed in the same way as a committee of the whole, as this example shows:

▶ A member says, "I move that the resolution be considered in quasi committee of the whole."

The motion must have a second. To bring the committee to an end, follow this procedure:

▶ The chair says, "The assembly, acting as if in a committee of the whole, has had under consideration [the task] and has made the following amendments [specific amendments]. The question is on the adoption of the amendments."

Term of office Quasi committees of the whole, like special committees, are disbanded when the particular task is completed. They may be re-formed at a later date, however, when the task once again presents itself.

Procedure A quasi committee of the whole is not a real committee but the assembly acting like a committee of the whole. The results of all votes are given to the entire assembly for final consideration, exactly like the committee of the whole. All members are allowed to speak as often as they like for as long as they like. Presiding officers are allowed to remain in the chair and to run the meeting.

The difference between a quasi committee of the whole and a traditional committee lies in the type of motions allowed. If any motion other than an amendment is accepted, the committee's term is automatically over.

Informal consideration of a question This is another, simplified version of the committee of the whole. It is designed for small meetings of regular organizations.

Term of office As with quasi committees of the whole, this variant is disbanded when the particular task is completed but may be re-formed later if the same charge once again presents itself.

Procedure By informally considering a question, the organization suspends the number of times a person can speak during a debate and the presiding officer runs the meeting, just as in a committee of the whole and a quasi committee of the whole. The primary difference lies in the voting procedure: with an informal consideration, the results of any votes are considered binding on the assembly and are not voted on again. While acting informally, the entire group can amend and adopt resolutions, and without further motion the chair can announce, as follows:

▶ The chair says, "The assembly, acting informally, has considered [the subject] and has made certain amendments, which the chair will report at this time."
At that point, the matter comes before the assembly as if reported by a committee. The chair's report becomes part of the regular minutes.

Establishing Committees

Committees can be established in five different ways:

1. Election by ballot
2. Open nomination
3. Nomination by the chair
4. Appointment by the chair
5. Appointment by adopting a motion

Election by ballot Some committees are formed in the same way officers are chosen—by ballot election. Since this is the most formal way to establish a committee, it is reserved for standing committees that have far-reaching powers. The committee chair can also be voted into office on the same ballot.

Open nomination Using this method, members are nominated from the floor, without a secret ballot. The following example demonstrates how to create a committee this way:

▶ The chair says, "Members will please nominate members for the ________ committee."

or

The chair says, "Nominations for the ________ committee are now in order."

Each member can nominate more than one candidate, but only after everyone has had the opportunity to make a nomination. If the prescribed number of people are nominated and no other nominations are forthcoming, the chair proceeds as follows:

▶ The chair says, "The following members [name individuals] have been nominated for the ________ committee. Are there any further nominations? [pause for response]. Since there are none, the committee has been formed with the members just named."

If more people are nominated than necessary, however, the presiding officer repeats all the names in the order they were nominated and puts the question on each nominee in turn, one at a time. The chair continues this procedure until the required number of committee members have been elected. The members nominated last usually have the slimmest chance of winning.

Nomination by the chair In this instance, the chair selects and names the members of the committee, naming the committee chair first.

▶ The chair says, "The chair nominates [member name] as chairperson, [member name], [member name], and [member name] to the ________ committee."

Other members are free to eliminate any candidate the chair names but are not allowed to name others, which remains the chair's prerogative. After all changes have been made, the chair once again states the motion, as follows:

▶ The chair says, "The chair nominates [member name] as chairperson, [member name], [member name], and [member name] to the ________ committee. Those members in favor of the committee as suggested please say aye [pause to tally]. Those opposed say no [pause to tally]."

This method of establishing a committee works best when the assembly trusts the chair's wisdom in selecting a committee.

Appointment by the chair The chair can only appoint committees when granted such power in the bylaws, as in this sample text: "The presiding officer shall appoint all committees."

The bylaws should be carefully drafted to allow for instances when it would not be desirable to have the chair appoint all committees, such as the nominating committee.

The chair announces those members who have been appointed to the specific committee, again naming the chair of the committee first. There is no vote when the chair appoints a committee.

Appointment by adopting a motion Using this method, the names of the committee members are included in a motion:

▶ A member says, "I move that the committee be composed of [member name], [member name], and [member name]."

The motion may or may not include the name of the committee chair.

Committee Size and Composition

The number of people on a committee depends on the task the committee has been assigned. It is important to realize that the size of a committee often influences its impact. While a large committee is more difficult to steer than a small one, its report is usually more persuasive because of the sheer number of members involved. This factor may influence people who are trying to block or to support specific issues.

Regardless of size, all committees should be composed of the best candidates for the specific task. In some instances, members should represent all points of view, with a balance of majority and minority viewpoints. In other cases, it is better to include only those members whose views are similar.

Investigation committees When the committee is charged with an investigative or deliberative mission, for example, it is important that all interests be fully represented. This will ensure that the rights of both the minority and majority will be protected. Such representation will also help cut down on divisiveness later on, when the committee delivers its report to the entire assembly. Therefore, these committees should have diverse membership and many members.

Action committees When a committee has to decide on an action, such as purchasing software or hiring a consultant, the number of members involved should be small. Further, unless the action is highly controversial, all members should support the action; those who do not should decline the nomination and excuse themselves from serving.

Running a Committee

Calling the first meeting The initial step in conducting business in a committee is calling the first meeting. This is the chairperson's responsibility. If the chairperson does not convene the committee, any two members can do so.

Electing or appointing a secretary The committee must next elect or appoint a secretary. In small committees this can be the chair, but if there is a great deal of business to accomplish, the chair may wish to delegate this responsibility to a secretary.

Taking complete minutes It is important that the secretary or clerk take accurate, detailed minutes of all committee meetings, for these minutes will be used later as the source for the committee report. Included in the minutes should be a record of the steps the committee took to arrive at its decisions. The secretary should also record members' opinions, facts researched and compiled, and committee actions. The minutes remain the property of the committee and can only be read by committee members.

Having a quorum As with any assembly, there must be a quorum to conduct business. Unless otherwise specified in the organization's bylaws or by a specific resolution, a quorum is a majority of members. The meeting is not considered legal unless all members have been notified; this task usually falls to the clerk of the organization as a whole. For subsequent meetings, the committee clerk will notify all members.

Chairing a committee The rules that govern assemblies are relaxed in committees. As a result, the chairperson can make motions and participate in debate without leaving the chair. The chair of a committee, like the presiding officer of any organization, guides the discussion rather than directs it. The chair must be able to explain the committee's goals to members, coordinate all suggestions, and make sure that all statements are clearly understood. Above all else, the chair must keep an open mind about the points that committee members raise.

Disciplining committee members A committee has no authority to punish its members. It can report to the assembly about what has transpired in the committee, however. The account must be in the form of a written report.

Adjourning a committee meeting If a committee intends to meet again, it need only adjourn or adjourn to meet at a later date. Absent members should be notified of the date of the next meeting, although this is not mandatory. When a special committee has completed its business, a member should make a motion that the committee *rise*. This is the same as a motion to *adjourn sine die* and empowers the chair to make a report to the presiding officer of the assembly. The motion to rise cannot be used in a standing committee, for it would signal the end of the committee.

First committee meeting checklist Use the following checklist to organize the initial meeting of a committee:

- List of committee members
- Copy of the resolution referred to committee
- Statement of the committee's task, if available
- Any special instructions
- Statement of the committee's powers
- Copies of any pertinent rules
- Copies of any relevant correspondence
- Copies of any previous decisions relevant to the issue
- Information about the report format
- Date the report is due to the membership

Making Committees Meaningful

Unfortunately many committees are misused. Too often they become burial grounds for unpleasant issues, a method of rewarding members and distributing titles to friends, or a device for giving everyone something to do. Occasionally they are even used to placate chronic troublemakers. "If we put these four disgruntled members on a minor committee," the argument runs, "they can vent their anger privately. We won't have to deal with them at the general meeting." But correctly used, committees serve an important and useful function within an organization. How can you make sure that the committees in your organization serve a real purpose?

Useful work First of all, no committee should be appointed unless it is needed. Members of a committee that have no real work will soon recognize this fact and lose interest in the committee. Busywork serves no one's best interests.

Timely agenda Set a reasonable time limit. Most people work better when they know that their work must be completed by a specific date. Place the committee's report on the assembly's agenda, so members will know that the end date is real.

Membership Try to select people who work together well. This is especially crucial if the committee is charged with a delicate task. This does not mean that everyone has to have the same personality, but try to match people whose personalities complement each other. For instance, you might match a detail-oriented member with someone who is more idea-oriented. This way, the committee will have someone to generate the ideas and someone else to fit them into the schedule.

Committee Reports

To complete its task, a committee must report to the entire assembly, describing its findings and including any resolutions. The entire committee submits a report. The report should be written, unless it is very brief. Except in certain instances noted below, the report can include only that information agreed to by the majority of the committee members. In most instances, a committee's report is accepted by the assembly, and this report determines what course of action the assembly will take on an issue. The minority, however, may submit its views in writing, but a minority report can be acted on only when the committee votes to substitute one for the majority report.

Committee Reports at a Glance

When to Make Reports	Who Makes Reports
Regular meetings	Only those committees that have reports to make: standing committees in the order they are listed in the bylaws, special committees in the order appointed

Annual meetings	All officers, boards, and committees
Specific Report	**Action to Take**
Minority report	May be submitted to the assembly by one or more committee members
Secretary's report or minutes	Circulated and read; may be approved by general consent or by a motion after any necessary corrections have been made
Treasurer's report	Does not require any action; filed for audit
Auditor's report	Must be adopted or rejected by the assembly
Nominating committee report	Does not require any action
Bylaws committee	As a main motion, usually requires a two-thirds vote for adoption
Adoption of all reports	The assembly can adopt all or part of a report. It is not necessary to make a motion to receive an informational report that has no recommendation.

Types of reports Committee reports can be divided into two types: annual reports and single-item reports. *Annual reports,* submitted according to the organization's bylaws, are most often for informational purposes only. They summarize the committee's work for the year and may or may not contain recommendations. *Single-item reports* can be submitted at any time, concern only one item of business, and may take different forms, depending on their function.

How to write a committee report As with nearly all group writing, a committee report is amassed in stages, as members contribute their opinions, phrases, and suggestions. This can be a cumbersome and time-consuming process, so the following steps are suggested to streamline the process:

Appoint one main writer To expedite the actual composition, have one member of the committee write the entire first draft of the report. Select a person who not only writes well but also is well-respected by the committee and represents the majority opinion. The person should know that the report is written in the third-person (not "I [or we] report," but rather "The committee reports").

Study the draft The draft of the report is reproduced and a copy given to every member. Allow ample time for the members to study the draft at their leisure. Every member of the committee reads the draft all the way through, marking it with specific suggestions, emendations, and corrections.

Edit the draft At a specified meeting, the committee chair then reads the draft aloud, one paragraph at a time. The chair should pause after each paragraph and say, "Are there any amendments any member would like to make here?" The members discuss proposed changes, and the clerk then makes the changes on his or her copy. This is most easily accomplished if the clerk makes the changes directly online on a desktop, laptop, or notebook computer.

Adopt or revise After the whole report has been read and discussed, the committee can adopt it at once if everyone is satisfied. If there have been many changes, the committee can have the clerk prepare a clean copy for the committee to reconsider. Or, if there is widespread dissatisfaction, the committee can reject the entire report and request a new one prepared in its place and then repeat the process.

Report contents Complete committee reports include the following items:

- Identification of the committee submitting the report
- Statement of the resolution given to the committee
- Summary of the methods of investigation the committee used
- Summary of the information the committee gathered
- Summary of the work accomplished
- Committee findings
- Committee recommendations or resolutions

Report format Committee reports are usually not addressed or dated. If the report is very important, all members should sign it. In other instances, only the chair need sign the report, adding the word *chair* or *chairperson* after the signature. Committee reports usually follow the form of the samples below:

Standing Committee
Report of the [name of committee]
The committee on [specific committee charge]
reports that [text of the report].
[Chair of the Committee]

Special or Select Committee
Report of the [name of committee]
The committee to which was referred
[specific committee charge], having considered
the matter, reports [text of the report].
[Chair of the Committee]

When the committee prepares its report, it should be careful to include the combined majority voice of the entire committee. This is in keeping with the aim of parliamentary procedure to reflect the voice of the majority while protecting the rights of the minority. What happens when a minority does not agree with the majority? In these instances, the minority can file its own report.

Minority reports Minority reports express the views of those committee members who do not concur with the committee report. A minority report is a privilege, not a right, since appointing a committee in the first place implies that the assembly is primarily interested in the findings of the majority of the committee members, not the minority. Check your bylaws: a minority report is usually allowed by the assembly when permission is requested.

Rights of the minority When committee members debate their report, any member of the committee who does not agree with the majority has the right to speak individually in opposition. The minority also has the right to recommend the following options with regard to the report:

- Rejection of the resolution
- Amendment of the resolution
- Adoption of some other suitable motion to dispose of the resolution appropriately
- Acceptance of part of the report

If a written committee report is signed by everyone on the committee who agrees and a committee member is in agreement with the entire report except for one or more items, the member can add a statement to the report. In the statement, the member should explain his or her agreement with the report except the part so specified and then sign the statement. This is done last, after every member in agreement has signed the report.

Format of a minority report A minority report may take the form shown in this sample.

> Report of the [name of the committee]
>
> The undersigned, a minority of the members of the [name of committee] appointed to [task of the committee] to which we were referred, not agreeing with the majority, desire to express their views in the case [text of the report].
>
> [Minority members]

Whether the views of the minority are formally presented or not, any member can move at a regular meeting of the entire assembly that the resolutions proposed by the committee be amended, postponed indefinitely, or that some other appropriate action be taken.

Confidentiality Whatever is said in committee cannot be repeated outside the confines of the meeting. No one can make reference to what occurred during the committee deliberations unless it is by report of the committee or by general consent.

Delivering the report After the committee report is completed and every member who concurs has signed it, the report follows a specific route, as explained below:

1. The committee chair or a member of the committee appointed for this purpose brings the report to a regular meeting of the entire assembly.
2. Standing committees report first, in the order in which they are listed in the bylaws. Then special committees report, arranged in the order in which they were appointed. Only those special committees who are prepared or instructed to report are called on.
3. Each speaker explains his or her report to the assembly and reads it to the entire group.
4. The representative hands the report to the clerk of the entire assembly.
5. When a report is very long, it is usually read when the group is ready to consider it formally.
6. The report will then lie on the table until the group is ready to consider it.
7. After the reading, the committee representative or another member can move that the report be accepted. Usually the assembly will not vote on accepting a committee report. However, if anyone objects, there must be a formal motion and vote.
8. The fact that the report has been read to the assembly indicates that the assembly has already received it. There is no need to make a motion to formally receive the report; that has already been accomplished through the reading.

If the committee wants to submit a minority report, it is read to everyone after the majority report is read. The minority report cannot be acted on by the assembly unless a motion is made to substitute it for the majority report. If the motion to substitute is passed, the minority report becomes the report of the committee and is the only one considered.

Acting on the report When the entire assembly is ready to formally consider a committee report, the assembly must decide what action to take on it. The organization can make one of the following decisions:

- File the report without comment
- Return the report to the committee for additional information

- Refer the report to another committee for study
- Give the report to an officer for study
- Give the report to a member for study
- Refer the report to an auditing committee
- Postpone consideration to a more convenient time
- Accept the entire report
- Reject the entire report
- Accept only part of the report
- Reject the report and substitute the minority report in its place

Implement recommendations When a report has recommendations, a member of the committee can make a motion that the organization accept the recommendations. In these instances, a second is not required. When the person making the motion is not a member of the organization, however, a second is required.

Adopt the entire report In some cases, the assembly may wish to adopt the entire report. This means that the membership accepts every single word of the report. A member can make a motion to *adopt, accept,* or *agree to* the report. All three terms mean the same thing; *adopt* is the word used most often. Even though these terms have the same definition as far as parliamentary law is concerned, they do carry shades of meaning that can affect their use; here are suggestions for using the terms:

- Adopt—For a report that contains opinions and facts but also includes resolutions
- Accept—For a report that contains statements of opinion and facts
- Agree to—For a report in any instance

A relatively infrequent action, the motion to adopt the report should not be made by the person giving the report. In addition, the motion requires a second. Adopting an entire report is not recommended except when the report will be published under the name of the entire organization.

When the motion is accepted, the report becomes part of the entire assembly's work. In effect, it is as though the committee had never existed. When the committee has completed its work, a committee member makes a motion for the committee to report to the chair of the assembly. This is called a *motion to rise;* it is the same as a motion to adjourn. After the committee makes its report, its work is finished; the committee is then disbanded.

Mass Meeting

A *mass meeting* is a meeting of an unorganized group which has been called to address a particular problem and is open to anyone interested in attending. It is understood that the people calling the meeting have the right to restrict the meeting to the subject at hand, but those in attendance have the right to decide what action will be taken on the issue.

Organizing a Mass Meeting

As with any meeting, successful preplanning is crucial to ensuring a productive mass meeting. Below are some suggestions for organizing a mass meeting.

Announcing the meeting The announcement is known as the *call of the meeting*. It must include the following information:

Date of the meeting
Time of the meeting
Place where the meeting will be held
Purpose of the meeting

Planning the meeting Because so many people are involved in a mass meeting and the potential for misrepresentation is great, the organizers should decide on the following items before the meeting:

- Who should chair the meeting
- Who should be the secretary
- Who should call the meeting to order and nominate the choice for chairperson
- Who should nominate the secretary
- What rules (if any) should be suggested
- Who should state the purpose of the meeting

Mass Meeting Rules

Most mass meetings use only parliamentary law as their rules. But if you anticipate conflict during the meeting, you may wish to have the assembly agree on an authoritative parliamentary guide and pass additional standing rules. (These standing rules are similar to those adopted at a convention, see page 87.) The call of the meeting functions as bylaws.

Running a Mass Meeting

Electing officers As with any first meeting, a mass meeting opens with the election of a presiding officer and a secretary. The election of officers should be the first order of business, directly after the meeting is called to order. Considering the number of people likely to be present, the most effective way to run the election is through a voice vote. To help ensure responsible leadership, the meeting planners should propose the candidates they have selected before the meeting. People attending the meeting are free to nominate additional candidates and to vote for anyone they choose, but in most instances the candidates selected by the meeting organizers will be elected. The nominations should follow the form below:

▶ A person says, "The meeting will come to order. I nominate [person's name] as presiding officer of this meeting."

The person who makes the nomination should run the election, calling for a vote on each nominee in turn.

After the chair is elected, he or she takes the floor and calls for nominations for secretary, as the following example illustrates:

▶ The chair says, "We will now accept nominations for secretary."

The election of secretary follows the same form as the election of the chair. After being elected, the secretary immediately begins to take the minutes of the meeting. Any additional officers are elected in the same way.

Opening business After the officers have been elected, the meeting turns to its purpose. The chair asks the secretary to read the *call of the meeting,* which includes the names of the people who arranged the meeting. Below is an example of this process:

▶ The chair says, "Will the secretary now read the call of the meeting."

Either the chair or a person designated for this purpose explains the reason for the meeting and what the sponsors hope to accomplish.

Drafting resolutions After discussion, it is time to offer one or more resolutions to achieve the purpose of the meeting. The resolutions can be offered at that time if they have been prepared in advance or a committee can be appointed to write the resolutions. If the resolutions have been prepared and everyone has read a copy of them, a member can move that they be adopted. The motion requires a second. As with any other main motion, a resolution is restated by the chair and opened to debate and amendment. Unless special rules have been adopted to the contrary, standard debate rules are in effect: No member can speak to the motion for more than 10 minutes, and there is no appeal from the chair's decision in assigning the floor.

All resolutions should be in writing and follow this format (see also page 91):

> ▶ "*Resolved,* That . . ."
> *or*
> "*Resolved,* That it is the sense of this meeting that . . ."

If the resolution has not been prepared in advance, a person in attendance can make a motion to establish a committee. The motion would be made as follows:

> ▶ A person says, "I move that the chair appoint a committee of [number] members to draft resolutions expressing the sense of this meeting on the issue of ________."

As a main motion, it requires a second, is debatable, and can be amended.

If the committee will need a great deal of time to draft the resolution, the meeting can recess. If not, the meeting can continue and the members can conduct other business or have a program. When the resolutions committee returns, the chair asks for its report. Below is a sample of this process:

> ▶ The presiding officer says, "Is the resolutions committee prepared to offer its report?"
> The committee chair answers, "Yes, we are."
> The presiding officer says, "If there is no objection, the chairperson will now offer the committee's report [pause]. The presiding officer recognizes the chair of the resolutions committee."
> The committee chair reports, "[Mr. or Madam] Chairper-

son, the resolutions committee recommends that on behalf of the committee I move the adoption of the following resolution(s): [committee chair reads the resolutions]."

The chair restates all the resolutions and, as with any main motion, they are open to debate.

Adjourning the meeting When all business has been completed, a member moves for adjournment. If no time has been set for another meeting, this motion will disband the assembly. The move to adjourn is a main motion and as such is open for debate and amendment. Or, a member can move to adjourn but set the time for another meeting, as in the following example:

▶ The member says, "I move that we adjourn until six o'clock Thursday evening."

While there is still business on the floor, a move to adjourn is not in order. If a member wants to call for adjournment while there is still pending business, the following rules are in effect:

- The motion to adjourn is privileged if the time for another meeting has already been set.
- Use the motion Fix the Time to Which to Adjourn if no time has been set for the next meeting. Then use the motion to Adjourn.

Convention

Organizing a Convention

A *convention* is an assembly of delegates selected specifically to represent a larger group of people in an assembly. In most cases, a local organization will select delegates to attend a national or international meeting of the group. Conventions can be large or small, brief or extended, educational or business-oriented.

Selecting Delegates

Each organization's bylaws should specify how delegates are selected to attend conventions. The presiding officer and other high-ranking officers are usually the authorized delegates, but each organization can select its delegates according to its own bylaws. The bylaws should include provisions for selecting alternates as well. Such provisions normally include a specific number of years of service, membership in good standing, and so on. It is important to select a sufficient number of alternates to make sure that the organization will be fully represented in case a delegate cannot attend the convention.

Hosting a Convention

Hosting a convention is similar to running any large meeting (see page 82). In addition, since conventions have special requirements, the host organization sets up specific committees to handle the preparations. The first three committees described below must be included, but any others may also be constituted, depending on the needs of the host organization. The committees and their duties are as follows:

Credentials Committee

- Distributes information about credentials to each organization entitled to representation at the convention
- Reads each application to verify its contents
- Notifies organizations if their delegates are not eligible
- Compiles membership and registration lists of officers, delegates, and alternates for the convention
- Runs the convention registration
- Prepares the committee's first report to the convention

Rules Committee

- Prepares rules specific to the convention
- Includes parliamentary and nonparliamentary rules

Program Committee

- Prepares an agenda for the convention
- Includes schedules of meetings, business matters, and special events

Arrangements Committee

- Selects the convention site
- Books the hall
- Arranges for hotel accommodations

- Selects the menu
- Books speakers and other entertainment
- Escorts dignitaries and honored guests from public transportation to the convention site
- Sets up the seating arrangements
- Staffs an information center

Resolutions Committee

- Drafts resolutions
- Screens main motions that come before the assembly

Conducting Convention Business

At the first business meeting (not the opening ceremonies) of a convention, the delegates form an official organization by accepting reports from the first three committees listed above—credentials, rules, and program committees. The chair of each committee gives his or her respective report, as the following examples show:

▶ The credentials committee chair says, "Enclosed is a list of the voting members of this convention and their alternates. On behalf of the committee, I move that the list of delegates submitted become the official list of the voting members of this assembly."

The rules committee chair says, "Enclosed is a list of the proposed rules for this convention. On behalf of the committee, I move that this list of rules become the official rules of this assembly."

The program committee chair says, "[Mr. or Madam] Chair, a printed copy of the proposed program has been distributed to every delegate. On behalf of the program committee, I move the printed program become the official program of this assembly."

While the committee reports can be debated and amended, in most instances they are accepted as offered, if the committees are reliable. Convention rules require a two-thirds vote for adoption. After these three reports have been accepted, the convention is officially organized.

When all business has been completed, a member moves

for adjournment. The correct motion is *adjournment sine die* (see page 88).

Parliamentary Rules of Order at Conventions

The following parliamentary procedures apply to most conventions:

- Convention business usually starts with the following three items: (1) adoption of credentials committee report, (2) adoption of convention rules, and (3) adoption of program.
- Delegates are expected to be aware of the feelings of the group they represent so they will know how to vote on certain matters.
- Unless otherwise specified by the bylaws, the convention quorum is a majority of the delegates who have registered, even though some of the members may have left.
- There are usually detailed procedures for submitting resolutions, with a resolutions (or reference) committee increasingly being used to review resolutions.
- Detailed procedures for nominations and elections usually apply, as do specific requirements for adopting amendments to the bylaws.
- The motion to reconsider an action can be made not only on the day the action was taken but also on the first business day following the day on which the action was taken.
- A main motion or resolution cannot be postponed to the next meeting, because it is usually a year away (the next annual convention).
- A tabled motion remains alive throughout the convention, but if it is not taken from the table before adjournment, it dies with adjournment. In this case, it may not be taken from the table at the next convention.
- All business that is unfinished when the convention adjourns *falls to the ground,* or expires.
- The only way to carry over business from one convention to the next is by referring it to committee, to the board of directors, and so on, with instructions to this body to report back at next year's convention.
- A main motion or resolution that is rejected at a convention may not be renewed at the same convention even though the convention takes place over several days.
- Convention minutes should not be held over for approval at next year's convention. Instead, they should be referred to a special committee or to a board of directors for approval.

- The motion to adjourn, when made to end a convention, is considered to be an incidental main motion. As such, it follows the rules of a main motion rather than the rules of a privileged motion to adjourn. It requires a second, and it can be debated, amended, and reconsidered. In addition, it must have a majority vote to pass.

Chapter 5

Motions

What Is a Motion?

A *motion* is a proposal for action by the group. Before meeting participants can consider any proposal, it must be placed before the assembly in the form of a motion. In most instances, motions are made in the following format:

▶ "I move that [specific content of motion]."

Kinds of motions There are two principal types of motions: main motions and secondary motions. Each of these kinds has subcategories, as follows:

Main Motions	*Secondary Motions*
Resolutions	Subsidiary motions
Original main motions	Privileged motions
Incidental main motions	Incidental motions

Each type of motion accomplishes a different action and is treated differently. Main motions are the most common type of motion, made most often in a parliamentary assembly.

Main Motions

TYPES OF MAIN MOTIONS AT A GLANCE

Motion	Description	Page
Resolutions	Stating a policy or principle	91
Original Main Motions	Presenting a new topic	94
Incidental Main Motions	Relating to assembly business	94

Definition of a Main Motion

A *main motion* introduces a new item of business, the matter to be considered by the assembly. It is a motion that brings business before the group. A main motion can also be called a *principal motion* or a *principal question,* and it can technically be on any subject. However, the motion can be ruled out of order if it conflicts with the organization's bylaws, constitution, standing rules, or any resolution already agreed upon by the assembly. If such a motion is introduced, it will be considered null and void. Since only one order of business can be considered at a time, only one main motion can be considered at a time.

Characteristics of a Main Motion

Rank Parliamentary motions have rank, which means that certain motions take precedence over others. The name *main motion* is somewhat misleading, the term *main* implying that these are the chief motions. In fact, main motions are the lowest-ranking motions and are superseded by the higher-ranking subsidiary motions, privileged motions, and incidental motions. A main motion cannot be made when another motion is being considered by the group, because it does not have precedence over any other motion. It yields to subsidiary, incidental, and privileged motions.

Use A main motion cannot be applied to any other motion. However, other motions can be applied to it. If a secondary motion is applied to it, the secondary motion stays with the main motion until both are voted on or the matter is resolved by the chair's ruling.

Further, a main motion is not in order when there is another motion on the floor.

A main motion has other specific qualities that distinguish it from other motions. A main motion can be:

- Amended in five different ways
- Debated
- Divided
- Laid on the table
- Objected to
- Postponed
- Reconsidered
- Referred to committee
- Renewed (if rejected)
- Rescinded (after approval)
- Seconded
- Terminated
- Voted on
- Withdrawn

Memorize this acronym to help remember the steps in handling a main motion and the order in which they can occur:

S D A M R

S Second
D Debate
A Amend
M Majority Vote
R Reconsider

In most instances a main motion requires a majority vote to pass, except when such a vote contradicts the organization's bylaws. In addition, a vote on a main motion is not valid when it supersedes the rights of members, in which case a two-thirds vote is needed.

Main motions can be classified into three different types: resolutions, original main motions, and incidental main motions. Each type is described below.

Resolutions

Resolutions are a type of main motion: resolutions and main motions differ only in their format. All resolutions are main motions, but not all main motions are resolutions. Resolutions usually state a policy, principle, feeling, or sentiment. As a result, they tend to have an explanatory preamble which is used to explain why the resolution is important and should be supported by the membership.

Each reason in the preamble usually begins with the word *whereas,* which serves as a bridge to introduce the explanation for the resolution. Although preambles have become customary, they do not have to be included in any resolution. Use one or more preambles only when the resolution truly requires a background statement. Unfortunately, some people believe that a preamble makes a resolution sound more official and so include one (or more), even when it is not necessary.

Be selective when drafting resolutions: include only that material necessary to convey the meaning fully. Brief, well-crafted resolutions are often more effective than long, windy ones. Further, it is usually better to divide a very long resolution into separate, smaller ones. Overloaded resolutions can be difficult to understand, which may predispose members to vote them down. Remember that a primary aim of parliamentary law is to clarify and streamline the process of decision-making, not to muddy it.

The list below shows the most common types of resolutions and gives a template for each. Notice the form used for preambles and resolutions. According to the conventions of parliamentary law, the word *Resolved* is capitalized in resolutions, and the word *Whereas* is capitalized in preambles. In addition, the word *Resolved* is usually italicized or underlined; it is always followed by the capitalized word *That*. The word *Whereas* may be followed by the capitalized word *The*. Each preamble begins a separate paragraph and ends with a semicolon.

- *Resolutions without a preamble*
  Resolved, That [text of the resolution]
- *Resolutions with a preamble of one "Whereas"*
  Whereas, The [text of the preamble];
  Resolved, That [text of the resolution]
- *Resolutions with a preamble of more than one "Whereas"*
  Whereas, [text of the preamble];
  Whereas, [text of the preamble];
  Resolved, That [text of the resolution]
- *Resolutions with more than one "Resolved"*
  Resolved, That [text of the resolution]
  Resolved, That [text of the resolution]
  Resolved, That [text of the resolution]
- *Resolutions with any combination of the above*
  Whereas, [text of the preamble];
  Whereas, [text of the preamble];
  Whereas, [text of the preamble];
  Resolved, That [text of the resolution]
  Resolved, That [text of the resolution]
  Resolved, That [text of the resolution]

The following sample texts illustrate resolutions with and without preambles.

Sample Resolutions

Resolution with a preamble:

Whereas, The Board of Trustees has voted to refurnish the district office on Smith Street to accommodate the merger with district #16, Fairway schools;

Resolved, That the Board of Trustees of the Hicksville School Board hereby awards the bid for office furniture in the base bid amount of Fifty Seven Thousand, Eight Hundred and Seventy Six ($57,876.00) dollars to Walder's, Milwaukee, Wisconsin, together with the following alternates:
Alternate #2—in the amount of Thirty Thousand Four Hundred ($30,400.00) dollars for seating;
Alternate #4—in the amount of Three Thousand Seven Hundred and Nine and 80/100 ($3,709.80) dollars for soft seating for waiting areas;
Alternate #6—in the amount of Eight Thousand Four Hundred and Twenty Four ($8,424.00) dollars for sofas;
Alternate #7—in the amount of Thirty Nine Thousand Five Hundred Seven and 60/100 ($39,507.60) dollars.

The total price of the base bid and four alternates thus being One Hundred Thirty Nine Thousand Nine Hundred Seventeen and 40/100 ($139,917.40) dollars, subject to the Bidder providing performance and payment bonds, insurance certificates, and fully executed contracts as required by the bid specifications, and subject to review and confirmation of Bid Award by the Board of Directors.

Resolution without a preamble:

Resolved, That the Board of Directors of the Tri-State Cultural Board will draft a position statement to be sent to the governor to protest the proposed drastic cutbacks in funding to the arts.

Resolutions tend to be longer than motions. Due to their length and complexity, resolutions are often presented in writing. It is recommended that members draft pivotal resolutions in committees to ensure that the language is clear, precise, and correct. Even less critical resolutions should be vetted by other members before being presented to the assembly. Such careful checking can help prevent careless errors from slipping through. Other than the differences described above, resolutions are treated in the same manner as other main motions.

Original Main Motions

An original main motion presents a new topic for debate. The most commonly used type of main motion, it may be made orally or in writing. Below are some examples of original main motions:

► A member says, "I move that the Society hold its annual holiday party at the Three Village Inn, on Saturday, December 18, at 8:00 to 11:00 p.m."

or

A member says, "I move that the Parent-Teacher Association sponsor a candy sale, the proceeds to be used to defray the cost of the new computer system."

or

A member says, "I move that the Club contribute $100.00 to support a visiting scholar from China."

Incidental Main Motions

An incidental main motion is tied into events before the assembly. Unlike a main motion or a resolution, it does not initiate business. Like these motions, however, an incidental main motion can only be proposed when there is no other motion on the floor. A motion to take a recess is an incidental main motion, because it is directly linked to what is happening in the meeting. In the same way, motions to accept a committee report or limit debate are incidental main motions. The following is a list of incidental main motions:

Adjourn
Adjourn to a future time
Adopt a matter previously considered
Adopt a report (accept, agree to)
Adopt bylaws (to form a new organization)
Adopt constitution (to form a new organization)
Adopt convention agenda
Adopt parliamentary standing rules in a convention
Adopt revised bylaws
Adopt special rules
Adopt standing rules

Amend convention agenda
Amend convention rules
Amend special rules
Annul (or rescind or repeal)
Approve the minutes
Confirm (or ratify)
Discharge a committee
Extend debate
Fix the Time to Which to Adjourn
Limit debate
Make a special order
Nominations
Order of the Day
Question of privilege
Recess
Refer a matter to committee
Repeal (or annul or rescind)
Rescind (or repeal or annul)
Voting

Notice of Main Motions

Specific main motions can be included in the call of the meeting to notify members that these motions will be introduced at the next meeting. The entire motion is included in the call of the meeting, worded exactly as it will be proposed. In this way, members will have prior notice that certain motions will be open for debate and know the exact content of the motion. Such notice can help members decide what positions they will take on the issues and to prepare their reasons. The notice can be sent via mail or transmitted electronically through E-mail or fax. For instance, the call of the meeting could include this sentence: "At the November 15, 1994, meeting Ms. Hyte will move to discharge the fund-raising committee."

In other instances, previous notice can be given orally at a meeting. In these circumstances, only the intention to propose the motion must be announced; the full text of the motion is not necessary. The member states his or her intention, and the chair repeats the statement. The following example illustrates this process:

▶ A member says, "I give notice that at the November 15, 1994, meeting I will move that the Society purchase three new computers and all necessary software."

> The chair says, "Notice has been given that at the November 15, 1994, meeting Member A will move that the Society purchase three new computers and all the necessary software."

When the notice is given orally, it should be included in the minutes as well. This helps ensure that all members will be notified, especially those who did not attend the meeting.

Whether or not the main motion is included in the call of the meeting in writing or given orally at a meeting depends on the nature of the motion itself. Any main motion can be included in the call of the meeting. In actual practice, the main motions that are most often included are those that change or cancel some previous action that the assembly has taken. The following main motions must have prior notice if they are to be ratified by a majority vote:

- Discharge a Committee
- Amend Something Previously Adopted
- Rescind

Other motions, such as that to adopt special rules, require a two-thirds vote as well as previous notice.

Subsidiary Motions

TYPES OF SUBSIDIARY MOTIONS AT A GLANCE

Motion	Description	Page
Amend	Tailoring a motion to be more specific and acceptable	98
Commit or Refer	Sending a motion to a committee for further study	106
Lay on the Table	Setting aside a main motion to deal with more urgent business	110
Limit or Extend Debate	Decreasing or increasing the amount of time to debate an issue	113
Postpone to a Certain Time	Moving consideration of the motion to a later time	115

Definition of a subsidiary motion A subsidiary motion is linked to a main motion to aid in its disposition. The need for subsidiary motions relates to the underlying principle of parliamentary law, to deal with business in the most fair and efficient way possible. As a result, only one question can be considered at a time. Once a motion is before an assembly, it must be adopted or rejected by a vote. If this cannot be accomplished, the assembly must deal with the motion through a subsidiary motion, which is applied to other motions. In this way, subsidiary motions can dispense with other motions.

Subsidiary motions can be made while a main motion is still being considered; this will not violate the rule of considering only one motion at a time. When a subsidiary motion is made, therefore, there will be two motions on the floor at once, as this example shows:

▶ Mr. Fishman offers a main motion when he says, "I move that the Society assess each member of the homeowners' association $500 to clean up the refuse in the Solovey yard." Ms. Witman makes a subsidiary motion when she says, "I move that this motion be postponed indefinitely."

There are now two motions on the floor, the main motion to assess each homeowner $500 and the subsidiary motion to postpone the main motion. The subsidiary motion is decided first, then the main motion.

Qualities of a subsidiary motion All subsidiary motions share four qualities that distinguish them from main motions:

1. Unlike a main motion, a subsidiary motion can never stand alone. As a *subsidiary* motion, it is always applied to another motion.
2. A subsidiary motion always changes the status of the motion to which it is applied by modifying it in some way.

3. The subsidiary motion must be decided before the assembly can act on the main motion.
4. Subsidiary motions are treated in a specific order, as explained below.

Types of subsidiary motions There are seven subsidiary motions, listed below in alphabetical order:

1. Amend
2. Commit or Refer
3. Lay on the Table
4. Limit or Extend Debate
5. Postpone to a Certain Time
6. Postpone Indefinitely
7. Previous Question

Order of precedence Subsidiary motions must be acted on before the main motion can once again be considered. This means that subsidiary motions supersede or take precedence over the main motion. Another way of saying this is that the main motion *yields* to the subsidiary motion. But a subsidiary motion gives way to privileged and incidental motions. Here is the order of precedence for subsidiary motions from lowest to highest rank:

1. Postpone Indefinitely (see page 118)
2. Amend (see page 98)
3. Commit, Refer, or Recommit (see page 106)
4. Postpone to a Certain Time (see page 115)
5. Limit or Extend Debate (see page 113)
6. Previous Question (see page 120)
7. Lay on the Table (see page 110)

The individual who has the floor can make any of these secondary motions except the one to Amend when a motion of lower order is being considered by the assembly. But a member cannot make a subsidiary motion if one of higher order is being considered. Each motion is explained below in detail.

Amend

If a member makes a main motion that is not clear or is too great in scope, the motion can be clarified or narrowed by being amended. The subsidiary motion to Amend allows members to tailor their main motions to their specific purpose. As a result, the main motion will be more likely to accomplish its intention and to receive a majority vote of the assembly. Since it is difficult to craft a main motion that is precise, the motion to Amend is used often. This motion does not allow members to substantially alter a main motion, however; the changes made must relate specifically to the original main motion.

Using a motion to Amend A motion to Amend can be applied to any main motion. In addition, it can be applied to any motion whose wording can be changed. The following lists illustrate which motions can and cannot be amended:

Motions that can be amended

- Amend an undebatable question
- Consideration by Paragraph
- Division of a Question
- Extend Debate
- Fix the Time to Which to Adjourn
- Limit Debate
- Nominations
- Recess
- Voting

Motions that cannot be amended

- Adjourn (when privileged)
- Amend an amendment to an undebatable motion
- Appeal
- Call for the Orders of the Day
- Calling a member to order
- Dispense with reading the minutes
- Division of the Assembly
- Lay on the Table
- Objection to the Consideration of a Question
- Parliamentary Inquiry
- Permission to Read Papers
- Permission to speak after being disciplined
- Permission to Withdraw a Motion
- Point of Information
- Point of Order
- Previous Question
- Raise a Question of Privilege
- Reconsider
- Reconsider an undebatable motion

- Request Permission to Modify a Motion
- Suspend the Rules
- Take from the Table

Voting As with all subsidiary motions, the motion to Amend is applied to a main motion and requires a majority vote to pass. But even if the motion to Amend is passed, the same vote does not pass the original main motion; it must be voted on separately. By not passing a motion to Amend, the members show that they prefer the original wording of the main motion. In the same way, members' votes on the motion to Amend are not in any way tied with their votes on the main motion; each is a separate vote.

If there is a motion to amend the main motion, the vote is taken first on the amendment and then on the original motion. If there are two motions to amend on the main motion, the vote is taken on the second motion to amend, then the first motion to amend, and then the main motion itself as it may or may not have been amended.

Kinds of amendments There are three kinds of amendments: friendly amendments, primary amendments, and secondary amendments; each is explained below. There are no third-degree amendments.

Friendly amendments These offer slight corrections to a motion but do not substantially change the motion. If members agree, friendly amendments are in order at any time during the process of making a main motion.

Primary (or first-degree) amendments A primary amendment must be germane to the motion to which it is applied. These amendments can themselves be amended.

Secondary (or second-degree) amendments A secondary amendment seeks to alter a primary amendment, to which it must apply. Secondary amendments do not apply directly to the main motion. There are no amendments permitted on secondary amendments.

• Guidelines for amending motions

1. If the amendment is simple and accepted by every member, it can be adopted by general or unanimous consent. In this way, it does not have to go through the formal process of being amended.

2. If a motion is complex and not accepted by the majority of members, amending it may simply confuse the issue and take up too much meeting time. In such cases, it is usually better to vote the motion down and then to propose a more precise and acceptable motion in its place.
3. Once a motion has been made, seconded, and repeated by the chair, a member does not need the permission of the mover to amend it. The motion has become the property of the assembly.
4. To be valid, an amendment must pertain to the motion and the specific change the member desires in its wording and meaning. An amendment that is not relevant should not be considered by the assembly.
5. A motion to amend may be hostile, but it may not be negative. For example, the motion to amend can change the word *praise* to *censure*. The motion cannot change *praise* to *not praise,* however.
6. A motion to amend is itself amendable.
7. The motion to amend can be debated when the motion to which it applies can be debated.
8. There is no limit to the number of motions to amend that can be applied to any main motion overall. However, no more than two motions to amend can be pending on a main motion at the same time.
9. Two amendments of the same degree (primary or secondary) cannot be considered at the same time.
10. In a resolution with a preamble, amend the resolution first and the preamble second.
11. The motion to amend can be reconsidered.
12. Presiding officers or secretaries may require that amendments be submitted in writing.
13. When an amendment has been adopted, the way it is phrased cannot then be changed unless the wording is so altered as to constitute an entirely new proposition. If the amended motion is substantially different from the original one and members will benefit from additional time to study the changes, a motion to Commit can be made (see page 106).

Methods of amending motions There are five ways to amend motions: by adding words, inserting words, striking out words, striking out and inserting words, and substituting a sentence or paragraph. Words added, inserted, or struck out should be consecutive and not scattered, to make it easier for members to understand the amended motion. Each of these methods is illustrated below, arranged from least to most complex. Select the method that most easily tailors the motion to its specific purpose.

By adding a word or words at the end of a motion One of the most common ways to amend a main motion is by adding words at the end of the sentence or sentences. For example, to amend the main motion "I move that we purchase a new sign," add the words "at a cost not to exceed $200" at the end of the motion. The amended motion would then read, "I move that we purchase a new sign at a cost not to exceed $200."

By inserting a word or words in the body of the motion A main motion can also be amended by inserting words within the sentence itself, not at the end. To amend the main motion "I move that we purchase a new sign," insert the word *club* between the words *new* and *sign*. The amended motion would then read, "I move that we purchase a new club sign."

By striking out one or more consecutive words In addition to adding and inserting words, motions can be amended by removing words, phrases, or clauses. To amend the main motion "I move that we hold our winter holiday party at the Fox Hollow Inn and our summer holiday party at the Crest Haven Country Club," strike out the words "and our summer holiday party at the Crest Haven Country Club." The amended motion then reads, "I move that we hold our winter holiday party at the Fox Hollow Inn."

By striking out one or more words and inserting others Two of the methods can be combined to make a motion as specific as possible. For example, to amend the main motion "I move that we hold our annual convention at the Marriott Hotel in San Diego, California," strike the phrase *San Diego* and insert the phrase *San Francisco*. The amended motion then reads, "I move that we hold our annual convention at the Marriott Hotel in San Francisco, California."

Replacing a pending motion in its entirety with another motion related to the same subject With this method, the mover is substituting another motion by replacing a sentence or paragraph. For this to be a valid amendment, it must be on the same subject as the original motion. Because this method usually requires the most substantive changes, the mover should write out the amendment before proposing it. For example, to amend the main motion "I move that we hold our annual membership dinner at the Bay

Ridge Country Club," substitute the following motion, "I move that we contribute $500 to a local charity in place of holding our annual membership dinner."

The following dialogue illustrates one possible way to amend a main motion to make it more acceptable to the majority.

▶ Ms. Bosso says, "Madam Chair."
The chair responds, "Ms. Bosso."
Ms. Bosso says, "I move that the Club donate $100 to the local shelter."
Mr. Ryan says, "I second the motion."
The chair says, "It has been moved and seconded that the Club donate $100 to the local shelter. The motion is now open for debate."
Ms. Bosso says, "With the cold weather coming on, there will be more and more people in need of hot meals. The shelter is going to be very crowded."
Mr. Henry says, "While I don't deny that the need is very real, I think we have already donated more than enough money to the shelter. What about the food pantry?"
Ms. Crissi says, "I move that we amend the motion by striking out the word *shelter* and inserting the phrase *food pantry*."
Mr. Henry says, "I second the motion."
The chair says, "It is moved and seconded to amend the motion by striking the word *shelter* and inserting the phrase *food pantry*. If the amendment is adopted, the motion will read: The Club should donate $100 to the local food pantry."

Amend—Summary

The motion to Amend yields to:

- All privileged motions
- All incidental motions
- Subsidiary motions to Limit Debate, Extend Debate, and Previous Question

One member cannot make a motion to Amend when another member has the floor. The motion requires a second and can be amended and reconsidered. It requires a majority vote to pass. The motion can be debated, but the debate must be confined to the amendment itself and cannot touch on the main motion to which it has been applied. In addition, the motion to Amend cannot be debated if the main motion that is being debated cannot be debated.

A member can amend an amendment, since the motion to Amend can be applied to itself. This will create an amendment to an amendment, a secondary amendment. The secondary amendment cannot be amended, because it would create a third-degree amendment, an unworkable situation. It is best to resolve each amendment at a time before offering new ones. This will help prevent confusion.

In addition, the motion to Amend must be treated before the main motion can be voted on. It also must be decided before any other subsidiary motion except the motion to Postpone Indefinitely; that must be decided first.

Unacceptable amendments The following amendments are unacceptable and cannot be proposed in a parliamentary assembly. An untenable amendment is one that:

- Changes a resolution by crossing out the word *Resolved,* essential for the motion to be in accordance with parliamentary law.
- Changes one motion to another, which could result in two main motions being on the floor at the same time.
- Is trivial and superficial or makes no sense, thus wasting valuable meeting time.
- Makes the main motion the same as a motion that had been voted down or approved previously during the meeting or session. If the main motion has already been voted down, it cannot then be reintroduced; if it has been passed, there is no reason to vote on it again.
- Does not pertain to the main motion on the floor.
- Negates the main motion, as the following example shows:

▶ Mr. Ruiz says, "I move that the Society support Senator Littenberg in her bid for reelection."
Ms. Finch says, "I second the motion."
Ms. Perretini says, "I move to amend the motion by adding the word *not* before the word *support*."
The chair says, "The motion to amend is out of order."

Filling in the blanks While not technically a kind of amendment, *filling in the blanks* serves much the same purpose by enabling members to make choices. It is an acceptable way to violate the rule that pertains to having only one primary and one secondary amendment applied to a main motion at one time. Filling in the blanks is different from a motion to Amend in the following ways:

- The number of choices offered to members is not restricted.
- Members can consider all choices before voting.
- Voting is less complex.

Parliamentary law allows for three ways to form a blank in a motion.

1. The chair can propose that a blank be inserted in a motion in place of a specific phrase, as shown below:

▶ Ms. Harris says, "I move that the Club donate $500 to the annual holiday parade and decorations on Main Street."
Mr. Kitter says, "I second the motion."
The chair says, "A motion has been made and seconded that the Club donate $500 to the annual holiday parade and decorations on Main Street. The chair proposes creating a blank by deleting *$500*. If no one objects to this change, the blank is created [pause for response]. Since no one objected, the blank is inserted in place of the specific sum."

2. The motion can include the blank, as the following example shows:

▶ A member says, "The Association shall purchase a new VCR at a cost not to exceed $_________."

3. A member can insert a blank in place of a specific section of a motion. If the motion to create a blank is passed, the blank is substituted for the original phrase in the motion, as this example illustrates:

▶ Mr. Joel says, "I move that we donate $100 to the Make a Wish Foundation."
Ms. Swenson says, "I second the motion."
Ms. Jefferson says, "I move that we create a blank in the motion by crossing out the phrase *$100*."
Mr. Williams says, "I second the motion."
The chair says, "A motion has been made and seconded to create a blank in the main motion by crossing out the phrase

$100. All those in favor of the motion please say aye [pause to count votes]. All those opposed please say no [pause to count votes]. The ayes have it and the motion is passed. The motion now reads: The Society should donate ________ to the Make a Wish Foundation."

Once the blank has been created by any of these methods, any member can provide the information for filling it in. The guidelines for filling in different information follow:

Money It is suggested that members arrange amounts to be filled in from least to most likely to be approved. This will vary according to the nature of the motion. If the organization wishes to *spend* money, for example, the numbers will be filled in from largest to smallest amount. If the organization is trying to *make* money, the numbers will usually range from the smallest to the largest amount. In this way, the motion will gather supporters toward the end of the process, making it easier to gain a majority.

Dates Members can vote on dates in the order in which they are proposed, in the order of their likely passage, or in the order of time. Select the method that is most likely to reflect the will of the majority.

Nominations Nominations can be completed if everyone agrees. In the absence of unanimous consent, the chair repeats each nomination and takes the vote in the same order.

Places Places can be voted on in the order of their likely passage or the order in which they are proposed.

Filling in the Blanks—Summary

As an incidental motion, the motion to Fill in the Blanks must have a second, but it cannot be amended or debated.

Commit or Refer

To Commit or Refer a main motion sends it to a committee for further study or action. Assemblies use this motion in the following instances:

- Additional time is required to study a main motion and consider its ramifications.
- Additional information is needed about the motion before making a decision about it.
- The motion is unclear as stated and more time is needed to hammer out the best possible wording.

Don't confuse asking a committee to consider a matter with a motion to Commit or Refer. To be a motion to Commit or Refer, the assembly must send a main motion to a committee. To recommit a motion means to send it to the committee once again. The committee may or may not be the same one that originally considered the motion.

As with all motions, a motion to Commit or Refer must include all relevant information to be effective. Depending on the specific nature of the motion, relevant information includes:

Name of the committee
Type of committee (special, standing, etc.)
Size of the committee
How the committee shall be formed
Any special instructions

The following examples illustrate the motion:

▶ A member says, "I move to refer the motion concerning office supplies to a committee of five members, to be appointed by the chair."

or

A member says, "I move to refer the motion to the convention committee, and respectfully ask that their report be delivered at the next regular meeting."

or

A member says, "I move that the motion be referred to the board of directors for further consideration."

or

A member says, "I move to refer the resolution to a committee of five to be elected by ballot."

Complete and clear motions If the motion is unclear, both the chair and members can offer the information that is missing. Below is a sample dialogue showing how the chair guides a member to complete the motion to Refer:

► A member says, "I move to refer the motion."
The chair says, "Which committee should the motion be referred to?"
The member says, "I move to refer the motion to a committee of five members."
The chair says, "How shall these members be selected to serve on the committee?"
The member says, "The members shall be appointed at the chair's discretion."
The chair says, "Does the member wish to specify a date by which the committee must complete its report?"
The member says, "No, sir."
The chair says, "A motion has been made to refer the issue to a committee of five members, to be appointed by the chair. Do we have a second to the motion?"

Uses In most instances, the motion to Commit or Refer is used to refer the main motion to a smaller committee for consideration; these are usually standing or special committees, including select and ad hoc committees.

The motion has another important use as well, for it can be used to debate the question with the entire assembly under committee rules. Such rules allow a relaxation of the accepted guidelines for debate. Under committee rules, members can speak to an issue as often as they are able to obtain the floor, although they cannot speak more than once until everyone has had a chance to speak to the issue. Further, when the assembly has become a committee of the whole or a variation, the presiding officer can then participate in the debate, make motions, and vote on all questions, actions which are not allowed in a general assembly. This is accomplished by making a motion to Commit or Refer as a motion to:

- Become a committee of the whole
- Form a quasi committee of the whole
- Consider informally

The motion to Commit or Refer must specify which of these methods is going to be used. Each use is explained briefly below:

Become a committee of the whole A committee of the whole, suitable for large organizations of over 100 members, can make only two motions: to amend and to adopt. An organization can create a committee of the whole when it wishes to debate a subject but not refer it to committee, or when the information on a specific subject is not yet fully clarified. To create a committee of the whole, a member should make a motion to commit, in the following form:

▶ A member says, "I move that the assembly does now resolve itself into a committee of the whole, to take under consideration [the specific resolution or subject]."

or

A member says, "I move to go into a committee of the whole to consider the pending question."

The motion needs a second. If the motion is carried, the presiding officer immediately calls another member to the chair and takes a place as a member of the committee. In large groups, the secretary also vacates his or her seat and the assistant clerk assumes it.

To close or limit debate in a committee of the whole, a member of the assembly makes a motion, as follows:

▶ A member says, "I move that the committee rise and report."

Since the motion to rise and report is the same as a motion to adjourn, it cannot be debated. After the motion is made, members vote. If the motion passes, the presiding officer immediately resumes the chair and the committee chair returns to the floor. The chair of the committee then rises to report, as follows:

▶ The committee chair says, "As chair of the committee of the whole, I report that the committee has gone through the business referred to it, and I am ready to make a report when the assembly is ready to receive it."

The assembly then votes on the recommendations. A committee of the whole is disbanded when its specified task is completed, but it can re-form at a later date, if necessary.

Form a quasi committee of the whole A quasi committee of the whole is appropriate for organizations of 50–100 members. It is formed in the same way as a committee of the whole and is disbanded when the particular task is completed. The committee may be re-formed later if the need arises.

Consider informally Informal consideration of a question is a further simplified version of the committee of the whole, designed for small meetings of regular organizations. With an informal consideration, the results of any votes are considered binding on the assembly and are not voted on again. While acting informally, the entire group can amend and adopt resolutions, and without further motion the chair can announce as follows:

▶ The chair says, "The assembly, acting informally, has considered [the subject] and has made certain amendments, which the chair will report at this time."

Then the issue comes before the assembly as if reported by a committee. The chair's report becomes part of the minutes. The committee is disbanded when the particular task is completed but may be re-formed later if the same charge once again presents itself.

Commit or Refer—Summary

The motion to Commit or Refer a motion to a committee takes precedence over the following:

- Main motion
- Subsidiary motions Amend and Postpone Indefinitely
- Incidental motions Division of a Question and Consideration by Paragraph

It yields to:

- Subsidiary motions Lay on the Table, Previous Question, Postpone to a Certain Time, Limit or Extend Debate
- Most incidental motions
- All privileged motions

The motion requires a second and can be amended, debated, and reconsidered. It is out of order when another person has the floor. It requires a majority vote to pass.

Lay on the Table

This motion allows the assembly to set aside (or *table*) a main motion to deal with pressing business. The matter that halts debate must be urgent. Otherwise, this motion is out of order, for it violates the members' parliamentary rights.

• Guidelines

1. The motion Lay on the Table does not establish a time for the debate to resume; rather, it enables the members to re-

sume the discussion at any point during the meeting. As a result, this motion can be used to manipulate the debate. For example, if a motion laid on the table at the beginning of the meeting is taken from the table at the very end, many members might have already left the meeting. This enables the remaining members—clearly the minority—to take any motions from the table and dispose of them in a manner that may not be in accordance with the wishes of the majority.

2. The motion Lay on the Table can only be applied to main motions. As a result, it cannot be applied to a committee report or any other entire portion of the agenda, such as new business.
3. A motion can be tabled more than once, but only if another emergency arises or the issues have been well debated between postponements.
4. While a motion is tabled, no member can make a motion that is substantially the same. Further, no member can make a motion that would conflict with the tabled motion.
5. The motions Orders of the Day and Question of Privilege can be laid on the table only when they are used as main motions.
6. Any subsidiary motions adhering to the tabled motion are postponed along with it. When the discussion resumes, the same motions are in effect. There are several exceptions, as follows:

    - The Previous Question expires at the end of a session. Thus, if the tabled motion is not resumed until the next session, the Previous Question is null.
    - An Appeal that is laid on the table in effect sustains the chair's decision for the time being. The original subject is not carried to the table with it.
    - When a motion to Reconsider a question is laid on the table, the original motion remains as it was before the motion to Reconsider. Only the motion to Reconsider is set aside.
    - If an amendment to the minutes is tabled, the entire minutes remain on the floor, not tabled.

The following examples illustrate the use of the motion:

► A member says, "I move to lay the question on the table."

or

A member says, "I move to lay the resolution on the table."

or

A member says, "I move the matter of [specific motion] be laid on the table."

or

A member says, "I move to lay the motion on the table."

or

A member says, "I move that the question of [specific motion] lie on the table."

The question is put to a vote as follows:

► A member says, "I move to lay the motion on the table."
Member B says, "I second the motion."
The chair says, "It has been moved and seconded to table the pending motion. All those in favor of tabling the pending motion say aye [pause to tally votes]. All those opposed please say no [pause to tally votes]."

Since a motion can be tabled only if pressing business arises, if such business is not readily apparent, the chair can ask the mover to explain the reason for the motion. The following dialogue illustrates this process:

► Member A says, "I move the matter of [specific motion] be laid on the table."
Member B says, "I second the motion."
The chair says, "For what reason does Member A make the motion?"
Member A says, "A majority of the membership must leave this meeting to attend the awards ceremony, to be held in 10 minutes."

Taking the motion from the table Resuming discussion on the tabled motion is called *taking the motion from the table*. The discussion cannot simply resume; a majority vote is required to continue with the debate on the tabled item. A motion can be taken from the table during any regular meeting if there is no other motion on the floor and if the motion fits with the type of business currently being discussed, such as new business or unfinished business. A motion cannot be taken from the table during a special meeting, however, unless prior notice has been given. The motion is made as follows:

► A member says, "I move to take the question of [specific motion] from the table."

or

A member says, "I move that we now consider the question of [specific motion]."

Lay on the Table—Summary

The motion to Lay on the Table takes precedence over:

- All subsidiary motions
- All incidental motions on the floor

It yields to:

- All privileged motions

The motion requires a second and is out of order when another has the floor. It cannot be amended, debated, or reconsidered. No subsidiary motion can be applied to it, and it requires a majority vote to pass.

Limit or Extend Debate

As its name suggests, this subsidiary motion serves to decrease or increase the amount of time that members can debate an issue.

• Guidelines

1. According to conventional parliamentary rules, each speaker is usually allocated 10 minutes to debate each motion. But if the agenda is unusually full or the debate is dragging on, members can use this motion to set a shorter time limit for each speech.

   Conversely, if the issues are highly complex and additional time is required to fully explore the subject, a member can use this motion to extend the duration and the number of speeches. For instance, speakers may be allowed to debate for 15 minutes rather than 10, and to make four speeches rather than two. The maker of the motion can restrict individual speakers as well as members of the entire assembly.
2. The motion does not contain guidelines for speech length; that is determined by the maker of the motion and the assembly.
3. The motion can only reduce or extend debate, not cut it off completely. The Previous Question is the motion to use in such an instance.
4. The motion can only be used in assemblies, not in committees.

The following examples illustrate various uses of the motion:

To limit the time that each speaker may have the floor

- ▶ A member says, "I move that the debate be limited to one speech of three minutes for each member."

To limit or extend the time that a specific member can speak

- ▶ A member says, "I move that the time that [name of member] be allowed to speak be limited to five minutes."

  or

  A member says, "I move that the time that [name of member] be allowed to speak be extended by five minutes."

To cut down on the number of speeches

- ▶ A member says, "I move that no member be allowed to speak more than once to the motion."

To limit the time for the entire debate

- ▶ A member says, "I move that debate on the pending motion be limited to 15 minutes [specific length of time]."

To set the time for stopping the debate and voting on the motion

- ▶ A member says, "I move that the debate be closed at 3:00 p.m. and the motion put to a vote at that time."

To combine purposes

- ▶ A member says, "I move that those individuals running for office be allowed to speak for 15 minutes each and that all other members be limited to one speech of no more than three minutes each and that all pending motions be voted on no later than 11:00 a.m."

The entire process of using this motion is illustrated below:

- ▶ Member A says, "I move that each speaker be limited to one speech each, not to exceed two minutes, and that the debate be closed no later than 6:00 p.m. and the motion put to a vote."

  Member B says, "I second the motion."

  The chair says, "It has been moved and seconded that each speaker be limited to one speech each, not to exceed two minutes, and that the debate be closed no later than 6:00 p.m. and the motion put to a vote. The motion to limit debate cannot be debated, but it can be amended. Are there any amendments to this motion? [pause for response]. There being none, are you ready for the question? All those in favor of the motion to limit each speaker to one speech each, not to exceed two minutes, and to close debate no later than 6:00 p.m., please rise [pause to count votes]. Thank you. You may be seated now. All those opposed please rise [pause to count votes]. Thank you. You may be seated now. The motion is carried by a two-thirds vote. Each speaker will therefore be limited to one speech each, not to exceed two minutes, and debate will be closed no later than 6:00 p.m. The motion before us now is [states the main motion on the floor]."

Limit or Extend Debate—Summary

The motion to Limit or Extend Debate takes precedence over:

- All main motions
- All motions that can be debated

It yields to:

- Subsidiary motions Lay on the Table and Previous Question
- All incidental motions
- All privileged motions

The motion requires a second and can be amended and reconsidered. It cannot be debated and is out of order when another has the floor. It requires a two-thirds vote to pass because it changes the rules.

Postpone to a Certain Time

The motion to Postpone to a Certain Time moves consideration of the question to a later time. Assemblies use this motion when:

- Members require more time to think about a motion but the debate has gone on too long already.
- Members realize that there are pressing reasons to put the debate off until a later time.
- It is late and people are growing weary. In such cases, the

motion may not receive a fair hearing unless it is postponed until people are rested.

Don't confuse this motion with the one to Postpone Indefinitely. The motion to Postpone to a Certain Time sets a specific time for the issue to be discussed. The debate must be set for a certain meeting, event, day, or hour. The issue is being deferred, not eliminated. The motion to Postpone Indefinitely, in contrast, serves to completely remove the issue from consideration.

• Guidelines

1. The motion must set a specific time for the debate on the issue to resume. Although the motion can be postponed more than once, it should not be postponed past the next meeting or the current session. If this guideline is violated, the move to Postpone could too easily become a move to Postpone Indefinitely. If the issue cannot wait until the next regular meeting, a special meeting must be called to accommodate it. Or, if members want to have an adjourned meeting in which to consider the subject, a member should make a motion to Fix the Time to Which to Adjourn before making a motion to postpone the issue until that time.
2. An item of business mandated by the bylaws, such as an election, cannot be postponed in advance. However, the motion can be postponed once it has been made. To do so, a member must make a motion to Fix the Time to Which to Adjourn.
3. When a main motion is postponed, it takes with it any subsidiary motions that are attached to it as well. The entire package—main and subsidiary motions—is therefore postponed. The most commonly attached subsidiary motions are Amend, Commit, Limit Debate, and Postpone Indefinitely. Conversely, when the motion is once again taken up, nearly all the attached subsidiary motions are in effect again as well. The sole exception is the motion to Limit Debate, which is automatically nullified. It would make no sense to keep this motion alive, since one of the primary purposes for postponing the motion in the first place is to allow additional time for further debate.

The following examples show how this motion is used:

To postpone the motion to the next regular meeting

▶ A member says, "I move to postpone the motion to the next meeting."

To discuss the motion after a specific event

- ▶ A member says, "I move to postpone debate on the motion until after refreshments have been served."

To set a specific time for the motion to be reconsidered

- ▶ A member says, "I move that debate on the motion be postponed until 7:30 p.m."

  or

  A member says, "I move that debate on the motion be postponed until the next regular meeting and then be discussed at 7:30 p.m."

  or

  A member says, "I move that the question be postponed until July 20, the next regular meeting, and be made a special order."

Taking up each postponed motion What happens when the postponed motion comes up for consideration again? Unless a subsidiary motion to Limit Debate has been attached, if the debate is being resumed during the same meeting, members pick up the debate where it left off. Members who have spoken once cannot again speak until everyone who so desires has a chance to speak. However, if the motion is being taken up at another meeting, the debate begins afresh. No matter who has spoken on the issue previously, the chair treats each speaker as a new contributor. All members can speak again after everyone has spoken once, even if they have already spoken to the question previously.

In what order are postponed items treated? A postponed item that is being resumed can be:

- Treated as an *order of the day,* giving it a specific place on the agenda.
- Reconsidered after every committee has given its report.
- Discussed under unfinished business.

If there is more than one postponed item to be discussed, each item should be considered in the order in which it was originally postponed. The first item that was postponed should be treated first, the second item should be treated second, and so forth. If time runs out before all the postponed items can be reconsidered, they all automatically become part of unfinished business for the next regular meeting.

Postpone to a Certain Time—Summary

The motion to Postpone to a Certain Time takes precedence over:

- The main motion
- Subsidiary motions Amend, Commit or Refer, and Postpone Indefinitely
- Incidental motions Division of a Question and Consideration by Paragraph

It yields to:

- Subsidiary motions Lay on the Table, Previous Question, Postpone to a Certain Time, and Limit or Extend Debate
- All incidental motions
- All privileged motions

The motion requires a second and can be amended, debated, and reconsidered. It is out of order when another has the floor. It requires a majority vote to pass. However, a two-thirds vote is required if members desire to vote on the motion before the specified time of the discussion.

Postpone Indefinitely

If a member has brought a main motion that could cause embarrassment or distress, the assembly would want to avoid bringing the motion to a vote. The motion to Postpone Indefinitely enables members to save face and avoid a potentially uncomfortable situation. A member can use the subsidiary motion to Postpone Indefinitely to remove the main motion from the floor, in effect removing it from consideration during the current meeting or session.

The motion to Postpone Indefinitely is disregarded, however, if a main motion carrying a motion to Postpone Indefinitely is referred to a committee. In these situations, the motion to Postpone Indefinitely is dropped, because by sending the main motion to a committee, the group indicates that they want to consider the main motion after all.

The following dialogue illustrates when and how this motion can be made:

▶ During a luncheon meeting at the Villa Doria restaurant, Dr. Callebro says, "I move that the Society henceforth hold our meetings at the Ristorante Edouard on Main Street in Westbury rather than at Villa Doria on Route 110 in Smithtown."

This motion creates an embarrassing situation, because the members are being served their lunch at the present time and are uncomfortable about debating the issue of moving the site of their meetings to another restaurant. Only a handful of members have expressed dissatisfaction with Villa Doria's prices, service, and selection. Therefore, to avoid dealing with the issue at the present time, another member takes the floor, as follows:

▶ Mr. Chrills says, "I move that the motion be postponed indefinitely."
Ms. Hartsdale, "I second the motion."
The chair says, "It is moved and seconded that the motion to change meeting sites be postponed indefinitely."

To decide whether the motion to move to a new restaurant should be debated or not, the chair asks first for debate on the motion to Postpone Indefinitely. Then the chair holds a vote on the motion, as follows:

▶ The chair says, "The question is on the motion to postpone indefinitely the motion that the Society henceforth hold our meetings at the Ristorante Edouard on Main Street in Westbury rather than at Villa Doria on Route 110 in Smithtown. Those in favor of postponing the motion please say aye [pause to count votes]. Those opposed please say no [pause to count votes]. The ayes have it and the motion is postponed indefinitely."

The matter ends here if the motion to Postpone Indefinitely is passed. However, if the motion to Postpone Indefinitely is defeated, the main motion is then considered. In such a case, the dialogue would follow the above format, up to the report of voting:

▶ The chair says, "The no votes have it and the motion to postpone indefinitely is defeated. The question before us is should the Society henceforth meet at the Ristorante Edouard on Main Street in Westbury rather than at Villa Doria on Route 110 in Smithtown."

Postpone Indefinitely—Summary

The motion to Postpone Indefinitely is the lowest ranking subsidiary motion, and it takes precedence over only the main motion. It yields to:

- All other subsidiary motions
- All privileged motions
- All relevant incidental motions

The motion requires a second and can be debated and reconsidered. It cannot be amended and must have a majority vote to pass. Further, it is out of order when another has the floor. Since a motion to Postpone Indefinitely can only be applied to a main motion, it must be made before the main motion has been decided. Otherwise, it is null and void.

Previous Question

This motion has a misleading name, for it has nothing to do with any question previously considered. Rather, moving the Previous Question closes debate and forces an immediate vote on a motion. At the same time, no other subsidiary motions can be made, except Lay on the Table.

• Guidelines

1. The motion replaces any previous motion to halt discussion.
2. The motion can be used with any motion that is on the floor.
3. When the motion is applied to a group of motions on the floor, the motions are voted on in reverse order, from the last to the first moved. The voting continues down the list unless a motion to Commit, Postpone, or Postpone Indefinitely is passed. In that instance, the voting is over and the motion is disposed according to the motion that carried.
4. The motion can be reconsidered before the voting on any of the motions that affect the order has begun.
5. If the motion to move the Previous Question carries, the chair immediately takes a vote on the motion on the floor.

The examples below illustrate the wording of the motion:

▶ A member says, "I move the previous question."

or

A member says, "I move the previous question to [describes the specific motion on the floor]."

or

A member says, "I demand the previous question."

or

A member says, "I demand the previous motion on all pending motions."

or

A member says, "I call for the previous question."

or

A member says, "I call the question."

The following dialogue shows how the motion is handled.

▶ Member A says, "I move the previous question."
Member B says, "I second the motion."
The chair says, "The previous question has been moved. All those in favor of moving the previous question please rise [pause to tally votes]. Please be seated. All those opposed to moving the previous question please rise [pause to tally votes]. Please be seated."

If the motion passes by a two-thirds vote

▶ The chair says, "The motion carries by a two-thirds vote and the previous question is called. The motion now on the floor is [states specific motion]. All those in favor of [specific motion] please say aye [pause to tally votes]. All those opposed please say no [pause to tally votes]. The ayes have it and the motion carries [*or* the no votes have it and the motion is defeated]."

If the motion does not pass by a two-thirds vote

▶ The chair says, "The motion did not carry by a two-thirds vote. The motion before us now is [states the previous motion on the floor]. The motion is now open for debate."

Previous Question—Summary

The motion takes precedence over:
- Every debatable motion

It yields to:
- Subsidiary motion Lay on the Table
- All incidental motions

- All privileged motions

The motion requires a second. It cannot be amended or debated. Since it cuts off debate, it requires a two-thirds rather than the more usual majority vote to pass.

Incidental Motions

TYPES OF INCIDENTAL MOTIONS AT A GLANCE

Motion	Description	Page
Appeal	Challenging the chair's ruling	123
Consideration by Paragraph	Separating a long document or motion into different parts and voting on each part separately	125
Division of the Assembly	Calling for retaking a vote	126
Division of a Question	Separating the main motion into different parts to vote on each part independently	127
Objection to the Consideration of a Question	Avoiding motions that are off the topic or disruptive	128
Point of Order	Compelling the chair to adhere to the rules of the assembly	129
Requests Parliamentary Inquiry Point of Information Reading Papers	Making inquiries about the business at a meeting and asking permission for meeting-related activities	131
Suspend the Rules	Temporarily setting aside the organization's rules	133

Definition of an incidental motion An incidental motion comes from another motion, which means that it is always directly related to the business on the floor. Unlike main motions, an incidental motion does not pertain to a main motion during the entire time that it is being debated. Members can make incidental motions as a result of a pending motion or an item of business that they wish to propose, as well as one that has been made but not stated by the chair or one that is pending.

Qualities of an incidental motion All incidental motions share five qualities that distinguish them from other motions:

1. They take precedence over main motions and subsidiary motions but yield to privileged questions.
2. In most cases, they must be decided before the meeting can continue.
3. They must be decided before other motions, in most instances.
4. They cannot be amended.
5. They cannot be debated, except for the motion to Appeal.

Types of Incidental Motions There are eight types of incidental motions:

1. Appeal
2. Consideration by Paragraph
3. Division of the Assembly
4. Division of a Question
5. Objection to the Consideration of a Question
6. Point of Order
7. Requests
   —Parliamentary Inquiry
   —Point of Information
   —Reading Papers
8. Suspend the Rules

Order of precedence Unlike subsidiary motions, incidental motions are not arranged in a strict hierarchy. Rather, they take precedence over other motions only when they are truly incidental to the business on the floor. As a result, incidental motions cannot be ranked. Each motion is described below in detail.

Appeal

An appeal challenges a presiding officer's ruling on a specific issue and thus refers the chair's decision to the members present at a meeting. It forces the chair to submit the matter to a vote by the membership. Members should freely make appeals in all instances where they feel the chair's ruling should be reconsidered. The chair should not feel threatened by the appeal; on the contrary, the chair should welcome the interplay, for it can often serve to strengthen an organization. Further, an appeal can even help a chair by alleviating blame in a difficult decision.

• Guidelines

1. Members can only appeal a chair's *ruling* on a specific issue. *Opinions* rendered during a discussion cannot be appealed.
2. An appeal must be made directly after the chair's ruling. It cannot be made after other business has transpired.
3. A member cannot appeal a chair's ruling unless there can be two opinions on the matter under dispute. Further, the motion would be considered out of order unless both sides of the issue were clearly logical.
4. Debate is allowed under all circumstances except if it pertains to the chair's behavior, a point of order, transgressions of the rules of speaking, or the order of business. The motion also cannot be debated if it is made while the Previous Question is being decided.
5. The presiding officer can speak to the motion without leaving the chair. Although every member can speak only once to the appeal, the presiding officer is allowed to speak at the beginning and the end of debate and should be given preference during the discussion.

The following dialogue illustrates when and how this motion can be made:

▶ Member A says, "I appeal the chair's decision."

or

Member A says, "I appeal from the decision of the chair."

Member B says, "I second the motion."

The chair states the issue under dispute and, if desired, explains the reasons for his or her ruling on the matter. Discussion ensues.

The chair then says, "Shall the chair's decision stand as the judgment for the organization?"

or

The chair then says, "Shall the decision of the chair stand as the judgment of the assembly?"

The appeal is then decided by vote. The chair says, "All those in favor of sustaining the chair's decision on the matter please say aye [pause to tally votes]. All those opposed please say no [pause to tally votes]." The chair then announces the decision.

Voting The appeal is decided by a vote of the assembly. The chair needs a majority vote to carry the decision, and if the vote is a tie, the chair's decision stands.

Appeal—Summary

The motion to Appeal yields to:

- All privileged motions
- All incidental motions that arise from it

The motion requires a second, which means that it requires two members to make an appeal. It is in order when another has the floor, but it cannot be amended. The motion can be debated under certain circumstances, explained above. If the motion can be debated, it yields to the subsidiary motions to Lay on the Table, Commit, Postpone Indefinitely, Previous Question, and Limit or Extend Debate. If the motion cannot be debated, it yields only to Lay on the Table. The motion can be reconsidered.

Consideration by Paragraph

This motion separates a long document or motion into different parts so that each part can be voted on independently of the others. The method is commonly used when an assembly is ratifying a long document such as its bylaws or constitution.

• Guidelines

1. This motion differs from Division of a Question in one crucial way: here, the document cannot clearly be divided into separate motions.
2. Separating the long document or motion into individual parts renews the debate. If each member is allowed 10 minutes to debate, members can only speak for 10 minutes on an entire document. But if the document is divided into three parts, for example, then members can speak for an additional 30 minutes each (10 minutes per section).
3. Any member, including the chair, can make this motion. In fact, it is often made by the chair.

Voting Members do not vote until the entire document or motion has been revised. There is only one vote, on the entire document, rather than individual votes on each section.

The following dialogue shows the motion in use:

▶ Member A says, "I move that we consider this document by paragraph."
Member B says, "I second the motion."
The chair then reads each paragraph in turn, asking at the end of each, "Is there any discussion on this passage?" If discussion ensues, the membership revises the passage. If not, the chair moves on to the next passage, reading it and then asking for discussion. When the entire document has been completed in this manner, the chair says, "Is there any discussion on the entire document?" Then the entire document is voted on.

Consideration by Paragraph—Summary

The motion to consider by paragraph takes precedence over:

- The main motion
- The subsidiary motion to Postpone Indefinitely
- An amendment

It yields to:

- Most subsidiary motions, except Amend, Limit or Extend Debate, and Postpone Indefinitely
- All incidental motions
- All privileged motions

The motion requires a second and a majority vote. It can be amended but not debated or reconsidered, and it requires a majority vote to pass.

Division of the Assembly

This motion calls for retaking a vote in instances where the first vote appears inconclusive. To make sure that the second vote is accurate, members usually revote by standing up.

• Guidelines

1. The motion is used when members have first voted by voice vote or by raising their hands.
2. The vote is retaken by having members stand up, to ensure a more accurate estimate. The votes do not have to be

counted, however. If a member wishes a count be taken, he or she has to make a motion. The motion requires a majority vote.

3. Any member can demand a division of the assembly. As a result, the motion is not voted on.
4. The motion to divide the assembly can be made even when another motion has been made and seconded. It must be made before the chair repeats the new motion, however.

The following examples illustrate the use of this motion:

▶ The chair announces the results of a vote, "The ayes have it and the motion is carried."
A member says, "I call for a division."
or
A member says, "Division!"
or
A member says, "I demand a division!"
The chair responds, "A division is requested." The chair then takes a rising vote.

Division of the Assembly—Summary

The motion to divide the assembly takes precedence over any main motion that has just been voted on. It does not yield to any motion and does not require a second. It cannot be debated, amended, or reconsidered. A member does not have to be recognized to call for a division.

Division of a Question

This motion separates a motion into different parts so that each part can be voted on independently of the others.

• Guidelines

1. The member making the motion to divide the question must describe how the question is going to be separated.
2. If someone at the meeting does not agree with the separation, he or she can move the amendment to suggest an alternate division.
3. Each part of the motion to be divided must be capable of

standing on its own. The division must not require any rewriting of the motion. If a motion cannot logically be separated into parts, a motion to divide the question cannot be used.

4. When a motion is divided, some parts can be approved and others defeated.
5. The motion to divide a question can be made at any time during the debate.

The following examples illustrate this motion:

▶ Member A says, "I move that the Society recognize Ann Adams' election to the position of President-elect of the Queens County chapter, and that a reception be given in her honor at Annabella's Restaurant on Tuesday, October 15, at 5:00 p.m."
Member B says, "I second the motion."
Member C says, "I move to divide the question so as to consider independently the question of holding the reception."
Member D says, "I second the motion."

Division of a Question—Summary

The motion to divide a question takes precedence over:

- The main motion
- The subsidiary motion to Postpone Indefinitely
- An amendment to which it may be linked

It yields to:

- Most subsidiary motions, except Amend, Limit or Extend Debate, and Postpone Indefinitely
- All privileged motions
- All incidental motions

The motion needs a second and can be amended. It is not in order when another has the floor. It cannot be debated or reconsidered, and it requires a majority vote to pass.

Objection to the Consideration of a Question

This motion enables members to avoid discussing motions that are off the topic or likely to disrupt the meeting. It is not intended to cut off debate; rather, it is intended primarily to prevent discussion of a pointless or potentially inflammatory topic.

- **Guidelines**

1. After a motion has been introduced, any member can raise an objection to the consideration of a question.
2. The motion must be made before the debate has begun.

Voting The motion to object to the consideration of a question can be adopted only by a two-thirds vote.

An example of this motion follows:

▶ A member says, "I object to the consideration of the question."
The chair says, "There is an objection to the consideration of the question. Shall the question be discussed? Those in favor of considering the question, please rise [pause to count votes]. You may be seated. Those opposed to considering the question, please rise [pause to count votes]. You may be seated. There are more than two thirds opposed and the question will not be considered."

Objection to the Consideration of a Question—Summary

The motion takes precedence over:
- The main motion
- Any attached subsidiary motions except Lay on the Table

It yields to:
- The subsidiary motion to Lay on the Table
- All privileged motions

The motion needs a second, and it cannot be debated or amended. It is in order when another has the floor. The vote can be reconsidered only if it supports the objection. In such an instance, there must be unanimous consent.

Point of Order

This motion forces the chair to adhere to the rules of the assembly. Any member can make the motion, for any rules.

- **Guidelines**

1. The motion must be made at the time of the suspected infraction. The motion cannot be made at any other time, even if the infraction is serious.
2. If the error continues for motion after motion and results in actions that violate the organization's bylaws or constitution, however, a member can rise to a point of order and mention previous instances of the same problem. It is important to point out past infractions in this instance because the previous rulings would be inaccurate.
3. While it is important to enforce the rules of parliamentary law, members should not raise points of order when the infraction is very minor. This serves only to slow down the meeting and create ill will.
4. If it is not clear whether the rules have been broken, a member is advised to make a parliamentary inquiry rather than a point of order.
5. After a member has raised a point of order, the chair may wish to briefly confer with the parliamentarian before rendering a ruling on the matter. This applies only in those instances when a parliamentarian is present at the meeting; business should not be disrupted unduly by seeking verification. The chair can also consult the parliamentary rules of order specified in the organization's bylaws.
6. The ruling must be made by the chair. If desired, the chair may speak briefly with members well-versed in parliamentary law, but the chair must be the one to approach the members. No matter how knowledgeable other members may be in parliamentary law, the decision must rest with the chair.

The examples below illustrate this motion:

▶ A member says, "Point of Order!"

or

A member says, "I rise to a point of order."
The chair says, "Please state your point of order."
The member says, "I make a point of order that [notes specific transgression of the rules]."
The chair says, "The point of order is well-taken because [explains specific violation of the rules]."

or

The chair says, "The point of order is not well-taken because [explains how the rules have been followed]."

If the chair is unsure of the decision, the members may be consulted as a group, as the following example shows:

▶ The chair says, "Member A raised a point of order that [suspected violation of the rules]. The chair asks the members for their input. The question is, [states the suspected violation of the rules]."

If the chair is unsure of the decision, he or she can put the matter to a vote, as shown below:

▶ The chair says, "All those who believe the motion is correct as stated, please say aye [pause to tally votes]. All those who believe the motion is out of order, please say no [pause to tally votes]. The no votes have it and the motion is out of order."

Point of Order—Summary

The motion yields to:

- The subsidiary motion to Lay on the Table
- All privileged motions

The motion does not need a second. In addition, it cannot be debated, amended, or reconsidered. A Point of Order is in order when another motion is pending. If the point is urgent, the mover can interrupt another speaker.

Requests

The motion allows members to make inquiries about the business that is transpiring at a meeting and to ask permission for meeting-related activities. There are three kinds of Requests: Parliamentary Inquiry, Point of Information, and Reading Papers.

Parliamentary Inquiry This motion allows a member to ask the chair a question about parliamentary law. The chair must respond to these questions when they have a direct bearing on the meeting. The member is not bound to follow the chair's ruling, however, and can appeal if subsequent actions are found to be in violation of parliamentary law. The following example illustrates this motion:

▶ A member says, "I have a parliamentary inquiry."
or

A member says, "I rise to a parliamentary inquiry."
The chair says, "What is the inquiry?"
The member says, "Does the motion to waive the reading of the minutes require a second?" [specific question about the way to conduct the business at hand].

Point of Information This motion asks a question about the proceedings not concerned with parliamentary law. A Point of Information must always be framed as a question, although it may really be a reminder, a rebuttal, or a response. Unlike a parliamentary inquiry, a point of information can be directed to any officer or member as well as to the chair. Neither members nor officers are obligated to respond to the point of information, especially since the time it takes for them to answer counts as part of their debate time. All responses must go through the chair; members should not address each other directly. Various methods of addressing points of information are shown below:

Point of Information addressed to an officer

▶ A member says, "Will the Secretary please explain when the correspondence was sent out?"

or

A member says, "Can the Treasurer please describe how these funds are going to be invested?"

Point of Information addressed to a member

▶ A member says, "Mr. Chair, I would like to ask the speaker a question."

Point of Information addressed to the chair

▶ A member says, "Mr. Chair, I rise to a point of information."
The chair says, "Please explain the point."
The member says, "How many people have responded to the survey thus far?" [specific point of information].

Reading Papers This motion is used to have documents read to the assembly before a vote is taken on them. Members can also use this motion to read small excerpts from documents to the assembly while a motion is being debated. The assembly must grant permission to have the material read. If even one member objects, the papers cannot be read aloud during the meeting without a majority vote. The motion does not apply to those members who were absent during a prior reading; if the document was read and people were not at the meeting, they cannot move to have the document read again for their accommodation. To make the motion, a member asks permission to read the information and explains its length and relevance to the debate, as shown in this example:

► A member says, "If there is no objection, I would like to read the following material. It is half a page long and bears directly on the matter of the proposed land acquisition [specific length and relevance of material explained]."
The chair says, "Is there any objection to the reading of this material? [pause for response]. There being none, permission to read the statement in debate is granted."
or
The chair says, "Is there any objection to the reading of this material? [pause for response]. There being objections, permission to read the statement in debate is denied." A vote can then be taken, requiring a majority to allow permission to read the statement.

Requests—Summary

A request takes precedence over:
- Any motion that sparked the request

It yields to:
- All other incidental motions
- All privileged motions

Members can make urgent requests when another motion is being debated, but they must obtain the floor to make less important requests. These motions do not require a second, and cannot be debated, amended, and, in most instances, reconsidered. Most requests do not have to be voted on. If a vote is needed, it is often taken by unanimous consent.

Suspend the Rules

This motion temporarily sets aside the organization's rules. The assembly uses this motion when it wishes to discuss an issue that violates its standing rules or rules of order. The constitution and bylaws of an organization are not involved because they cannot be suspended under any circumstances. Rules that guard any member's rights are also protected from this motion.

• Guidelines

1. The motion does not have to list the specific rule, but it does have to provide a reason for suspending the rule.
2. If the motion achieves passage by a two-thirds vote, the assembly can discuss the new motion at once.
3. If the motion does not pass, it cannot be made again during the same meeting for the same purpose unless all members agree. It can be made again during the next meeting, however.

• Voting

1. A motion to suspend the rules of order requires a two-thirds vote and previous notice to be adopted.
2. Any rule that does not relate to parliamentary law requires a majority vote to pass.
3. When the matter is not controversial and all members are in agreement, unanimous consent can be used to pass the motion more quickly.

The examples below illustrate the motion in use:

▶ A member says, "I move to suspend the rules that interfere with [specific matter at hand]."

or

A member says, "I move that the rules be suspended that interfere with [specific matter at hand] because [gives specific reason for the move to suspend]."

or

A member says, "I move to suspend the rules to discuss [specific issue]."

or

A member says, "I move to suspend the rules to discuss the membership drive, since it is only a week until the convention."

or

A member says, "I move to suspend the rules and to adopt the following motion [specific motion]."

Suspend the Rules—Summary

The motion to Suspend the Rules takes precedence over:

- Any motion it affects

It yields to:

- The subsidiary motion to Lay on the Table
- All privileged motions except Call for the Orders of the Day

The motion requires a second and cannot be debated, amended, reconsidered, or made while another motion is being debated.

Privileged Motions

TYPES OF PRIVILEGED MOTIONS AT A GLANCE

Motion	Description	Page
Adjourn	Ending the meeting	136
Call for the Orders of the Day	Requiring the agenda be followed	137
Fix the Time to Which to Adjourn	Setting the time for the next meeting	138
Question of Privilege	Allowing members to make urgent requests about the rights of the assembly and its members	139
Recess	Taking a short break in a meeting	141

Definition of a privileged motion A privileged motion deals with a special matter of pressing importance. Unlike main, subsidiary, and incidental motions, privileged motions do not deal with business on the floor. This class of motions can also be called *privileged questions* but should not be confused with *questions of privilege,* as explained on page 139.

Qualities of privileged motions All privileged motions share two qualities that distinguish them from other motions: (1) they are the highest ranking motions, taking precedence over all other motions, and (2) they can interrupt any business on the floor, without requiring debate or discussion.

Types of privileged motions There are five types of privileged motions, listed below in alphabetical order:

1. Adjourn
2. Call for the Orders of the Day
3. Fix the Time to Which to Adjourn
4. Question of Privilege
5. Recess

Order of precedence As the highest ranking motions, privileged motions take precedence over all other motions. They follow this order of precedence from lowest to highest rank:

1. Call for the Orders of the Day (see page 137)
2. Question of Privilege (see page 139)
3. Recess (see page 141)
4. Adjourn (see page 136)
5. Fix the Time to Which to Adjourn (see page 138)

Adjourn

This motion ends the meeting.

- **Guidelines**

1. This motion can function in two ways: as a privileged motion or as a main motion. A privileged motion to adjourn is made when there is no set time for adjournment and another meeting has been set up. It becomes a main motion when a time for adjournment has already been set, is included in the motion, or when another meeting is not set. It is a main motion when it functions to end all business.
2. As long as the time for the next meeting has been set previously, any member can call for an adjournment, even in the middle of a debate. The motion cannot be made in the middle of a vote, however.
3. If the motion closes business at the end of one of a series of meetings in a session, business resumes at the point where it left off at the next meeting.
4. The following actions can be taken while a privileged motion to adjourn is on the floor: giving notice of a motion that will be made at subsequent meetings; moving to set a time for an adjourned meeting; and making announcements.
5. The chair must announce that the meeting is adjourned.

Until that time, the meeting is still officially in session, even if the vote has been tallied to adjourn.

The examples below illustrate this motion:

▶ A member says, "I move that the meeting be adjourned at this time."

or

A member says, "I move to adjourn."
Another member says, "I second the motion."
The chair says, "It has been moved and seconded that the meeting now adjourn. All those in favor of immediate adjournment please say aye [pause to tally votes]. All those opposed please say no [pause to tally votes]. The ayes have it and the meeting is now adjourned."

Adjourn—Summary

The motion to Adjourn takes precedence over:

- All main motions
- All subsidiary motions
- All incidental motions
- All privileged motions except Fix the Time to Which to Adjourn

The motion is out of order when another has the floor, and it requires a second. It cannot be debated, amended, or reconsidered. The motion must have a majority vote to pass. No other motion can be applied to it, and it cannot be applied to any motion.

Call for the Orders of the Day

If the agenda is not being followed, or a specific motion is supposed to be debated at a certain time and has not been taken up, any member can call for the orders of the day.

• Guidelines

1. Use this motion if the presiding officer has skipped an item on the agenda.
2. It can also be used when a *general order* is ignored.
3. This motion requires that the agenda be followed, unless the members decide by a two-thirds vote to set aside the orders of the day.

4. When the orders of the day are requested, the chair lets anyone who is speaking complete a thought and then turns the meeting to the skipped item from the agenda or to the neglected special order. At the completion of that item, the chair returns to the speaker who was interrupted by the call for the orders of the day.

The examples below show the motion in use:

▶ Member A says, "Madame Chair, I request the regular orders of the day."

or

Member A says, "Mr. Chair, I call for the orders of the day."
The chair responds, "The chair recognizes Member A."
Member A says, "Madam Chair, the assembly was supposed to consider the financial shortfall at this time."
The chair responds, "Thank you, Member A. Member B will now yield the floor, and the assembly will discuss the financial shortfall at this time."

Call for the Orders of the Day—Summary

The motion to Call for the Orders of the Day takes precedence over:

- All main motions
- All subsidiary motions
- Most incidental motions

It yields to:

- Other privileged motions
- A motion to Suspend the Rules

The motion does not require a second and cannot be amended, debated, or reconsidered. It can be made when someone else has the floor, even if that person is speaking.

Fix the Time to Which to Adjourn

This motion sets the time for the next meeting.

• Guidelines

1. This motion does not affect the adjournment of the present meeting.

2. For this motion to be privileged, two conditions must be met: the motion must be made while another motion is being debated, and another meeting has not been set. If these conditions are not met, Fix the Time to Which to Adjourn becomes a main motion.
3. The motion can be made even after the members have voted to adjourn, but not after the chair has declared the meeting adjourned.
4. The motion can be amended to include such information as the place of the next meeting as well as the time.

The example below shows the wording of this motion:

▶ Member A says, "I move that when this assembly adjourns, it adjourns to meet at 4:00 p.m. on Tuesday, June 1 [a specific time]."
Member B says, "I second the motion."
The chair says, "It has been moved and seconded that the meeting fix the time to which to adjourn to 4:00 p.m. on Tuesday, June 1. All those in favor of the motion please say aye [pause to tally votes]. All those opposed please say no [pause to tally votes]. The ayes have it. When the meeting adjourns this morning, it will adjourn to meet at 4:00 on Tuesday, June 1."

Fix the Time to Which to Adjourn—Summary

The motion to Fix the Time to Which to Adjourn takes precedence over:

- All main motions
- All subsidiary motions
- All incidental motions
- All privileged motions

The motion requires a second and can be amended and reconsidered but not debated. It requires a majority vote to pass.

Question of Privilege

A Question of Privilege allows any member to make an urgent request about the prerogatives and rights of the assembly and its members.

• Guidelines

1. There are two types of questions of privilege: those that pertain to individual rights, and those that pertain to the prerogatives of the entire assembly. If both are made at the same time, the rights of the assembly take precedence over the rights of the individual.
2. To raise a question of privilege means that a member obtains the floor while business is in progress to make an urgent request. Then the chair must rule on the request. For instance, this motion can be used if there is something wrong with the meeting hall, such as a faulty heating or air-conditioning system.
3. The motion is also applicable if the rights of the assembly are in danger of being transgressed. This might occur if a member raises a confidential organizational matter before a guest, for example.
4. The motion can be used if a member feels that his or her comments were incorrectly recorded in the minutes.
5. If the situation cannot be resolved informally (adjusting the heat or air-conditioning, going into executive session), the chair must then rule whether the matter is a question of privilege and should be considered before business can be resumed. When business is once again taken up, it recommences at the point where it was interrupted.
6. The motion can be made even when someone is speaking, but it cannot interrupt a vote.

The following examples illustrate this motion:

▶ A member says, "I rise to a question of personal privilege."

or

A member says, "I rise to a question of privilege pertaining to the entire assembly."

or

A member says, "Madam Chair, a question of privilege!"
The chair responds, "Please state your question."
The member says, "[stating the specific problem] The light from the window is creating a glare, making it impossible to see the podium."
The chair says, "Will the sergeant-at-arms please close the drapes behind the podium."

Question of Privilege—Summary

A Question of Privilege takes precedence over:

- All main motions

- All subsidiary motions
- All incidental motions
- Most privileged motions, except those with higher rank: to Adjourn, Fix the Time to Which to Adjourn, and Recess

The motion can be made when someone else has the floor, but only if the matter is urgent. If possible, it should not interrupt a speaker. The motion does not require a second and cannot be amended, debated, or reconsidered. No vote is taken, as the chair rules on the motion.

Recess

A recess is a short break in a meeting.

• Guidelines

1. Don't confuse the privileged motion to recess with the main motion to recess. The privileged motion allows a recess while a motion is on the floor. A main motion allows the assembly to take a recess when there is *no* motion on the floor. As a result, the privileged motion only applies when a motion is on the floor.
2. The motion to recess is especially useful when it is necessary to take a short break in the debate, affording members a chance for a brief "cooling-off" period. A recess is also helpful during an election when the tellers are busy counting the ballots. In addition, a brief recess can give officers an opportunity to complete some necessary executive business.
3. After a recess, business is taken up exactly where it was left off.
4. If the agenda specifies a recess, there is no need to make a motion for one. In these instances, the chair need only declare the recess when it is reached on the agenda. It takes a two-thirds vote to postpone a scheduled recess.

The following examples describe the motion's use:

▶ A member says, "I move that we take a 15-minute recess."

or

A member says. "I move that the meeting recess until reconvened by the chair."

or

A member says, "I move that we recess until [specified time]."

A vote is taken, and if the motion carries, the chair says, "The motion is carried and the meeting is in recess for 20 minutes."

At the end of the recess, the chair says, "The recess is over and the meeting will now come to order."

Recess—Summary

A motion to take a recess takes precedence over:

- All main motions
- All subsidiary motions
- All incidental motions
- Most privileged motions except those of higher rank: Adjourn and Fix the Time to Which to Adjourn

The motion requires a second, and it cannot be debated or reconsidered. It can be amended and requires a majority vote to pass.

Illegal Motions

The following list highlights the most common illegal motions made during a meeting. If made, they will be denied by the chair. The illegal motions are arranged in alphabetical order by category.

- **Adjourn**

  1. A motion to adjourn at a specific time cannot be made while a motion is on the floor.
  2. A member cannot call out, "I move to adjourn," without first obtaining the floor. The motion is allowed, however, if the speaker obtains the consent of all members present at the meeting.

- **Appeal**

An appeal on an issue that cannot have two sides is out of order. In order for an appeal to be valid, the issue being appealed must have two logical sides.

- **Commit or Refer**

Any motion to Commit or Refer that is clearly foolish or abuses the motion is out of order. It would be out of order, for example, if a member made a motion to Commit that served to defeat the main motion.

- **Division of the Assembly**

This motion for retaking a vote is out of order if it is clear that the original vote was properly taken and tallied.

- **Lay on the Table**

1. While a motion is tabled, no member can make a motion that is substantially the same.
2. No member can make a motion that would conflict with the tabled motion.
3. A motion can only be tabled if the assembly has to deal with urgent business. A motion cannot be tabled simply for the convenience of the assembly.
4. The motion cannot be used to suppress debate or kill a motion.

- **Parliamentary Inquiry (Request)**

1. A presiding officer does not have to answer a parliamentary inquiry about a supposed situation.
2. The question must pertain directly to the matter at hand.

- **Point of Order**

While it is important to enforce the rules, members should not raise points of order when the infraction is minor.

- **Postpone to a Certain Time**

A motion to Postpone to a Certain Time that kills the main motion is not permitted. The following example illustrates such an instance:

► A fund-raising ball is being held on January 3. On December 15, the assembly receives an invitation to purchase a table of tickets. Ms. Draghi says, "I move that we purchase a table of tickets to the Museum Grand Ball on January 3, for a total cost of $1,000."
Mr. Heller says, "I second the motion."
The chair says, "A motion that the Society purchase a table of tickets to the Museum Grand Ball on January 3, for a total cost of $1,000 has been made and seconded."
Mr. Malone says, "I move that we postpone discussion of the motion until our next regular meeting, on January 14."

> The chair says, "Your motion is out of order. The issue is open for discussion."

If Mr. Malone still wishes to kill the motion, he can make a motion to Postpone Indefinitely.

• Reading Papers

The motion to read papers cannot be used as a delaying tactic.

Chapter 6

How To Make Motions

It is much more material that there should be a rule to go by, than what that rule is; that there may be a uniformity of proceeding in business, not subject to the caprice of the Speaker, or captiousness of the members. It is very material that order, decency, and regularity be preserved in a dignified public body.

Thomas Jefferson, *Manual of Parliamentary Practice,* 1801

The Chapter at a Glance

The Process of Making Motions

Listed below are the basic steps in making any motion:

1. A member stands up and addresses the chair.
2. The chair acknowledges the individual.
3. The member states the motion.
4. Another member seconds the motion.
5. The chair repeats the motion.
6. The chair calls for discussion on the motion.
7. The chair puts the motion to a vote.
8. The chair announces the results of the vote.

Addressing the Chair

In a small meeting, a member does not have to rise to address the chair. In a large meeting, however, the member must rise. If the meeting is very large, such as a convention, members may have to walk to a microphone to address the chair. Regardless of the size of the meeting, when addressing the chair the member need only give the chair's title, in the form the individual prefers. Traditionally the person leading the meeting was called the *chairman*. Today the presiding officer is more often called the *chair*, to make the term free of gender bias. Ask the chair or someone else in authority for the preferred term, or listen carefully to the conversation to find out the preferred term of address. Below are two examples:

▶ A member says, "Madam Chair."

or

A member says, "Mr. Chair."

Acknowledging the Individual

In a small meeting, the chair might simply nod in the member's direction to show acknowledgment. In a larger meeting, the chair will normally repeat the person's name, as the following example shows:

▶ The chair says, "The chair recognizes Carly Meyer."

The individual must wait for this acknowledgment before speaking.

Stating the Motion

Motions are often introduced with the words *I move that*. Below are several examples of ways to state the motion.

▶ Mr. Ling says, "I move that we adopt the Maxwell proposal."

or

Ms. Perez says, "I move that we establish a task force to examine the merger in greater detail."

or

Ms. Smith says, "I move that we recommend the Bradley group be retained for this project."

Since the main purpose of any motion is to communicate an idea to the assembly, all motions should be stated in concise, clear language that is appropriate to the assembly. Clarity is especially important when the motion is long or contains complex ideas. Many people jot down their main motions before offering them to the assembly to make sure that their ideas are ordered correctly and that the language is as precise as possible. The following example shows how an unclear motion can be effectively reworked:

▶ *Weak:* "I move that we should keep the club's trophies in a bookcase that we had won in the golf tournament." [Did the club win the trophies or the bookcase?]
Effective: "I move that we should keep the club's trophies that we won in the golf tournament in a bookcase."

It is equally important that the main motion be worth making. No matter how well-phrased a motion may be, it will serve only to obfuscate business and slow down the agenda if it does not serve a useful purpose. Below is an example of a main motion that does not have to be made.

▶ *Weak:* "I move that the assembly not answer the letter from Congressman Byrd."
Effective: [Why make the motion at all? Without the motion, there would not be a response, which is just what the motion proposes to accomplish.]

While it is true that all motions should be carefully crafted, it can be a challenging process to precisely capture the sentiments of an individual or an assembly in a motion that has not been written out ahead of time. As a result, parliamentary procedure allows for motions to be reshaped at several points in the procedure. At this stage in the process, it is simple to tailor the motion more precisely. Before the motion has been seconded, members can offer changes that fine-tune or slightly alter the speaker's meaning.

Shaping motions Suggestions to reshape motions should generally be minor adjustments to the motion, not major revisions. A motion that requires major revising would be voted down by the assembly. A new motion that more closely expresses the will of the majority would then be made.

The person who has offered the motion to the assembly has the option to accept or reject these suggestions. If so desired, the member can then restate the motion to include the suggestions. The following two examples demonstrate this process:

▶ Mr. Ling says, "I move that we adopt the Maxwell proposal."
Ms. Dorans says, "Perhaps you wish to add that we favor the *second* Maxwell proposal, the one offered on June 25th of this year."
Mr. Ling says, "Thank you for that suggestion. I agree that the word *second* should be included in the motion, but I do not think it necessary to mention the date the proposal was made. At this time, I would like to restate my motion as follows: I move that we adopt the second Maxwell proposal."

or

Ms. Smith says, "I move that we recommend the Bradley group be retained for this project."
Ms. Smith says, "Madam Chair, I wish to modify the motion by inserting the word *strongly* before the word *recommend*."

Withdrawing a motion At this point, the person who made the motion also has the option of withdrawing it from consideration. The motion can be withdrawn even after the motion has been seconded. After the chair states the motion, however, the motion must be disposed of by the assembly. The following dialogue illustrates this process:

▶ Ms. Perez says, "I move that we establish a task force to examine the merger in greater detail."
Ms. Perez says, "Mr. Chair, on second thought, I wish to withdraw the motion."
The chair says, "The motion has been withdrawn from consideration."

or

Ms. Padden says, "Madam Chair, I ask permission to withdraw my motion."
The chair says, "If no one objects, the motion is withdrawn."

Withdrawing Motions—Summary

A motion can be withdrawn up until the time that the voting has begun. The process is the same at any time after the chair has stated the motion. The maker of the motion must ask permission, and if no one objects, the motion can be withdrawn. If there is an objection, however, the motion must stand. It can be voted on or disposed of in another manner in accordance with parliamentary law.

Seconding the Motion

After the motion has been stated, in most instances another member must second it, as the following illustrates:

▶ A member says, "Madam Chair, I second the motion."

or

A member says, "I second the motion, Mr. Chairman."

Procedures that do not need a second are nominations and committee recommendations. Motions that do not require a second include the following:

- Division of the Assembly
- Nominations
- Objection to the Consideration of a Question
- Orders of the Day
- Parliamentary Inquiry
- Point of Information
- Point of Order
- Point of Personal Privilege
- Question of Privilege
- Requests
- Withdrawing a Motion

Repeating the Motion

After the motion has been made and seconded, the chair repeats the motion for the entire assembly. In this way, the chair can make sure that everyone has heard the motion.

▶ The chair says, "A motion has been made to adopt the Maxwell proposal."

or

The chair says, "A motion has been made to establish a task force to examine the merger in greater detail."

or

The chair says, "A motion has been made to recommend the Bradley group be retained for this project."

At this stage in the process, the members have another chance to reshape the motion before it is put to a vote. Once the chair has restated the motion, however, its revision is no longer in the hands of the person who originally made the motion. Now the membership controls how the motion is stated. If the member who made the motion wishes to revise it, he or she must receive unanimous consent.

Calling for Debate on the Motion

The chair then opens the discussion on the motion, as these examples show:

▶ The chair says, "The motion that the assembly adopt the Maxwell proposal has been seconded. It is now open for discussion."

or

The chair says, "The motion that the society establish a task force to examine the merger in greater detail has been seconded. It is now open for discussion."

or

The chair says, "The motion that the organization recommend the Bradley group be retained for this project has been seconded. Is there discussion on the motion?"

The motion can be revised at any point. At this stage in the process, however, the motion requires a motion to Amend to be altered (see page 98).

Putting the Motion to a Vote

After everyone who so desires has had an opportunity to speak to the motion, the chair takes a vote. It is important to wait until the discussion has subsided to be sure that everyone has had a chance to address the issue. The following examples illustrate how to put a motion to the vote:

▶ The chair says, "It has been moved and seconded that the assembly adopt the Maxwell proposal. Those in favor of the motion raise their hands now [pause to count votes]. Those opposed raise their hands now [pause to count votes]."

or

The chair says, "You have heard the resolution. Those in favor of its adoption please raise their right hands [pause to count the yes votes]. Those opposed please raise their right hands [pause to count the no votes]."

or

The chair says, "Those in favor of the motion say aye [pause to count votes]. Those opposed to the motion say no [pause to count votes]."

Announcing the Results of the Vote

The chair always announces the results of any vote. Below are some ways to accomplish this:

▶ The chair says, "The motion is carried, and the resolution is adopted."

or

The chair says, "The ayes have it; the motion is passed."

or

The chair says, "The motion is defeated."

Complete Process of Making a Motion

The following dialogue illustrates the entire process of making a motion when the matter is relatively clear-cut and the majority of the membership is in agreement with the motion:

▶ Ms. Bosso says, "Madam Chairwoman."
The chair responds, "Ms. Bosso."
Ms. Bosso says, "I move that the Club serve refreshments at all subsequent meetings."
Mr. Ryan says, "I second the motion."
The chair says, "It has been moved and seconded that the Club serve refreshments at all subsequent meetings. The motion is now open for debate." [The chair looks at Ms. Bosso. As the person who made the motion, she is entitled to speak first. Since she made the motion, she must speak in favor of it.]
Ms. Bosso says, "I think that refreshments add to the fellowship and help create a collegial atmosphere. We do not need anything elaborate, perhaps some cake and coffee."
Ms. Hynes says, "Who is going to supply these refreshments?"
Mr. Ryan says, "We can call the local bakery to bring over some cakes."

Ms. Meyer adds, "They can also supply coffee and tea."
Mr. Swanket says, "Sounds great to me. I could sure use a little dessert around now."
The chair says, "It has been moved and seconded that the Club serve refreshments at all subsequent meetings. Those in favor of the motion say aye [pause to count votes]. Those opposed say no [pause to count votes]. The motion is carried, and the motion is adopted."

Order of Precedence

The order in which motions are made and treated depends on their order of precedence. If a motion is made out of order, it is null and void. The following chart illustrates the order of precedence of motions.

Highest Rank (Takes precedence)	**Privileged Motions** Fix the Time to Which to Adjourn Adjourn Recess Question of Privilege Call for the Orders of the Day **Incidental Motions** [Incidental motions take precedence over other motions only when they are truly incidental to the business on the floor and thus cannot be ranked.] **Subsidiary Motions** Lay on the Table Previous Question Limit or Extend Debate Postpone to a Certain Time Commit or Refer Amend Postpone Indefinitely
Lowest Rank (Yields to all)	**Main Motion**

Making Main Motions

The steps described above hold for making all motions, but there are special rules that apply to making main motions. These rules are as follows:

1. An assembly cannot deal with any matter that falls outside its scope. Thus, an organization cannot pass a main motion that is not covered by its bylaws. However, this rule can be overturned by a two-thirds vote of the entire membership.
2. A main motion must be in accord with the rules of the organization and the rules of the state where the organization is chartered. When a nonvalid motion is passed by the assembly, it is automatically invalid, no matter how large a margin it received.
3. A main motion cannot contradict a motion that has already been approved by the assembly.
4. Similarly, a main motion cannot contradict a motion that is before the assembly but has not yet been voted on. If the motion is still alive but has not yet been disposed of, a new motion cannot work against it.
5. A member cannot make a main motion that repeats a main motion that has already been voted down by the assembly in the same meeting or the same session. This holds true even if the main motion has been reworded. If it is substantially the same motion, it is invalid. However, the same main motion can be made once again at a new meeting or a new session.

Applying Secondary Motions

Subsidiary, incidental, and privileged motions are called *secondary motions,* as they are applied to main motions to aid in their disposition or to draw the members' attention to matters of pressing importance. Under most circumstances, each main motion must be decided before the assembly can consider another order of business.

Privileged Motions

Two privileged motions, Call for the Orders of the Day and Question of Privilege, can be brought up at any time during a debate on a main motion because each must be addressed at once.

Call for the Orders of the Day Under parliamentary law, it takes only one member to point out that the agenda is not being followed. To do so, the member makes a Call for the Orders of the Day. This motion demands that the order of items be followed. The assembly can set aside the agenda only through a two-thirds vote. (See also page 137.)

Question of Privilege In the same way, only one member is needed to interrupt a meeting to point out a problem with the physical surroundings—the heat, light, noise, and so on. The problem must be of pressing importance, however. In most cases, the chair resolves the problem informally.

Even though a Call for the Orders of the Day and a Question of Privilege are both privileged and not main motions, they are disposed of as main motions in that they must be resolved before the assembly can once again consider the main motion. (See also page 139.)

Subsidiary and Incidental Motions

Subsidiary and incidental motions can be applied to main motions to shape their disposition. In most instances, subsidiary and incidental motions are applied to main motions while the motion is being debated.

What happens if more than one subsidiary or incidental motion is applied to a main motion? In such cases, the assembly can deal with each subsidiary or incidental motion in turn so that only one such motion is applied to the main motion at a time. Or, the membership can decide to allow the motions to continue and deal with them all at once. Each motion then can be disposed of according to the order in which it was made, voting from the last motion to the first; the final motion to be voted on would be the main motion itself.

The manner in which the membership decides to deal with subsidiary and incidental motions depends in part on the motions themselves. In some instances, it is more sensible to deal with each motion as it is made, for the disposition of the secondary motion can affect the main motion substantially. In other cases, the motions can be voted on after they have all been made.

Motion Format

The following examples demonstrate possible ways to make various motions. During an actual meeting, the wording of each motion will vary with the nature of the specific motion, the degree of formality of the assembly, and the speaker's style. Use the following examples as guidelines. In all cases, motions should be as specific and clear as possible; many speakers jot down their motions before offering them to the assembly. The motions, with their examples, are arranged in alphabetical order.

Adjourn

▶ Member A says, "I move that the meeting be adjourned at this time."
Member B says, "I second the motion."
The chair says, "It has been moved and seconded that the meeting now adjourn. All those in favor of immediate adjournment, please say aye [pause to tally votes]. All those opposed, please say no [pause to tally votes]. The ayes have it and the meeting is now adjourned."

Amend

Adding specific words at the end of the motion

▶ A member says, "I move to amend the motion by adding [specific words]."

Inserting words in the body of the motion

▶ A member says, "I move to amend the motion by inserting [specific word or words] before/after the word [specific words in the motion]."

Deleting words in the motion

▶ A member says, "I move to amend the motion by crossing out [specific word, sentence, or paragraph]."

Deleting and inserting words in the motion

- ▶ A member says, "I move to amend the motion by crossing out [specific words] and inserting [new material]."

Replacing a pending motion in its entirety with another motion relating to the same subject

- ▶ A member says, "I move to substitute the pending motion with the following new motion: [body of the new motion]."

Filling in the Blanks

The chair creates a blank in a motion

- ▶ The chair says, "The chair proposes creating a blank by deleting [material to be deleted]. If no one objects to this change, the blank is created. Since no one objected, the blank is inserted in place of [specific material]."

A member creates a blank in a motion

- ▶ A member says, "The Society shall sponsor an exchange student at a cost not to exceed $ ________."

A member inserts a blank in place of a specific section of a motion

- ▶ A member says, "I move that we create a blank in the motion by crossing out the phrase [specific phrase]."

Appeal

- ▶ Member A says, "I appeal the chair's decision."
  Member B says, "I second the motion."
  The chair states the issue under dispute and, if desired, explains the reasons for his or her ruling on the matter. Discussion ensues. The chair then says, "Shall the chair's decision stand as the judgment for the organization?"
  The appeal is decided by vote. The chair says, "All those in favor of sustaining the chair's decision on the matter say aye [pause to tally votes]. All those opposed say no [pause to tally votes]." The chair then announces the decision.

Call for the Orders of the Day

- ▶ A member says, "Madam Chair, I request the regular orders of the day."
  The chair responds, "There has been a call for the orders of the day." The chair then treats the skipped item.

Commit or Refer

Refer to a committee

- A member says, "I move to refer [specific matter] to the [specific name of committee] for further study."

  or

  A member says, "I move that the motion be referred to a committee of four members to be appointed by the chair."

Consider as a committee of the whole

- A member says, "I move that the Society now resolve itself into a committee of the whole to consider the matter of [specific matter]."

Consider as a quasi committee of the whole

- A member says, "I move that the Society now resolve itself into a quasi committee of the whole to consider the issue."

Consider informally

- A member says, "I move that the issue be considered informally."

Consideration by Paragraph

- Member A says, "I move that we consider this document by paragraph."

  Member B says, "I second the motion."

  The chair then reads each paragraph in turn, asking at the end of each, "Is there any discussion on this passage?" If discussion ensues, the membership revises the passage. If not, the chair moves on to the next passage, reading it and then asking for discussion. When the entire document has been completed in this manner, the chair says, "Is there any discussion on the entire document?" Then the entire document is voted on.

Division of the Assembly

- The chair announces the results of the vote. "The ayes have it and the motion is carried."

  A member says, "I call for a division."

  or

  A member says, "I demand a division!"

The chair responds, "A division is requested," and then takes a rising vote.

Division of a Question

▶ Member A says, "I move to divide the question so as to consider independently the question of [specific issue] and [second specific issue]."
Member B says, "I second the motion."

Fix the Time to Which to Adjourn

▶ Member A says, "I move that when this assembly adjourns, it adjourns to meet at 4:00 p.m. on Tuesday, June 1 [a specific time]."
Member B says, "I second the motion."
The chair says, "It has been moved and seconded that the meeting fix the time to which to adjourn to 4:00 p.m. on Tuesday, June 1. All those in favor of the motion please say aye [pause to tally votes]. All those opposed please say no [pause to tally votes]. The ayes have it. When the meeting adjourns this morning, it will adjourn to meet at 4:00 p.m. on Tuesday, June 1."

Lay on the Table

▶ A member says, "I move that the question of [specific motion] lie on the table."

Taking the motion from the table, resuming debate on the tabled motion

▶ A member says, "I move to take the question of [specific motion] from the table."

Limit or Extend Debate

To cut down on the number of speeches

▶ A member says, "I move that no member be allowed to speak more than once to the motion."

To limit the time that each speaker may have the floor

▶ A member says, "I move that each speaker be limited to one speech of two minutes each."

To limit or extend the time that a specific member can speak

▶ A member says, "I move that the time that [name of member] be allowed to speak be limited to two minutes."

or

A member says, "I move that the time that [name of member] be allowed to speak be extended by two minutes."

To limit the time for the entire debate

▶ A member says, "I move that debate on the pending motion be limited to [specific length of time]."

To set the time for stopping the debate and voting on the motion

▶ A member says, "I move that the debate be closed at 1:00 p.m. and the motion put to a vote at that time."

To combine purposes

▶ A member says, "I move that the members in charge of the fund-raising drive be allowed to speak for five minutes each and that all other members be limited to one speech of no more than two minutes each and that all pending motions be voted on no later than 5:00 p.m."

Main Motion

▶ A member says, "I move that the Society hold its annual holiday party at the Three Village Inn, on Saturday, December 18, at 8:00 to 11:00 p.m."

or

A member says, "I move that the Parent-Teacher Association sponsor a candy sale, the proceeds to be used to defray the cost of the new computer system."

Objection to the Consideration of a Question

▶ A member says, "I object to the consideration of a question." The chair says, "There is an objection to the consideration of the question. Shall the question be discussed? Those in favor of considering the question please rise [pause to count votes]. You may be seated. Those opposed to considering the question please rise [pause to count votes]. You may be seated. There are less than two-thirds opposed and the question will be considered."

Parliamentary Inquiry

▶ A member says, "I have a parliamentary inquiry."
The chair says, "What is the inquiry?"

The member says, "Is it [specific question about the way to conduct the business at hand]."

Point of Information

Addressed to an officer

▶ A member says, "Will the Secretary please explain when the correspondence was sent out?"

Addressed to a member

▶ A member says, "Mr. Chair, I would like to ask the speaker a question."

Addressed to the chair

▶ A member says, "Mr. Chair, I rise to a point of information."
The chair says, "Please explain the point."
The member says, "How many people have signed up for the convention planning committee? [specific point of information]."

Point of Order

▶ A member says, "Point of Order!"
The chair says, "Please state your point of order."
The member says, "I make a point of order that [notes specific transgression of the rules]."
The chair says, "The point of order is well-taken because [explains specific violation of the rules]."
or
The chair says, "The point of order is not well-taken because [explains how the rules have been followed]."

If the chair is unsure of the decision, the members may be consulted as a group, as the following example shows:

▶ The chair says, "Member A raised a point of order that [suspected violation of the rules]. The chair asks the members for their input. The question is, [states the suspected violation of the rules]."

If the chair is unsure of the decision, he or she can put the matter to a vote, as shown below:

▶ The chair says, "All those who believe the motion is correct as stated, please say aye [pause to tally votes]. All those who believe the motion is out of order, please say no [pause to tally votes]. The no votes have it and the motion is out of order."

Postpone to a Certain Time

To postpone the motion to the next regular meeting

▶ A member says, "I move that we postpone this motion to the next regular meeting."

To discuss the motion after a specific event has occurred

▶ A member says, "I move to postpone discussion on the motion until after we present the scroll and plaque to Mayor Carman."

To set a definite time for the motion to be reconsidered

▶ A member says, "I move that debate on the motion be postponed until 9:00 p.m."

Postpone Indefinitely

▶ Member A says, "I move that we purchase six copies of Henry Rusk's new book of photographs for the Society's library."
Member B responds, "I move that the motion be postponed indefinitely."
Member C says, "I second the motion."
The chair says, "It is moved and seconded to postpone indefinitely the motion that the Society purchase six copies of Henry Rusk's new book of photographs for its library. Those in favor of postponing the motion please say aye [pause to count votes]. Those opposed please say no [pause to count votes]. The ayes have it and the motion is postponed indefinitely."

If the motion to Postpone Indefinitely is defeated, the dialogue would follow this format:

▶ The chair says, "The question is on the motion to postpone indefinitely the motion that the Society purchase six copies of Henry Rusk's new book of photographs for its library. Those in favor of postponing the motion please say aye [pause to count votes]. Those opposed please say no [pause to count votes]. The no votes have it and the motion to postpone indefinitely is defeated."

Previous Question

▶ A member says, "I move the previous question."

Question of Privilege

▶ A member says, "I rise to a question of personal privilege."
The chair responds, "Please state your question."
The member says [stating the specific problem], "The noise from the next meeting room is very distracting."
The chair says, "Will the sergeant-at-arms please close the door between the two rooms."

Reading Papers

▶ A member says, "If there is no objection, I would like to read the following material. It is half a page long and bears directly on the matter of the proposed land acquisition [specific length and relevance of material explained]."
The chair says, "Is there any objection to the reading of this material? [pause for response]. There being none, permission to read the statement in debate is granted."

or

The chair says, "Is there any objection to the reading of this material? [pause for response]. There being objections, permission to read the statement in debate is denied."

Recess

▶ A member says, "I move that we take a 15-minute recess."
A vote is taken, and if the motion carries, the chair says, "The motion is carried and the meeting is in recess for 15 minutes."
At the end of the recess, the chair says, "The recess is over and the meeting will now come to order."

Suspend the Rules

▶ A member says, "I move to suspend the rules that interfere with [specific matter at hand]."
A member says, "I move to suspend the rules to discuss the membership drive, since it is only a week until the convention."

Handling a Motion for Passage or Defeat

At any meeting, members will be confronted with a series of motions and resolutions, some of which they will support and some which they will oppose. How does parliamentary procedure affect a member's personal reactions to specific motions and resolutions? Parliamentary procedure can be used to help members ensure that a motion passes or is defeated. This is entirely ethical, when used within the following boundaries:

To help pass a motion	To help defeat a motion
Do not let a motion be postponed by voting against the motion to delay.	Move to postpone the motion until the next meeting.
Do not let a motion be referred to a committee. Vote against the motion to refer to committee.	Move to refer the motion to a committee. This will help prolong or delay its passage.
Vote for the motion.	Vote against the motion.
Rise and speak in favor of the motion.	Rise and speak against the motion.
Have all your supporters at the meeting and convince them to stay until the end. Remember: voters decide the question.	Have all your supporters at the meeting and convince them to stay until the end. Remember: voters decide the question.
Defeat unfriendly amendments and propose useful ones.	Amend the motion to make it more complex and less useful.
Vote against indefinite postponement to bring the motion back to the floor.	Move to postpone the motion for an indefinite period of time; this will in effect kill it outright.
Second the motion when it is made.	Do not second the motion; remain silent in your seat.
Vote against tabling the motion.	Move to table the motion to remove it from consideration.

Defeat the motion to recess. This will prevent opponents from gathering the support they need.	Move to take a recess. This will help members gather the support they need to pass the motion.
Vote to defeat the previous question. This will give members more time to fully discuss the motion's good points.	Move the question. This will stifle discussion of the motion's valid points.
Defeat adjournment.	Make a motion to adjourn the meeting. This removes the motion for consideration that day.
Graciously accept the results of the vote to uphold the organization's dignity and maintain its unity.	Graciously accept the results of the vote to uphold the organization's dignity and maintain its unity.

Motions in Review

The table below summarizes the main features of various commonly used motions. A brief example of a motion's wording is followed by its need for a second, whether it can be debated or amended, and the size of the vote required for its passage.

How to Make Motions

Motion	What to Say	Second	Debate	Amend	Vote
Adjourn	"I move that we adjourn."	Yes	No	No	Majority
Adjourn at a future time	"I move that we adjourn at [specific time]." *or* "I move that we adjourn to reconvene at [specific time]."	Yes	Yes	Yes	Majority

Motion	What to Say	Second	Debate	Amend	Vote
Adopt a report	"I move that the report be adopted."	Yes	No	No	Majority
Amend a motion on the floor	"I move to amend by adding . . ." *or* "I move to amend by striking out . . ." *or* "I move to amend by inserting the word . . . before [or after] the word. . . ."	Yes	Yes	Yes	Majority
Avoid debating an improper motion	"I object to consideration of this motion."	Yes	No	No	Two-thirds
Complain about the physical conditions	"I rise to a question of privilege."	Yes	No	No	None
End debate	"I move the previous question."	Yes	No	No	Two-thirds
Give closer study	"I move to refer the matter to committee."	Yes	Yes	Yes	Majority
Introduce business	"I move that [insert specific motion]."	Yes	Yes	Yes	Majority
Postpone discussion	"I move to postpone discussion until . . ."	Yes	Yes	Yes	Majority
Protest a breach of rules or conduct	"I rise to a point of order."	No	No	No	None

Motion	What to Say	Second	Debate	Amend	Vote
Recess	"I move that we recess for . . ."	Yes	No	Yes	Majority
Reconsider an action	"I move to reconsider the vote on [specific issue]."	Yes	If debatable	No	Majority
Request information	"Point of information."	No	No	No	None
Suspend an issue	"I move to table the motion."	Yes	No	No	Majority
Suspend the rules	"I move to suspend the rules so that [specific issue]."	Yes	No	No	Majority
Take up a tabled issue	"I move to take from the table [specific issue]."	Yes	No	No	Majority
Verify a vote by asking members to rise	"I call for a division." *or* "Division!"	No	No	No	None
Vote on the chair's ruling	"I appeal the chair's decision."	Yes	Yes	No	Majority

Chapter 7

Mock Meeting

THE MEETING AT A GLANCE

The following mock meeting illustrates how motions are made to accomplish business smoothly and efficiently. You can use this sample meeting script in several different ways. First, you can read through it as a way to reinforce what you learned about making motions in the previous chapters. Or, you may wish to use it as a way to refresh your memory before you chair or attend a meeting. It is also useful during a meeting; follow the script to help you dispose of business in the proper order.

Sample Meeting Script

[This is the biweekly meeting of the Anytown School Board. The meeting has been called for 7:30. The chair is presiding.]

CHAIR:

This is the 7:30 meeting of the Anytown School Board. A quorum is present, so the meeting will come to order. [The chair raps the gavel once.]

The minutes of the previous meeting have been distributed. Does everyone have a copy of the minutes? [Brief pause.]

Are there any corrections to the minutes? [Note: The chair should use the term *corrections* rather than the terms *additions* or *deletions* because *corrections* covers both these instances. Otherwise, the chair will have to call first for additions and then for deletions, clearly taking too much time on this matter.]

1st MEMBER:

I have a parliamentary inquiry. [The chair recognizes the 1st Member.] The minutes show every approved and defeated amendment as well as a summary of the discussion. Is it necessary that minutes be written in such detail?

CHAIR:

Detailed minutes are not necessary. When a motion is amended and adopted, the minutes should read, "A motion by Maria Sanchez was amended and adopted as follows: . . . ." Also, debate is not summarized. Would the clerk please revise the minutes in this regard for approval at the next meeting.

2nd MEMBER:

At the last meeting, there was a long discussion and a resolution on the installation of the new heating system. Later in the meeting, the motion was withdrawn. Should mention be made in the minutes of the fact that a motion was made and then withdrawn without being voted on?

CHAIR:

Such mention is not necessary; withdrawn motions do not appear in the minutes. At this time, would the treasurer please give a report.

TREASURER:

As of January 1, cash in the EAB money market account was $213,639.17. Cash in the NW money market account was $233,202.87. Cash in the Bank of NY money market account was $150,931.40. Cash in the Citibank money market account was

$150,840.65. Cash in the checking account was $10,122.67. In addition, we have a $100,000.00 Certificate of Deposit at NWB due 10/21/94 @ 2.90% interest. This gives a total of $858,736.76.

Our receipts are as follows: $153,631.00 for a partial tax levy and $479.86 for December interest. Our liabilities are as follows:

Accounts Payable	$187,485.00
Donations	286.00
Accrued Wages	431,907.98

This means that our total liabilities are $619,678.98. This leaves a total fund balance of $239,057.78, subject to the annual audit.

CHAIR:
Are there any questions on the treasurer's report? Hearing none, the treasurer's report will be filed for audit.

3RD MEMBER:
A point of order. [The Chair recognizes the 3rd Member.] We failed to take any action on the treasurer's report.

CHAIR:
The treasurer's report is received or filed for audit. No action is necessary. The next item of business on the agenda is the report of the transportation committee. In the absence of the chair of that committee, will a member of the committee please give the report.

4TH MEMBER:
At our last meeting, on December 15, we authorized the hiring of a new bus company, KayCor Incorporated, to transport students. On December 17, the company was hired to handle the late run, scheduled at 4:30 p.m. At the same time, we also issued a memo to all district residents with school-age children. The memo concerns the bus policy and specifically stresses student behavior and pick-up times on all routes.

CHAIR:
Thank you for your report. The next standing committee report is the curriculum committee.

2ND MEMBER:
Point of order. We did not take action on the transportation committee's report. Nor did we make a motion or second on the report.

CHAIR:
Committee reports without recommendations are for information only and do not require any action on the part of the membership or the chair. Further, the only time a committee report would be seconded is when it is a committee of one. Now we will have the report of the curriculum committee.

5TH MEMBER:
The committee recommends that the district host an informational night for parents. We recommend that the program include seminars on the science, math, English, reading, and social studies programs. In addition, we would like to include workshops on study skills, attendance, and behavior problems. At the same time, we would like to screen very young children for learning disorders.

3RD MEMBER:
A point of information. I have a number of questions. First of all, who is going to run this program? Would it be offered during the day or at night? And then, how will it be funded? Do parents really want such a program? What attendance can we reasonably expect?

CHAIR:
[Speaking to the 5th Member] Would you answer these questions?

5TH MEMBER:
We will ask subject-area chairpersons to volunteer to run the seminars and workshops. We will invite the school psychologists and the

guidance department to test the three- and four-year-olds for learning disorders. The program would be offered at night, from 7:00 p.m. to 9:30 p.m., with each seminar or workshop 45 minutes in length, reserving the rest of the time for passing in the halls, brief opening and closing ceremonies, and refreshments. Parents or other interested parties would then be able to take one or two seminars or workshops. The learning-disability screening will continue throughout the evening. The Parent-Teacher Association has agreed to fund the program, but we anticipate the only costs to be refreshments and publicity. Parents have expressed an interest in such a program; to date, about 100 people responded in the affirmative to our preliminary survey.

CHAIR:
Is there any discussion on the motion to host an informational night for parents? [Remember that the chair states every motion, second, and outcome of the vote.]

4TH MEMBER:
I move to divide the question so we can consider and vote on the two questions separately.

1ST MEMBER:
Second.

CHAIR:
All those in favor of dividing the question say aye [pause to count votes]. Those opposed say no [pause to count votes]. The chair is in doubt of the outcome and will take a standing vote. All those in favor of dividing the question please rise. Thank you [pause to count votes]. Be seated. All those opposed please stand. Thank you [pause to count votes]. Be seated. The motion to divide is defeated. The question before us is that the curriculum committee host an informational night for parents including workshops on study skills, attendance, and behavior problems and simultaneously screen very young children for learning disorders. Is there further discussion on the question?

2ND MEMBER:
I move to postpone further discussion on the matter to the next meeting.

3RD MEMBER:
Second.

CHAIR:
It has been moved and seconded to postpone further discussion on the informational night project until the next meeting. Is there any discussion on this motion?

2ND MEMBER:
I move to refer the whole matter back to the curriculum committee for further study.

CHAIR:
The motion to refer to committee is out of order. [The motion to refer is of lower rank.] Is there any discussion on the motion to postpone further discussion on the informational night project until the next meeting? [pause]. Hearing none, all those in favor of the motion say aye [pause to count votes]. All those opposed say no [pause to count votes]. The motion to postpone is defeated.

The pending question is that the curriculum committee host an informational night for parents including workshops on study skills, attendance, and behavior problems and simultaneously screen very young children for learning disorders. Are you ready for the question? All in favor of hosting an informational night for parents including workshops on study skills, attendance, and behavior problems and simultaneously screening very young children for learning disorders say aye [pause to count votes]. All those opposed say no [pause to count votes]. The motion is defeated.

6TH MEMBER:
A point of personal privilege. I noticed that Dr. Brock has just arrived. I suggest that we interrupt our regular business to permit her to speak to us about the state budget.

CHAIR:

With your general consent, we will have Dr. Brock speak now. [Consent is obtained and Dr. Brock delivers her speech.] Thank you, Dr. Brock. When the last meeting adjourned, a motion was pending to spend $500 for a Whole Language consultant. The question is now before you for consideration under Unfinished Business. Is there any discussion to this matter? [pause].

Since there is no discussion, are you ready for the vote? All those in favor of the motion say aye [pause to count votes]. All those opposed say no [pause to count votes]. The ayes have it and the motion is carried.

We will now proceed to New Business. Is there any New Business?

1st MEMBER:

At our last meeting, we approved the purchase of several pieces of furniture for the Head Start room at a cost not to exceed $4,000. I have since learned that several members are willing to donate the furniture that we need and that it is in excellent condition. I therefore move to rescind the purchase of the office furniture.

4th MEMBER:

Second.

CHAIR:

Is there any discussion?

7th MEMBER:

I call the previous question.

3rd MEMBER:

Second.

CHAIR:
The question has been called. All those in favor of the motion raise their right hands [pause to count votes]. All those opposed raise their right hands [pause to count votes]. The motion to call the question has been approved by a two-thirds vote.

Now to vote on the motion to rescind the motion to purchase the office furniture. All those in favor of the motion say aye [pause to count votes]. All those opposed say no [pause to count votes]. The no votes have it and the motion to rescind is defeated. Is there any further New Business?

2ND MEMBER:
I move that we have refreshments at the conclusion of all board meetings.

3RD MEMBER:
Second.

5TH MEMBER:
I move to amend the motion by adding the words "the refreshments to be donated by members" at the end of the motion.

4TH MEMBER:
Second.

CHAIR:
Is there any discussion? If not, we will vote on the amendment first and then the motion as amended. All those in favor of the amendment say aye [pause to count votes]. All those opposed say no [pause to count votes]. The motion to amend has been approved.

We are now voting on the motion as amended to have refreshments at the conclusion of all board meetings, the refreshments to be donated by members. All those in favor of the amended motion say aye [pause to count votes]. All those opposed say no [pause to count votes]. The ayes have it and the motion to serve refreshments, as provided by members, has been approved.

2ND MEMBER:
Earlier this evening we defeated a motion that the district host an informational night for parents and simultaneously screen very young children for learning disorders. I voted against that motion. I now move to reconsider that action.

4TH MEMBER:
Second.

CHAIR:
It has been moved and seconded to reconsider the proposal to host an informational night for parents and simultaneously screen very young children for learning disorders. Is there any discussion? [Discussion ensues.]

1ST MEMBER:
I move the previous question.

3RD MEMBER:
I second the motion.

CHAIR:
The previous question has been moved. All those in favor of moving the previous question please rise [pause to tally votes]. Please be seated. All those opposed to moving the previous question please rise [pause to tally votes]. Please be seated. The motion did not carry by a two-thirds vote. The motion before us now is to reconsider the proposal to host an informational night for parents and simultaneously screen very young children for learning disorders. The motion is now open for debate.

Are you ready for the question? All those in favor of the motion say aye [pause to count votes]. All those opposed say no [pause to count votes]. The motion is defeated. Is there any other business? [pause].

2ND MEMBER:
I move that in response to recent surveys and a demonstrated need, we institute a full-day kindergarten program, district-wide.

4TH MEMBER:
I second the motion.

CHAIR:
It has been moved and seconded that the school district institute a full-day kindergarten program, district-wide. Is there any discussion to the motion?

1ST MEMBER:
The hour being late, I move to postpone the motion until 7:30 p.m. at our next regular meeting.

3RD MEMBER:
I second the motion.

2ND MEMBER:
This is an extremely important issue and should be considered at once. Many people in the district are agitating for a full-day kindergarten program, and standardized test scores indicate that our kindergarten students are falling behind those whose schools offer a full-day program.

4TH MEMBER:
This motion is urgent, but it will require a great deal of discussion on our part, as well as a significant outlay of funds. This issue deserves our full and fresh attention and it is very late. As a result, I support the motion to postpone.

2ND MEMBER:
The arguments are well-taken. As a result, I will move to amend the motion to postpone, by adding "and make it a special order."

5TH MEMBER:
I second the motion.

CHAIR:
It is moved and seconded that the motion be amended to postpone the motion until the next regular meeting by adding "and make it a special order." Is there any debate on the motion? [pause]. Since there is no comment, the question before us is to amend the motion to postpone the motion until 7:30 p.m. at our next regular meeting by adding "and make it a special order." Are you ready for the question? All those in favor of the motion say aye [pause to count votes]. All those opposed say no [pause to count votes]. The ayes have it and the amendment is adopted.

The question is now on the amended motion to postpone the motion until 7:30 p.m. and make it a special order. The motion needs a two-thirds vote to pass. Are you ready for the question? All those in favor of postponing the motion until 7:30 p.m. at our next regular meeting and make it a special order please rise [pause to count votes]. Thank you. You may be seated now. All those opposed please rise [pause to count votes]. Thank you. You may be seated now. The motion is carried, by a two-thirds vote. The motion is a special order for 7:30 p.m. at our next regular meeting.

Is there any further new business? There being none, we stand adjourned. [The chair raps the gavel.]

Chapter 8

How To Run a Meeting

> The great purpose of all rules and forms is to subserve the will of the assembly, rather than to restrain it; to facilitate, and not to obstruct, the expression of their deliberate sense.
>
> Luther Cushing, *Manual of Parliamentary Practice,* 1845

The Chapter at a Glance

Effective Organizations

You have spent the last week on the road, attending different shareholders meetings. Some were so interesting and effective that you were astonished at the end of the meeting to realize that you had been sitting around a table for two hours; other meetings, in contrast, were so tedious that you kept stealing glances at your watch. Or perhaps you have been invited to consult at another division of your volunteer service organization. The topic is highly controversial and you are anticipating trouble. The grapevine buzzes for a week about the hot issues and the fiery personalities involved.

To your amazement, the meeting runs smoothly and the matter is settled equitably and amicably.

Qualities of an effective meeting It is not your imagination; some meetings *are* more efficient than others. At these meetings, a great deal of business gets accomplished and people remain composed. How do they do it?

Effective organizations share a number of qualities in common. First, there is a high level of trust, as people feel that they can rely on each other to deal with issues fairly and honestly. Second, there is a concern for the welfare of co-workers, especially for the weakest or least-assertive members. There is a sense that each individual's feelings will be respected, and not be used as ammunition when issues are being decided. Third, authority is shared, which fosters a sense of collective responsibility and a respect for the work the organization seeks to accomplish. Expectations are high, as people believe they will work together to produce the best possible product and decisions. Lastly, time is used carefully, and people exert a high level of discretionary effort.

It is not smoke and mirrors, moreover! There are some clear-cut prerequisites for effective teamwork and group leadership. Read the following characteristics and see how many apply to your organization—and how many you would like to see become a part of it.

- **Characteristics of successful organizations**

1. The group has a clear understanding of its purpose and goals.
2. Members of the group are able to see beyond the immediate goals to the long-range effects.
3. As a result of careful planning and long-range vision, members take changes in stride.
4. There is a high degree of intercommunication in an atmosphere that allows people to freely express their reactions and opinions.
5. Although there is a high degree of cohesiveness and solidarity, the group is able to be objective about its own functioning.
6. Members can face problems and make whatever changes are necessary to achieve the group's goals, heading off small difficulties before they become large problems.
7. There is a suitable balance between the group's productivity and the individual's satisfaction, largely because people communicate with each other well and share leadership responsibilities.

These strengths of a successful group also appear in the details of effective meetings. Here the group's members make progress toward a meeting's goals with a maximum of efficiency and a minimum of wasted time and effort.

As this chapter describes, the group is guided through a successful meeting by a combination of capable officers and a clear agenda, which is drawn from the order of business.

Order of Business

The *order of business* deals with the order in which matters are considered before the assembly. The arrangement of items can also be called *orders of the day* or the *agenda.* Arranging items in a specific ranking helps members and officers deal with all the business they must resolve because they can be assured that each item will be treated fully in its turn. Groups that meet at regular times, such as once a month, will normally follow the same order of business at every meeting. Special meetings and conventions, in contrast, will set up a special order of business for each meeting. Most organizations divide the business into six sections, as follows:

1. Reading and approval of the minutes
2. Reports of officers, boards, and standing committees
3. Reports of special committees
4. Special orders
5. Unfinished business
6. New business

Notice that the amount of time devoted to each item is left open, since it may vary from meeting to meeting. Effective chairpersons study the order of business carefully before every meeting and keep it close at hand during the proceedings. Below is a table that describes the order of business. The first column describes what happens; the second, what is said.

- **Call to Order**

Chair rises, raps the gavel once, and calls the meeting to order. Optional opening ceremony, with invocation and/or pledge.	The chair says, "The meeting will now come to order."

- **Reading and Approval of the Minutes**

The clerk reads the minutes.	The chair says, "The clerk will read the minutes of the previous meeting."
The chair asks for any necessary corrections to the minutes.	The chair says, "Are there any corrections to the minutes?"

- **Treasurer's Report**

The treasurer's report does not have to be adopted, unless the report is a financial audit.	The chair says, "We will now have the treasurer's report."
After the report, the chair asks for questions.	The chair says, "Are there any questions? If not, the the report will be filed for audit."

- **Correspondence**

In most instances, the clerk summarizes the correspondence, unless a letter is very brief or a member requests that a letter be read. The clerk also reads the correspondence that does not require any action on the part of the board. Letters that do require board action are treated in the chairperson's report or under New Business.	The chair says, "Is there any correspondence?"

- **Committee Reports: Executive Board**

The clerk gives a brief report of any business that has been transacted. No action is taken on this report.	The chair says, "We shall now hear the executive board report by the secretary [or clerk]."

If there are any recommendations, the members vote on them at this time. This helps the assembly deal with business in a more timely manner.

The chair says, "You have heard the recommendations of the executive board. What is your pleasure?" [The members then make the appropriate motions.]

- **Committee Reports: Standing Committees**

Before the meeting, the chairperson should contact the chairs of the standing committees to see who wishes to make a report. Chairs should be reminded to keep their reports brief. Members do not have to make a motion for adoption unless the committee makes recommendations for action by the assembly.

The chair says, "We will now hear the report of the ________ committee given by the chair of that committee [or a member who may be substituting for the chair]." The chair then says, "Are there any questions or discussion in regard to this committee report? If not, the report will be filed as read."

The chair makes a motion to adopt the recommendations in the report. The motion does not have to be seconded.

The chair thanks all the members of the committee for their work. The chair then says, "The ________ committee moves that the organization [specific recommendation]. Is there any discussion to the motion?" [Complete the motion process.]

- **Committee Reports: Special Committees**

Recall that special committees are automatically disbanded when their work is completed. The reports describe the progress of their committees.

The chair says, "We will now have the report of the ________ special committee."

After the report, the chair says, "Are there any questions? What is your pleasure concerning this information?"

- **Unfinished Business**

The chair and members can look at the agenda to see what business has been left unfinished. In addition, the clerk will have prepared a list of items carried over from the previous meetings. Each item is dealt with in order.

The chair says, "Under unfinished business, the first item is [specific motion]."

- **New Business**

The chair or any member can bring new business before the group for consideration. A motion must be made before discussion and vote.

The chair says, "New business is now in order. Is there any new business?"

- **Announcements**

The chair announces the date, time, and location of the next meeting.

The chair says, "The next regular meeting will be held on [date] in the usual meeting room [or any other location]."

- **Program**

The program for the evening begins.

The chair calls on the program chairs or the program committee to introduce the program. At the end of the program, the chair thanks all participants.

- **Adjournment**

No motion is necessary for adjournment; the meeting may be ad-

The chair says, "If there is no further business at this meeting [pause

journed by general consent.	to allow people to respond], the meeting will stand adjourned." The chair taps the gavel once.

Establishing an Agenda

The Agenda at a Glance

Agenda planning Successful meetings are not a result of chance or good fortune; rather, they are the result of thorough, complete planning. It is important to plan all meetings carefully, most especially those meetings that appear likely to become divisive.

Items for inclusion Be sure that members and officers submit agenda items in ample time to allow the clerk to prepare the document. You may wish to have the clerk actively request agenda items. The clerk can write to officers (and members, if the membership is small enough to make this practical), stating that the agenda is being prepared and requesting that any materials that need to be included must be submitted by a specific date.

Modern technology It is especially helpful to prepare the agenda on a computer or word processor, since it is much easier to make changes and print out clean copies through this method rather than with a typewriter. Some organizations take this technology one step further, sending members copies of the agenda before the meeting by modem or fax.

Nonbinding consideration The agenda is for informational purposes only; it is not formally binding until it is adopted, except in the standard arrangement of items. Organizations whose meetings are more than three months apart often formally adopt their agendas.

Sample Agenda

Below is a sample agenda for the regular meeting of a hypothetical organization, The Sierra Group. See how closely this agenda meets your organization's needs.

Sample Agenda

The Sierra Group
Board of Trustees
Regular Meeting
October 6, 1994

I. Call to Order
II. Reading and approval of the minutes of the September 10, 1994 meeting
III. Reports

A. Treasurer's report
B. Officers' reports
C. Executive committee reports
D. Standing committee reports

Building and grounds
Finance and budget
Personnel

E. Special committee reports

Design
New building legal

IV. Unfinished business

A. Sale of Main Street site
B. Central database installation
C. Annual convention planning
D. Fund raising
E. Donations

V. New business

A. Fire-alarm system
B. Security system
C. Meeting attendance

VI. Adjournment

Arrangement of Items

Do not think of an agenda as a monolithic and frightening document; it is simply one more tool for handling business smoothly, efficiently, and fairly. Think of an agenda as carved in sand, not granite. Any item on the agenda can be considered at any time during the meeting. For instance, if some order of business appears to be unusually urgent, it can be considered earlier in the meeting. To do this, a member makes a motion to suspend the rules, as follows:

▶ A member says, "At this time, I move that we consider the donation of the medical van to the town's outreach program."
If a member anticipates an objection, or another member does indeed object, the first member can say, "I move to suspend the rules that interfere with the introduction at this time of the motion to consider the donation of the medical van to the town's outreach program."

The motion must be carried by a two-thirds vote. If the motion is carried, the order of items on the agenda is rearranged and the motion is considered at that time, out of the original order. If only a few items stand in the way of considering the issue, they can be laid on the table (see page 110) or postponed (see page 115). Note that the chairperson cannot disregard the agenda; the agenda can only be set aside by a two-thirds vote. However, if the chair wishes to consider an item out of its original order, the following example illustrates the format:

▶ The chair says, "The chair will entertain a motion to suspend the rules to take up the matter of [the topic]."
If no one objects, the chair then says, "If there is no objection, the chair proposes at this time to take up [the topic]."

Moving items on an agenda Moving items around on an agenda can usually help the assembly treat each order of business more fully and fairly. However, this practice can also be used unscrupulously to manipulate the passage or ensure the blockage of certain items. For example, a member or the chair may wish to manipulate an issue by having it considered when the members most opposed to it are not present at the meeting to raise their objections. Conversely, a chair or certain members may try to pack a meeting with their supporters and present a motion when they have the strongest support. This is why the motion to suspend the rules must be passed by two-thirds of those present at a meeting; unanimous consent is even better. (The use of parliamentary law to manipulate motions is treated more fully on page 163.)

Order of the Day

An order of the day is a particular item of business that is given a predetermined point in the agenda. There are two kinds of orders of the day: *special orders* and *general orders*.

Special orders This type of order of the day suspends any rules that interfere with its consideration except those concerned with adjournment, recess, or questions of privilege. This means that the special order interrupts any debate on the floor at that moment. It requires a two-thirds vote for passage.

General orders This type is any order of the day that is not a special order.

There are three ways to make an order of the day:

1. Postpone a pending question to a specific time; this requires a majority vote. Or, by a two-thirds vote, make it into a special order.
2. Pass a motion to postpone a question that has not yet been considered by the assembly. This requires a two-thirds vote.
3. Assign an item of business to a specific place on the agenda. The item is then a general order of the day unless it is assigned to a specific hour, which then makes it a special order for that hour.

The following examples illustrate the way to make an order of the day:

▶ The member proposing a special order says, "I move that the following resolution be made a special order for the next meeting: *Resolved,* That [the motion]."

> *or*
>
> The member says, "I propose the following resolution be made a special resolution for [a specific time on the agenda]." If the resolution concerns a committee report, the person would say, "*Resolved,* That the report of the committee on [topic] be made a special order for [date and time.]"

Unless the assembly reconsiders the vote that set the order of the day or suspends the rules, the order of the day cannot be considered before the time for which it is placed. In instances where more than three months will pass before the next regular meeting, the order of the day cannot be made for a time beyond the end of the current session.

Creating Your Own Agenda

A combination of general and specific orders of the day creates the agenda. Items that have no specific times are general orders; those with specific times are special orders. After an agenda has been adopted by a group, it can be changed only by a two-thirds vote or by unanimous consent.

The items you place on your agenda depend on the type of meeting and its objectives. If you are preparing the agenda for an annual meeting, for example, you will probably include items for selecting officers and establishing committees, which would not be on the agenda for a regular meeting. Look carefully at your organization's bylaws and consider your current needs to see what items should be included in the agenda for each meeting.

As you create an agenda for your next meeting, you may also wish to consider some of the following optional categories, if they pertain to your organization's business:

Opening ceremonies Many organizations open their meetings with the pledge of allegiance and the singing of the national anthem. If you choose to do so, be sure to have the American flag prominently and correctly displayed. You may wish to invite a member or a guest to play the piano or to provide some other appropriate musical accompaniment. While the chair most often leads these ceremonies, some organizations invite guests to participate as well. You may also wish to open the meeting with an invocation or with a ritual that reminds members of the organization's ideals.

Roll call Some organizations follow the opening ceremonies with a roll call of officers, to make sure that they are in attendance. In small organizations, the names of members may be called as well. To conduct a roll call, the chair says, "Now, the clerk will call the roll of officers."

Consent calendar If your organization is large and you have a great deal of business to accomplish, you may wish to include a *consent calendar* on your agenda. The calendar is called at a special place in the agenda, before the reports of the special committees. The items listed in the consent calendar are considered in order, unless someone objects. In that instance, they are placed back in the regular position on the agenda. In addition, items placed on a consent calendar must be taken together, without debate or amendment.

Good of the order (also called *general good and welfare* or *open forum*) Placed on the agenda after all new business has been completed, the good of the order refers to the general welfare of the group. The heading allows members to talk about what the organization is doing, in which direction it appears to be heading, its reputation, and so on. Unlike regular motions, which allow members to talk only about the specific issue on the floor, the good of the order allows general observations on the organization as whole.

Announcements Under this heading, officers and members can share information of concern to the entire group. Placing an item on the agenda in this position, however, does not prevent the chair from making an urgent announcement at any time during the meeting.

Program The program is usually presented after all other business is completed, but it may be placed before business is taken up, for the convenience of the guest speaker or the members. For instance, if a speaker has only limited time and wishes to speak early in the meeting, it is customary to accommodate the guest.

The program may also be placed earlier on the agenda if it seems likely that the assembly may wish to act on the information presented in the program. For example, if the program concerns a sales presentation, the assembly would need time after the program to consider the message and any action they may wish to take. By suspending the rules, the program may be presented at any time during the meeting, even before the minutes have been read.

The example below introduces the program:

► The chair says, "If there is no objection, we will have our program at this time."

Agenda Checklist

Use this checklist to help you create your own meeting agendas:

1. Call to order
2. Opening ceremony
3. Approval of the minutes
4. Reports of officers
5. Treasurer's report
6. Correspondence
7. Reports of standing committees
8. Reports of special committees
9. Unfinished business
10. New business
11. Program for the meeting
12. Adjournment

Quorum of Members

A quorum in a meeting is the number of people needed to conduct business. The concept of a quorum is vital because it helps protect a small group acting without the will of the majority. Unless the organization's bylaws state otherwise, a quorum is a majority of all members, the largest number that can be depended on to attend a meeting under normal circumstances. Many groups, however, often decide that a smaller number of members can constitute the quorum. This percentage may be as small as one-twentieth of the members. Below are some guidelines to follow about quorums under different circumstances:

- **Quorum guidelines**
  1. In a mass meeting, the quorum is the number of people present.
  2. In groups without a reliable membership roster, a quorum consists of those who attend a properly called meeting.
  3. In a body of delegates, a quorum is a majority of the people who have registered, whether or not they are currently attending the convention.
  4. In other groups whose bylaws do not specify a quorum, it is a majority of all members.

Although a quorum can carry out any business, it is usually advisable not to transact important business unless the meeting has a significant number of members present. Many organizations give ample prior notice of the meeting to ensure good attendance; often the notice is in writing and transmitted through E-mail, interoffice memos, postings in a central location, or regular mail. To pass a motion unanimously, a quorum must be present.

Required Officers in Attendance

In addition to a quorum of members, certain officers must be present for an assembly to conduct business. The officers are counted toward the quorum. The two officers who must be present are:

1. The chair, who leads the meeting and makes sure that the correct procedures are observed.
2. The clerk (or secretary), who makes a written record of business, called the *minutes*.

Business conducted without a quorum present is not valid. Even if everyone present votes to conduct business, the vote is null and void. In the absence of a quorum, those members in attendance can adjourn, recess, fix a time at which to adjourn, or take measures to establish a quorum. When vital business must be conducted, the members present can act at their own risk with the hope that their actions will be held up at a later meeting that does have a quorum.

What happens if a meeting opens with a quorum but then the members leave, destroying the quorum? At that point, the chair must declare that the quorum has been lost and that no other business can be conducted during that meeting. The meeting is then adjourned.

Officers

Officers at a Glance

What officers are necessary to keep the meeting running smoothly and to accomplish all the necessary business? Most members know who is in charge of their organization and what duties and responsibilities each person has within it. The company you work for may have relatively few people in charge, with each person performing clear-cut tasks within the hierarchy. Or, you might be associated with an organization that has a large number of officers, with many of their duties arranged on a flowchart. People may rotate jobs and titles, or they may stay in the same track during their tenure with the organization, group, or club.

Parliamentary procedure allows for a specific number of officers. Traditionally the minimum essential officers are the chair and the clerk (secretary). The officers your organization elects will vary with the amount of work and its specific nature, and they should be clearly spelled out in the organization's bylaws. In addition, the bylaws should state the qualifications for office, how the officers are elected, and the duties of each officer. A description of the traditional officers according to parliamentary practice appears in the following sections.

Chair or President

The person who runs the meeting is usually called the *chair* or *presiding officer*. Other terms used are *chairperson* or *president,* depending on the will of the majority. While the title *chair* comes from the term *chairman,* the title has another derivation as well. The presiding officer must be placed where he or she can see all the members at all times. This central location is called *the chair,* because it is a chair or a high stool. As the meeting is being conducted, the presiding officer is *in the chair.*

Chair's rank The specific rank of the chair varies, depending on the nature of the organization. Within a company, for example, the presiding officer may be the president, the vice president, the executive director, or the director. In a college or university, the chair of a meeting may be the president, a dean, a department head, or a faculty member elected for that purpose. Within a club, the chair is most often the presiding officer.

Duties of the chair The chair has a number of specific duties, as follows:

- Seeing that a quorum is present.
- Opening the meeting at the specified time by calling the members to order.
- Announcing the business of the assembly and the order in which it will be considered.
- Acknowledging members who are entitled to speak.
- Stating all motions and putting them to vote.
- Announcing the results of all votes.
- Making sure that the debate proceeds in an orderly fashion, using the rules of parliamentary law.
- Enforcing decorum.
- Saving time by refusing to recognize obviously frivolous motions.
- Enforcing the rules about debate procedure.
- Making the business of the meeting run as smoothly as possible.
- Deciding all questions of order.
- Informing the participants about a point of order or specific parliamentary practice when requested.
- Authenticating the proceedings with his or her signature.
- Representing the assembly by obeying its rules.

- Declaring the meeting adjourned when all business has been concluded.

To carry out the duties of office, the chair should have the following materials at every meeting:

- Copy of the organization's bylaws
- Book of parliamentary law
- List of all committees and their members
- Agenda

Guiding the discussion The rules of parliamentary law guide chairpersons to be effective leaders by maintaining their impartiality. First and most important, the chair cannot participate in the debate. (Note: This rule is often set aside in small boards and committees, where chairs *are* allowed to participate fully in the debate. See page 61 for information about this exception.)

Further, the chair cannot interrupt another speaker as long as the speaker has not violated any rules of debate; this helps prevent abuse of power. Nevertheless, some chairs will give their opinions on questions before the assembly, even interrupting a member who is speaking. The chair should not be someone who wants to take a vigorous part in the debate. A chair cannot control others unless he or she has self-control.

A chairperson sometimes asks another member to assume the chair temporarily so he or she can participate in the debate. This is not advisable and should never be done when the member objects or when the substitution might make it difficult to keep order in the assembly. When a chair gives up his or her objectivity, the ability to control the opposition is weakened.

Maintaining decorum As part of effective leadership, the chair should maintain decorum; one way is through demeanor. In large, formal meetings, the chair stands up to put questions to a vote. In small or less formal meetings, such as committees or boards of trustees, the chair remains seated. The same rule is followed on questions of order.

One of the most effective techniques for maintaining decorum is to use the rules of parliamentary law consistently. Another technique is for chairs to season their judgments with tact and common sense. In congenial meetings, for example, chairs often will not insist that routine motions be seconded; this helps save time and move the agenda along briskly. But when the meeting is not smooth or disagreements are anticipated, it is important to adhere closely to the rules of parliamentary law. In this way, the chair can help head off disagreements and cool down simmering resentments.

Assisting members Effective chairs help their colleagues accomplish the purpose of the meeting. If a member makes an incorrect motion, for example, it is more effective to suggest the best way to make the motion rather than just ruling it out of order. Here are some examples:

▶ Member A says, "I move that we Lay the question on the Table until the next meeting."
The chair says, "Perhaps you mean that we should Postpone the question until the next meeting."

or

Member B says, "I move that we Postpone the question."
The chair says, "Do you want to specify a time? If not, perhaps you wish to Lay the question on the Table?"

or

Member C says, "I move that we reject the resolution."
The chair says, "I believe that the question should be Postponed Indefinitely, since that is the parliamentary form of the question."

Another technique to help maintain decorum is for the chair to refer to himself or herself in the third-person, as *the chair* rather than *I*. For example, the chair would say, "The chair has called for [*not* I have called for]."

Knowing parliamentary procedure Parliamentary procedure can be used to hinder as well as help accomplish business. Beware of people who use the rules of parliamentary debate to stand in the way of getting things done. Chairs can refuse to entertain motions that serve only to slow the proceedings. If the opposition appeals the chair's ruling, the matter can be brought to a vote. If the chair is supported by a majority, he or she can then refuse to recognize any delaying tactics the opposition makes during the rest of the meeting. Effective chairs recognize the difference between a faction seeking to obstruct business and a group with legitimate concerns.

One of the surest ways to run a meeting successfully is to be completely familiar with the business on the agenda and the rules of parliamentary law. It is astonishing how many chairs and other officers come to meetings without ever having read the agenda—much less having refreshed their memories about parliamentary law. The more information the chair has about parliamentary law, the more easily he or she will be able to accomplish the order of business and earn the respect of those at the meeting. At the very least, the chair should be thoroughly versed in the basic rules of parliamentary law, but a more thorough grounding in the complete rules of order will make it much easier for the chair to expedite the agenda and ensure that the interests of all members are met.

Absence What happens if a chair knows that he or she will be absent from a future meeting? Can the chair just call a member and arrange for a substitute? No! If the chair is absent from a meeting or has to leave the meeting for any reason, the appointment of a temporary chair depends on the structure of the organization. If there are vice presidents, the most senior one present at the meeting becomes the acting chair if the presiding officer is not present. The vice president should always be called to fill in for an absent president. If there is more than one vice president, they should be called to assume the chair in order of seniority, the most senior vice president called first, then the next, and so forth.

If there is no vice president, however, the chair may appoint a temporary chair, called a *chair pro tem*. The appointment is valid only for the duration of the meeting or for a clearly specified period of time. In addition, the assembly may end the appointment earlier by electing another chair. If the chair is not present to appoint a chair pro tem, the task falls to the clerk. In the clerk's absence, any member can call the meeting to order and see to it that a chair pro tem is elected. The chair pro tem would then be in charge of the meeting unless or until the regular chair returned.

Voting Chairs are allowed to vote in certain instances: when the voting is done by ballot, and when the chair's vote would alter the outcome of the election. For example, suppose that a simple majority vote is needed to pass a motion; if the chair voted with the majority, the motion would pass. In this case, the chair is allowed to vote because the vote would change the outcome of the election. Following the same guideline, assume that a two-thirds vote is needed to pass a specific motion. Here the chair may vote with the minority to create a tie vote, causing the motion to fail.

No matter what the circumstances of the issue and the required number of votes needed to pass or defeat a motion, the chair must vote before the tellers have begun the tally. If not, the chair must obtain the assembly's permission to vote. To avoid conflicts of interest, if a member makes a motion that refers to the chair, the chair should not call for the vote. Instead, the clerk or the member making the motion should put it to a vote.

Below is a list of guidelines for chairpersons: Familiarize yourself with these suggestions to help you run more productive meetings.

DO	**DO NOT**
Have a written agenda.	Arive at a meeting without being fully prepared.
Call the meeting to order on time.	Get sidetracked and arrive late.
Entertain one piece of business at a time.	Let the issues become muddy.
Protect the rights of the minority.	Speak for a member because you believe that you do it better.
See that the will of the majority is preserved.	Let a small group monopolize the debate.
Refer to yourself in the third-person, as in "The chair thinks."	Use the first-person pronoun *I*, as in "I think."
Maintain decorum at all times.	Allow members to involve personalities in the debate.
Keep a quorum at all times.	Start or run a meeting without a quorum.
Encourage everyone to participate fully.	Favor a minority or faction.
Control yourself in order to control others.	Lose your temper.
Take a vote correctly.	Lose track of the vote.
Use tact when enforcing rules.	Be pedantic about enforcing rules of order.
Be impartial.	Try to make people bend to your will.
Say, "The motion is out of order."	Say, "You are out of order."
Preserve order and decorum at all times.	Use your office for personal gain.

Insist that members follow the rules of the organization.	Change everything because you are in charge.
Step down graciously when your term of office is over.	Associate yourself with the office of chair.

Managing meetings Parliamentary rules enable a group of people to arrive at the majority opinion of those present in an accurate, impartial, and timely way. These rules will help you as chair to maintain order, ensure equality and fairness, and expedite business. Follow these guidelines to help your meetings run smoothly.

• Meeting Guidelines

1. Recognize that the power of the organization is vested in its members.
2. Act in a fair, tactful, and polite way.
3. Make sure that all members have equal rights and privileges: to introduce new business, to participate in discussions, and to vote.
4. In large gatherings, encourage people to identify themselves before they address the group.
5. Help members adhere to the rules of parliamentary law.
6. Be sure that a motion has indeed been made before the discussion starts on an issue. Just raising the issue is not sufficient; the issue must be framed as a motion. As the presiding officer, you can ask someone to make a motion.
7. Make sure that every member knows that he or she is entitled to speak once to a motion that can be debated.
8. Encourage everyone at the meeting to participate fully in the discussion. This will also help prevent individual members from monopolizing the meeting.
9. Consider only one main motion or question at a time. Resolve the motion before moving on to another main motion.
10. Remember that the person who makes the motion is entitled to speak first and cannot speak against the motion.
11. Give only one person the floor at a time.
12. Restrict the debate to the merits of the pending question.
13. Check to see that everyone knows, at all times, the question that is before the assembly. This will help the meeting stay on track and run smoothly.
14. Make sure that personalities do not enter into the issues. The motion can be attacked or denounced, but never the person.

15. Do not allow anyone to speak a second time in a debate until everyone who wants to speak has had a chance.
16. Exercise care to prevent the abuse of such motions as Point of Order, Point of Personal Privilege, and Point of Information.
17. If necessary, limit the debate on the question. With the approval of the members, the presiding officer can restrict the number of speakers and the amount of time, as well as call the question to end debate.
18. To save time, use general (unanimous) consent when everyone is in agreement.
19. Refer complex issues to committees for further discussion and study.

Chairing a difficult meeting Despite all your organization, some meetings will be more difficult to chair than others, due to the issues and the personalities involved. Perhaps some board members are upset about a debate not being decided in their favor and so decide to form a faction to impede other business. Or maybe the issue before the board carries great emotional impact, and feelings are running high. It is possible that during a previous meeting personalities became entangled with issues and tempers flared, and during the upcoming meeting you will have to deal with the spillover. No matter what reason you have for anticipating an explosive meeting, there are ways that you can defuse the situation. Below are some ideas for you to consider when you have to chair a difficult meeting.

- **Before the Meeting:**

1. Think about the meeting with your officers and committee members before everyone arrives to brainstorm ways to deal with the situation. The goal is not to silence the opposition, but rather to allow everyone to participate fully and freely.
2. Remove yourself from the fray. Look at the situation as objectively and coolly as you can.
3. Set the tone for the meeting. If you stay in control, you have a much better chance of ensuring those in attendance will also act in a professional way.
4. Prepare a detailed agenda for the meeting, including all items that you think are important to the discussion. Make sure everyone understands that these issues will be raised in the meeting.
5. Arm yourself with facts about the issues to be considered at the meeting. You may wish to appoint a committee to gather

relevant information and report to the group before the meeting. Be sure you have considered the issue from all sides.

6. Consult your organization's bylaws to make sure you fully understand your obligations and limitations as a chair.

- **During the Meeting:**
  1. Run the meeting as formally as possible.
  2. Maintain the rights of the individual only so long as they do not infringe on the rights of the group.
  3. Use the rules of parliamentary procedure as fully as you can. In general, the more difficult the meeting, the more closely the rules of parliamentary law should be followed.
     - If members raise petty or inflammatory points of order, try to seize the floor, interrupt others, or refuse to yield the floor when their time has run out, you may rise to a Point of Order.
     - If you or other members are being verbally attacked, abused, or insulted, you may rise to a Point of Personal Privilege.
     - If order has disintegrated and there is much side conversation, you may rise to a Point of General Privilege.
     - If a speaker strays from the agenda, offers personal comments unrelated to the subject of the debate, interrupts another speaker, or in any way abrogates another speaker's rights, call the speaker *out of order*.
  4. It is easier to handle people who belong at your meeting; eject those who do not have the right to be present. Ask people to identify themselves as they speak to see who has the right to be at the meeting.
  5. Remember that the chair cannot do it alone; all members share the responsibility for maintaining order and decorum.
  6. If your group is willing, institute a special set of rules for the meeting. For example, you may wish to limit the number of times a person can speak on an issue, or set time limits for all speakers.
  7. Keep the meeting impartial and level. For instance, you do not have to recognize a speaker who would monopolize the floor. If you think that your own feelings about the meeting or the issues will get in the way of your acting impartially, step down for the meeting and let the vice president assume the chair so you can participate in the debate.
  8. Do not criticize those who address the meeting; this can exacerbate an already adversarial or hostile situation.

9. Prevent disagreements whenever you can. One way to keep things professional is to make the most of areas of agreement between individuals or groups.
10. Insist that all remarks be addressed to the chair, not to the audience or to other members.
11. Do not permit abusive, defamatory, or insulting language. Keep the focus on the issues, not the personalities of the speakers. Make sure that other members do not attack speakers or their motives. At the first sign of disorder, act promptly to restore order and attention. Use the rules of parliamentary law rather than trying to silence someone with your voice or the gavel.
12. If there is extensive disagreement, suggest that the matter be referred to a committee. If the motion to refer to committee is passed, appoint people to the committee who feel strongly about the issue. Set a time for their report to be delivered to the group as a whole.
13. If matters get out of hand, call a recess to give tempers a chance to cool off.
14. If you feel that a motion is inflammatory and should not be considered by the group, you may object to it being considered, but you must do so directly after it is made. If the motion is made anyway and does indeed create discord, you can move to table it, postpone it, or refer it to committee.
15. During the meeting, you may wish to display the agenda to keep people focused on the issues. Some chairs use an overhead projector or a large board for this purpose. You may also wish to enlarge the agenda and display it on an easel.
16. Be courteous, tactful, and firm in your dealings. Maintain your self-control, no matter how great the provocation.
17. Use technology to your advantage. If you are using a microphone, for example, be familiar with its operation. If a speaker becomes abusive or insulting, you can disconnect the microphone at your discretion.
18. Do not monopolize the meeting. Try to give everyone's ideas precedence over your own. As the chair, you should be a listener rather than a talker.

Special techniques to ensure effective meetings There are other ways to help make sure that a meeting will run smoothly. These suggestions can be adapted to your own specific needs.

1. To establish an air of collegiality from the outset, invite all members to introduce themselves at the first meeting. Start

with yourself, and then go around the table or the room. Use this technique any time you have newcomers attending your meetings, for it will help put everyone at ease. You may also wish to use nametags, nameplates, or other professional markers to help people identify each other.

2. Make advance preparations well ahead of the start of the meeting. If you intend to use a video recorder, for example, check that it is working before the meeting begins. Be sure that any material you wish to distribute has been copied and collated.
3. Consider copying different documents on different colored paper stock, for this makes it much easier to distribute and refer to various documents during the meeting. You may wish to copy the agenda on white paper, the bills on yellow paper, and the membership list on blue paper, for instance.
4. Be sensitive to the needs of your members. For example, if someone asks a question, repeat it to make sure that all the members heard it. Asking members to stand when they give a report or make a motion ensures that voices will carry to all members. You may also wish to pause during the discussion to summarize what has been said thus far.
5. Do not monopolize the meeting yourself. Talk no more than is necessary. If the chair of a committee is absent, for example, do not give his or her report. Instead, ask another member to deliver it in the committee chair's absence.
6. Stay organized. As you complete items on the agenda, check them off. This will help you keep track of what you have to cover during the meeting.
7. Keep order by asking the group for its attention. Do not let any one person dominate the meeting; see that everyone gets a chance to speak. Avoid lengthy and senseless discussions that are off the topic. To help cut down on such time-wasting tactics, you can also asks members and participants to hold their questions and statements—if they are not part of the issue—until the discussion is completed. If you anticipate a fractious meeting, you may wish to have all motions submitted in writing. If you have a gavel, use it only as a last resort and to start and end a meeting.
8. If a special committee is appointed, set a date by which time their report must be submitted. This will help you complete business in a timely fashion.
9. Be flexible. If the meeting is running longer than anticipated and some members are leaving and others seem anxious to move on to other matters, try to move the agenda along. If necessary, table items that can wait until the next meeting.

President-elect

Definition In some organizations it is common practice to elect a chair or president one term in advance. In these instances, the elected official is called the *president-elect*. After the president-elect has served a term in this capacity, the individual automatically becomes the presiding officer for the following term.

Advantages There are a number of advantages to having a president-elect. It clearly provides for someone to fill the office of the chair if the current chair is not present at specific meetings, resigns, or becomes unable to complete the term of office. Without a president-elect, the vice president would usually be tapped to fill the vacated office until a new election could be held, or until the matter was resolved according to the organization's bylaws. Depending on the organization, the president-elect may or may not have specific responsibilities. If the organization is very large and has a great deal of business to complete, the president-elect might serve in an advisory position for the term of office. Well-run organizations spell out these matters in their bylaws with great care.

Vice President

Definition and succession The vice president's primary function is to lead the meetings in the president's absence. Some organizations elect a number of different vice presidents in order of responsibility, such as first vice president, second vice president, third vice president, and so on. In these instances, the vice presidents take over for the presiding officer in order of precedence: i.e., the first vice president is the initial choice to chair the meeting if the president is absent. The vacated offices are then filled in succession; if the first vice president is absent or unable to serve, the second vice president takes over, and so on. If the first vice president becomes the president, the second vice president becomes the first vice president, and so on. In most businesses, the vice presidents have specific administrative duties as well.

Some organizations prefer to have just one vice president serve in that office at a time. In these instances, the vice president would be the officer to assume the chair if the president could not run the meeting because of absence or incapacity.

Secretary or Clerk

Definition The person who records what happens at meetings is called the *secretary* or *clerk;* the two terms are used interchangeably. The record of what happens at a meeting is called the minutes. Depending on the nature of the organization, the number of meetings, and the amount of work, there may be two secretaries. In these cases, the secretary who records the minutes is called the *recording secretary,* while the one who handles the correspondence is called the *corresponding secretary.*

Responsibilities What are the secretary's duties? While specific responsibilities vary with different organizations, the secretary is generally responsible for the following duties:

- Keeping the minutes
- Having the minutes available to all members
- Filing all committee reports
- Taking attendance
- Having officers and members supply needed documents
- Providing delegates with credentials
- Signing official documents, as required by the bylaws
- Maintaining records of the organization, including all bylaws, special rules, and minutes
- Notifying members of all meetings, known as the Call of the Meeting
- Carrying out all needed correspondence for the organization
- Preparing an order of business before every meeting, which the chair uses during the meeting
- Calling the meeting to order in the absence of the president and the vice president

In most instances, the secretary sits near the chair during meetings. This helps the secretary record events accurately and fully; it is also helpful if the secretary has to call the meeting to order in the absence of the chair or vice president. In such cases, the secretary runs the meeting until a chair pro tem can be elected.

Nearly all large organizations tape-record their meetings. If desired or necessary, the secretary can listen to the tape when preparing the minutes. However, the secretary cannot transcribe the tape to serve as minutes. (The minutes are explained more fully on pages 217–225.)

Fiscal responsibility In some organizations, the secretary also handles financial matters in addition to other duties. In these instances, the secretary is in effect functioning as a financial officer and would report to the organization all money received and disbursed. In most organizations, the secretary (or any other officers handling money) is bonded to protect the company against the possibility of financial loss.

If the financial duties are extensive, the company may decide to appoint a *financial secretary,* whose responsibilities include maintaining accounts, giving financial reports, and related activities. In these instances, the company would have two or three different secretaries, each with the specific duties outlined above.

Executive Secretary

Duties Unlike the clerk or secretary described above, an executive secretary is paid to serve as a record keeper for the organization. This individual works full time to manage the paperwork for the company. The executive secretary reports to the board of directors and is responsible for making sure that the board's directions are carried out. The precise nature of the executive secretary's duties depends on the company's bylaws, but this job can carry with it responsibility for hiring, firing, and setting salaries for the employees.

Treasurer

Duties The treasurer's responsibilities will be determined by the needs of each organization. In some cases, the treasurer may simply keep track of all the funds; in other instances, he or she may take a more active role by paying invoices, mailing checks, and receiving receipts. Regardless of specific duties, the treasurer must submit periodic reports that summarize the organization's financial transactions.

Most treasurers of large businesses prepare monthly or bimonthly reports and submit these to members for their information, but all organizations prepare an *annual report* that summarizes the year's financial transactions. If the treasurer is serving only as a repository for funds, the annual report might just list the amount of money in the account at the start of the fiscal year, the money dispersed and received during the year, and the amount of money in the account at the end of the year. If the treasurer has a more active role in the business, the annual report will have to account for all the money in detail. (See also page 210.)

In some organizations, the secretary is the person who actually pays the bills; in these instances, the secretary should also prepare the monthly and annual report, unless an outside auditor is retained for these purposes. The monthly treasurer's report requires no action by the assembly.

Directors

Many organizations have directors, who may also be called *trustees* or *managers*. These officers are part of the executive board. Their duties vary according to the kind of business but are clearly stated in the bylaws. For instance, directors may function as auditors or policy makers.

Parliamentarian

Some organizations hire a professional versed in parliamentary law to serve as an adviser. This person is paid a salary to assist the organization and its board of directors in understanding how to run a meeting under parliamentary rules. Unless meetings are unusually fractious, small organizations rarely need a parliamentarian, but in larger organizations with more complex business matters to resolve, such an adviser can often help move agenda items along briskly and smoothly. It can also be extremely helpful to have such an outside adjudicator to assist with any questions that may arise about policy matters.

Experienced parliamentarians are often able to anticipate problems that may affect a member's rights. In these instances, the parliamentarian can quietly call such situations to the president's attention and help redirect the meeting to avert problems. In addition to advising during a meeting, a parliamentarian can also help set up meetings and offer useful preplanning suggestions. Parliamentarians can also offer classes in parliamentary law as well as brief consultations to members of the organization.

Sergeant-at-arms

The sergeant-at-arms (also called the *warden* or *warrant officer*) is responsible for helping the chair keep order. The nature of the duties varies with the type of meeting and its atmosphere. At a shareholders meeting, for example, the sergeant-at-arms may help set up the hall, making sure that the chairs and tables are in place and the audiovisual equipment and telephones are functioning. In this instance, the sergeant-at-arms would also be in charge of ushers and some security matters. At a service meeting such as Rotary International, for example, the sergeant-at-arms would likely be the member to display the pledge, hang the banners, and make sure that the American flag was in place.

In organizations that have the power to command attendance, the sergeant-at-arms has the authority to serve warrants or levy monetary fines. In general, the sergeant-at-arms helps to make sure that the meeting functions smoothly.

Historian

Some organizations want a more personal, narrative account of their business transactions. In these instances, they may elect a historian to prepare a chronological version of events. This would become a lasting part of the company's records. These records are often bound into handsome books and displayed in a prominent place. This is especially common when a major event is taking place within a company, such as the passing of power into new hands.

Librarian

Many organizations have a collection of documents relating to their history. Magazine publishers, for example, keep back issues of their publications. Organizations may also have letters, original manuscripts, illustrations, caricatures, photographs, and other printed materials to catalog and store. Increasingly, organizations are storing printed matter on computer disk. No matter what form the documents take, the librarian is in charge of arranging, storing, and accessing these materials. This office is increasingly important today, since there is much more information to keep track of and catalog.

Curator

The curator is in charge of objects of value that the company may own. Library holdings are not included in this category. Instead, included are such items as trophies, statues, sculpture, models, awards, and original artwork, for example.

Doorkeeper

Some organizations have a doorkeeper, an officer who makes sure that only authorized people enter the meeting. To do so, the doorkeeper checks a person's credentials and either permits or denies entrance. The sergeant-at-arms may function in this capacity as well.

Honorary Officers

The title says it all: these individuals are rewarded for loyal service or great distinction, but they do not govern within the organization. As with an honorary university degree, honorary officers are singled out for special accolade. Nonmembers as well as members of an organization can be granted honorary offices, depending on the bylaws of the organization.

An honorary office is usually bestowed on a member upon his or her retirement from the company or organization. The honorary office matches the office the person once held. Thus the retiring president can be elected to the position of *honorary president* or the former chair to the office of *honorary chair*. The title stays with the person for life, unless modified according to the company's bylaws.

Honorary officers are accorded the privilege of attending and speaking at all meetings, but they are usually not allowed to make motions or vote on issues, unless this ruling is modified in the bylaws. The offices do not carry with them any responsibilities, but that does not prevent the individual from holding another office that does entail actual duties. Honorary officers may be invited to sit on the dais and have their names and titles listed in any literature produced by the organization. It is not uncommon for the deceased honorary officers to be listed in the literature as well.

Number of Officers

The number of officers your organization has and how clearly their duties are stated affects the smooth operation of a group. In general, elect just those officers you need to get the work done. Having too few officers will overburden members with jobs and make it difficult to get through what has to be accomplished; having too many officers can make it just as hard to get the work done. State the duties of all officers in the organization's bylaws. Make sure that the bylaws are kept up-to-date to reflect the company's changing needs.

Reports of Officers

REPORTS AT A GLANCE

When are reports made? In small organizations, officers and committees usually give brief reports at every regular meeting, or when there is important information to share with the members. In large organizations, reports from all officers, boards (such as executive boards or boards of directors), and committees are usually made only at annual meetings.

Most organizations require officers to make reports every year. In addition, officers may wish to make more frequent reports to keep members up-to-date on their activities. All these reports are given the same place on the meeting agenda, directly after the minutes are read and approved.

Officers' Reports

If an officer has a recommendation to make during a report, the officer should not move the implementation on his or her own. Rather, such a motion should be made by any member as soon as the officer's report is completed. In committees, by contrast, the chair or other reporting member should make the motion for implementation.

Treasurer's Reports

The treasurer gives a brief verbal summary of the organization's financial dealings at every regular meeting. The members of the organization do not have to take any action on this report.

The treasurer must also prepare a full, written financial report every year. The scope of the report is the company's fiscal year, most often January 1 to December 31, but this varies with the specific needs of the organization.

The primary goal of the written report is to give members the financial information they need in a simple, readable manner. Even if the report is very long, it must be easily understood by those not trained in financial matters. As a result, the most successful annual financial reports omit details such as dates that checks are signed, the purpose of invoices, and other such details that would obscure the essential facts of the report.

The form of financial reports varies with the needs of the organization, although all such reports contain standard financial information. It is a good idea to match the form of your organization's financial report to those of similar organizations. Large organizations with significant financial dealings will most likely use an online bookkeeping system and employ one or more accountants to keep these records. Below are two possible forms that could be used, depending on the individual needs of your organization.

Treasurer's report format The first sample, for "Kelly Harris Creations," could be used as an annual financial report for a small organization with relatively simple bookkeeping chores. The second sample, for "Signet Enterprises," is better suited to a large organization with significant revenues and expenditures. Adapt either sample to the needs of your organization.

Treasurer's Report

The undersigned, treasurer of Kelly Harris Creations, hereby submits the following annual financial report:

> The balance on hand at the beginning of the fiscal year was $4,764.00. There was received from all sources $5,543.00; during the same time, expenses amounted to $1,000, leaving a balance on hand of $9,307.00.
>
> The attached statement of receipts and expenditures shows in detail the source of income and various expenditures.

Charles Lin,
Treasurer, Kelly Harris Creations

Kelly Harris Creations, Charles Lin, Treasurer

Receipts		**Expenditures**	
Direct sales	$2,000.00	Rent	$ 400.00
Catalog sales	3,543.00	Stationery	50.00
		Advertising	150.00
		Utilities	400.00
Total	$5,543.00		$1,000.00

Signet Enterprises
Uniondale, New York
Treasurer's Report

September 30, 1994

Cash in FL Money Market Account	$483,363.43
Cash in NW Money Market Account	227,083.12
Cash in Checking Account	26,454.35
Due 10-22-94 @ 3.575%	98,049.00
TOTAL FUNDS	$834,949.90

T'Aysha Wilson-George
Treasurer

Signet Enterprises
Uniondale, New York
Treasurer's Report

Treasurer's Report for **FL Money Market Account, September 30, 1994**

Balance reported at the end of the previous month: $471,797.45

RECEIPTS DURING THE MONTH:

Source	**Amount**
Deposits	$ 150,370.00
Interest	$ 1,195.98
Total Receipts	**$151,565.98**
Total Receipts including balance	**$623,363.43**

DISBURSEMENTS MADE DURING THE MONTH:

Transfers to checking account	**$140,000.00**
Cash balance per records	**$483,363.43**

RECONCILIATION WITH BANK STATEMENTS:

Balance as given on bank statement end of month	**$483,363.43**
Less outstanding checks (list attached)	**0**
Reconciled bank balance	**$483,363.43**

Received by the Board and entered as part of the Minutes of the Board meeting held on

______________________________ 19________

____

Treasurer of the Board

Signet Enterprises
Uniondale, New York
Treasurer's Report

Treasurer's Report for **NW Money Market Account, September 30, 1994**

Balance reported at the end of the previous month:	**$226,553.28**

RECEIPTS DURING THE MONTH:

Source	**Amount**
Interest	$ 529.84
Total Receipts	**$ 529.84**
Total Receipts including balance	**$227,083.12**

DISBURSEMENTS MADE DURING THE MONTH:

Cash balance per records	**$227,083.12**

RECONCILIATION WITH BANK STATEMENTS:

Balance as given on bank statement end of month	**$227,083.12**
Less outstanding checks (list attached)	**0**
Reconciled bank balance	**$227,083.12**

Received by the Board and entered as part of the Minutes of the Board meeting held on

____________________________ 19_______

____

Treasurer of the Board

Signet Enterprises
Uniondale, New York
Treasurer's Report

Treasurer's Report for **Checking Account, September 30, 1994**

Balance reported at the end of the previous month: $9,242.92

RECEIPTS DURING THE MONTH:

Source	**Amount**
Transfers MM	$ 140,000.00
Greenhouse dismantling	8,262.00
Sundry	2,164.44
Travel	1,176.00
Entertainment	1,011.30
Training	582.95
Total Receipts	**$154,486.04**
Total Receipts including balance	**$163,728.96**

DISBURSEMENTS MADE DURING THE MONTH:

From check No. 14822 to 14903	**$137,274.61**
Cash balance per records	**$ 26,454.35**

RECONCILIATION WITH BANK STATEMENTS:

Balance as given on bank statement end of month	**$ 31,164.90**
Less outstanding checks (list attached)	**4,710.55**
Reconciled bank balance	**$ 26,454.35**

Received by the Board and entered
as part of the Minutes of the Board
meeting held on

____________________________ 19________

____

Treasurer of the Board

Signet Enterprises
Uniondale, New York
Treasurer's Report

Treasurer's Report for **Checking Account, September 30, 1994**

Balance reported at the end of the previous month:	**$0**

RECEIPTS DURING THE MONTH:

Source	**Amount**
Deposits	$ 39,944.73
Payroll	37,972.82
Total Receipts	**$77,967.55**
Total Receipts including balance	**$77,967.55**

DISBURSEMENTS MADE DURING THE MONTH:

From check No. 5756 to 5760	**$77,967.55**
Cash balance per records	**0**

RECONCILIATION WITH BANK STATEMENTS:

Balance as given on bank statement end of month	**$3,114.44**
Less outstanding checks (list attached)	**3,114.44**
Reconciled bank balance	**0**

Received by the Board and entered
as part of the Minutes of the Board
meeting held on

____________________________ 19______

____

Treasurer of the Board

Auditors In most organizations, the treasurer submits the annual financial report to an outside auditor or to an internal auditing committee. Whoever is auditing the report carefully studies the document and any required backup materials (invoices, vouchers, check stubs, bills, and so forth) to verify that the accounts are correct. The auditor or auditing committee then submits a report to the organization, which is the equivalent of a resolution stating that the treasurer's report is correct.

Treasurers should insist on audits to make sure that any errors are quickly picked up and corrected before they have a chance to magnify. Once the organization accepts the auditor's report that the financial report is correct, the treasurer or other officer who prepared it is relieved of any responsibility for errors in computation. Below is a sample of an auditor's statement:

Auditor's Statement

We do hereby certify that we have examined the above account and find it to be correct. We certify that the balance in the account is ______________________________.

Sincerely,

____

for Hersan and Mandall, Auditors

Committee Reports

At meetings other than annual meetings, the chair calls on only those committees that have reports to make, in the following order:

1. Standing committees (in the order listed in the bylaws)
2. Special committees (in the order listed in the bylaws)

Minority reports When committee recommendations are moved, they become main motions and can be disposed of in the same manner as any main motion or resolution. One or more committee members, if they wish, can submit minority reports to the assembly for its information (see also page 77).

Reference reports Because of the sheer volume of business that has to be transacted at many conventions, the use of *reference* (or *resolutions) committees* is becoming increasingly popular. The chair appoints one or more reference committees to hold hearings early in the convention on resolutions that have been submitted. The committees then recommend appropriate action to those attending the convention.

Further information on reports Below are some additional guidelines on committee reports:

1. To help members move quickly and fully through the agenda, all major reports should be written and, if possible, distributed to members ahead of time. Any recommendations for action by the group should also be included and placed at the end of the report.
2. An organization can adopt an entire committee report verbatim, but this is usually not recommended unless the report is going to be published in the name of the organization. It is especially crucial in these instances to have other members read through the report for matters of grammar, mechanics, and style.
3. It is not necessary to make a motion to accept reports given solely for information, especially when they do not have any recommendations.
4. Other officers, such as the librarian or historian, may also need to report to the assembly. These reports are usually informational, but in some instances they may contain recommendations for action.

Minutes

MINUTES AT A GLANCE

Definition The record of a meeting is called the *minutes*. The minutes are a nonbiased account of the business accomplished at the meeting. As such, the minutes should not show any member's individual bias nor should they record only what each member said. The clerk should never use the minutes as a forum to comment on something said at the meeting.

Style Effective minutes succinctly summarize what happened at the meeting in a straightforward narrative style. The writing avoids jargon, overly technical terms, and loaded or biased language. The document is in standard written English, free from errors in grammar, spelling, usage, or punctuation.

Production Most minutes are done on computer with an standard and up-to-date word processing program, which makes it easy for the clerk to make any necessary corrections. Such technology also makes transmission possible through fax, modem, and E-mail.

Content

Although the specific form and content of the minutes varies with each individual organization, the minutes must follow the arrangement of items on the agenda, as shown below:

1. Call to order
2. Reading and approval of the minutes of the previous meeting
3. Executive committee reports
4. Standing committee reports
5. Special committee reports
6. Unfinished business
7. New business
8. Adjournment

Some organizations include the headings for each of these categories in their minutes; other groups number the items. Still other organizations simply run the items one after the other. The choice is yours, but maintain a consistent style. Below are guidelines for preparing each section of the minutes.

First paragraph The first paragraph of the minutes contains the following information, not necessarily in this order:

- Name of the organization
- Date, time, and place of the meeting
- Description of the type of meeting, such as *regular, special,* or *emergency*
- Names of the officers present
- Whether the minutes of the previous meeting were read and approved

Below are two examples of opening paragraphs. In the second instance, the clerk was absent from the meeting and a clerk pro tem had to be appointed:

► "At the regular monthly meeting of Supra International held on July 20, 1994, at 9:00 a.m. at the Cleveland, Ohio, conference center, the minutes were read by the clerk of the board and approved with no corrections. Ms. Geraldine Schmidt presided, with Vice President Fred Schneider and Board Clerk Alana D'Alnoise present."

or

"An emergency meeting of Meadville Volunteers was held on June 15, 1994, at 5:00 p.m. at the Meadville, Pennsylvania, Community Center with Jim Stephens presiding. The clerk being absent, Marie Lilly was appointed clerk pro tem. The minutes were then read and approved."

Body The body of the minutes contains a summary of the essential events of the meeting. Each subject is treated in its own paragraph. The body includes the following information, again not necessarily in the order specified below:

- All main motions
- Disposition of each motion
- Secondary motions
- All points of order and appeals

Here are some additional guidelines for the body of the minutes:

Voting When the voting is by ballot or there is a division in the outcome, in some organizations the secretary enters the number of votes on each side of the issue. When the vote is by voice, the secretary should enter a list of those voting on each side as well.

Motions In most instances, the name of the person who seconded a motion should not be included in the minutes. Any exceptions would be noted in the bylaws.

Committees The proceedings of a committee should not be part of the minutes, but the report should be included. When the committee report is very important and is likely to have an influence on the organization's future actions, it can be entered in its entirety.

Conclusion The conclusion of the minutes contains the following information, again not necessarily in the order specified below:

- Time the meeting was adjourned
- Secretary's signature

Sample Minutes

The following sample of completed minutes includes headings for each category.

Signet Enterprises
Board of Trustees Meeting
May 11, 1994

The regular monthly meeting of the Board of Trustees of Signet Enterprises was held on Tuesday, May 11, 1994, at the company's western headquarters. Present at the meeting were:

Dr. Fitzpatrick, President	Ms. Simon, Director
Mrs. Ulrich, Vice President	Mr. Arangio, Secretary
Mr. Jorge	Mrs. Nizzi, Treasurer
Mr. Reddy	Ms. Jordan, Clerk

Absent: Ms. Hendrix, Judge Lester Brown, Ms. Clara Bennett (all with prior notice).

Guests: Mr. George Trepp, Director, Apex Consolidated; Ms. Adrienne Flick, Marketing Manager, SGG, Inc.; Ms. Dina Nayer, Past Vice-President, Habso Co.

Call to Order

Dr. Ellen Fitzpatrick called the meeting to order at 2:30 p.m.

Approval of the Minutes

On a motion by Mr. Reddy, the minutes of the last meeting were read and approved as corrected.

Correspondence

The Board acknowledged receipt of a letter from Ms. Shirley Lang, chief counsel for Lang and Schwartz. The letter raised questions concerning Signet Enterprises' audits of 1990, 1992, and 1993. The President directed the Secretary to keep the letter on file.

The Board acknowledged receipt of a letter from Pastor Harris of Grace Cathedral. The letter requested that Signet Enterprises consider donating property to Grace Cathedral. By consensus, the Board's response is to request that the church make a responsible offer to purchase the property.

Treasurer's Report

The treasurer reported $214,081.06 in the EAB money market account, $231,922.13 in the GGH money market account, $23,805.55 in the checking account, and $100,000.00 in a certificate of deposit (due 10/21/94 @ 2.90%) for total funds of $569,808.74. The Treasurer read the following bills:

Number	*Amount*
15857-60	$ 1,169.34
15861	44,922.37
15862	43,423.99
15863	673.99
15864	22,241.11
15865	7,899.17
15866	6,311.00

Director's Report

The Director reported that at the new building site, the first-floor slab is completed and only one section remains to be completed in the basement. The block walls are being erected next week and some of the exterior-finish brick has been delivered to the site. The prep work has begun on the peaked portions of the roof and the boiler is ready to be shipped, but the manufacturer will not release it until they have assurance that payment will be prompt, within four weeks. The lawyer is settling the matter this week.

Reports of Standing Committees

Prior to the meeting, the following reports were distributed to the Board: Special Services, Media Services, Technical Services, Personnel.

The reports were accepted for filing on a motion by Mr. Arangio.

The chair of the New Building Committee, Mr. Reddy, reported that the architect has offered the Board a previously owned 21-foot wood and leather conference table and 16 leather chairs at a cost between $10,000 and $15,000. On a motion by Mrs. Ulrich, the Board authorized the Director to open negotiations for a walnut and leather conference table and set of 16 chairs, for a price not to exceed $11,000. The motion passed unanimously.

Mrs. Ulrich moved "that the Board approve the following change order for the new building: Add additional treated wood blockings at the roof eaves around the entire structure as per BHA sketches and the architect's report of April 1993." On a motion by Mr. Jorge, the motion was referred to the Design Committee with instructions to have their report ready by next month. The committee consists of Mrs. Ulrich, Mr. Arangio, and Mr. Jorge.

On a motion by Mr. Reddy, the Board approved the following change order for the new building: "Substitute Terne-coated stainless steel metal roofing material for the zinc material as specified in the original contract."

Yes votes	*Opposed votes*
Mrs. Ulrich	Mr. Reddy
Mr. Arangio	
Mr. Jorge	

Motion passed.

Reports of Special Committees

The special committee appointed to investigate the situation with Summit Roofing reported that after we notified Summit of our intention to place them in default, they returned to work last week. The prep work on the roof is almost completed and the air-conditioning is scheduled to be reinstalled on Friday. The roof should be completed by this time next week, weather permitting. The entire job should be completed in three weeks.

Unfinished Business

The resolution relating to the appraisal of the Main Street facility, which was postponed from last month's meeting, was taken up. After amendment and further debate, the resolution was adopted as follows: "*Resolved,* That Signet Enterprises hire Stuart DeRosa at a sum of $1,500 to appraise the property at 56 Main Street."

New Business

Mr. Arangio moved that the Board approve the following resignation: "William Olsen, Driver, at the annual salary of $18,500, effective July 1, 1994." The motion passed unanimously.

By consensus, the Board agreed that a special meeting should be held on May 18, at 4:00 p.m., at the Merrick Country Club, to discuss the company's goals and missions.

Program

Mr. Sidney Pochriss, a representative from AT&T, spoke about the latest telephone technology. Mr. Jorge, chair of the Program Committee, thanked Mr. Pochriss for his informative and entertaining presentation.

Adjournment

The meeting was adjourned at 10:00 p.m.

Ms. Jordan
Clerk

Reading and Approving the Minutes

After the clerk completes the minutes, he or she presents them for approval to the membership at the next regular meeting. The actual approval takes place directly after the call to order. The chair calls for the minutes to be read, asks for any corrections, accepts the corrections if valid, and then declares the minutes approved. The following example shows how to ask for corrections:

► The chair says, "Are there any corrections to the minutes? [pause to allow members to answer]."

At this time, members have a chance to correct the minutes. Only factual errors should be corrected; under no circumstances should members be allowed to recast events to present themselves in a more favorable light. It is not unknown for some members to try to rewrite history, to switch their allegiance on key issues, or to otherwise try to change someone's perception of their actions. If necessary, the clerk can use the tape recording or transcript of the previous meeting to establish the veracity of the minutes. The following examples show what the chair would say under these circumstances:

If there are no corrections

- ▶ The chair says, "If there are no corrections, the minutes stand as read."

If there are corrections

- ▶ The chair says, "If there are no further corrections, the minutes are approved as corrected."

The approval is usually by unanimous consent.

Special meeting minutes Special meeting minutes are handled differently. Since special meetings are called for specific purposes, the minutes are not approved at these meetings; rather, the approval takes place at the next regular meeting.

Distributing Drafts of the Minutes

Many organizations send a draft of the minutes to all members before the meeting. Most often the minutes of the previous meeting are sent with the notice for the upcoming meeting. This gives the members a chance to read and study the minutes at their leisure. Further, this practice can be helpful for keeping members informed of all events. The minutes are then approved at a regular meeting in the manner described above. The copies previously distributed to members are not authoritative; only the formal copy entered into the minutes book has that status.

The practice of distributing drafts can be a double-edged sword, however. Having the minutes ahead of time may result in confusion, as some members add more corrections than others. These incorrect copies may then become confused with authorized versions. Several months later, members may become confused about which copies are correct and which are not. The practice of distributing minutes ahead of time also encourages members to make unnecessary corrections that waste time and fray tempers.

If the majority consents in a vote without debate, the reading of the minutes can be postponed—not eliminated. In these instances, the minutes can be read later in the meeting or at a subsequent meeting. The rules must be suspended to approve the minutes without having read them at all.

Publishing the Minutes

In some cases, the minutes are published in full. This will most often occur at a convention or other major meeting. In these cases, the minutes will also contain a list of those who spoke on each side of an issue and a summary of what every speaker said. When this is the case, it is important that every speaker clearly state his or her name and affiliation, as shown in the following example.

▶ The speaker says, "I am Gregory Skrocki, speaking on behalf of Interstate Asphalt Paving, based in Rhode Island."

Many companies ask speakers to spell as well as state their names to prevent misspellings in the minutes. It is also common practice to use a microphone or public-address system to further prevent misunderstandings. To expedite this process and ensure accuracy, the organization usually retains a stenographer or someone else trained in making transcripts. Committee reports are included in the minutes as well, printed exactly as submitted.

Debate

Debate at a Glance

Rules of Debate

Debate is the heart of a meeting. With the skillful use of parliamentary law, debate allows members to exchange their ideas freely and to come to a consensus that reflects the will of the majority yet protects the rights of the minority. This is the essence of an effective gathering of people.

Recognizing a member A person who wishes to participate in a debate should rise (in a large, formal meeting), address the chair, and wait for the chair to acknowledge his or her presence in some manner. If necessary, the person can state his or her name and affiliation to gain the chair's attention. In a small, informal meeting, the chair might simply recognize the person with a nod; in a larger, more formal meeting, the chair often states the speaker's name and affiliation. The examples below show two methods of recognizing a member:

▶ The member says, "Madam Chair" or "Mr. Chairman."
The chair says, "Ms. Swerfnosky, president of Automatic Tellers."

or

The member says, "Madam Chair" or "Mr. Chairman."
The chair looks at the member and indicates that the member has the floor.
The member says, "Ms. Swerfnosky, president of Automatic Tellers."

The member then addresses the assembly. The chair must recognize any member who is entitled to speak. Nonetheless, the chair is entitled to ask the member the purpose for speaking, as shown below:

▶ The chair says, "For what purpose does the speaker address the chair?"

or

The chair says, "For what purpose does the speaker address the assembly?"

Opening the Debate

To open the debate, the member then makes a motion. Only the person who was recognized by the chair can make a motion at that point in the meeting.

If two or more people rise and try to claim the floor at the same time, the one who spoke to the chair first after the floor was yielded is recognized. If the chair recognizes the wrong person by error, another member can rise to a point of order.

The same person who opens the debate is given the opportunity to close the debate, but only after everyone who wants to speak has been given the chance.

Amount of Debate

The amount of debate on an issue will depend on its importance to the group or how strongly people feel about it. Whether an issue is debated for five minutes or five hours, every member of the group has a right to speak on all issues that come before the group.

For an issue to be debated before a group, the member who was recognized by the chair must make a motion, another member must second it, and the chair must read the motion to the assembly. Except for the person who made the motion, no one may speak more than twice on the same question and only once to a question of order. The person who made the motion must support it. Every other member can speak for or against the motion, but all remarks must be confined to the motion itself—not to any other topic. In addition, the amount of time a person may speak is limited, usually to 10 minutes, but the time limit varies according to the organization's rules.

When a motion is amended, however, it changes. As far as the rules of debate are concerned, then the amendment becomes an entirely new topic. As a result, those members who have spoken on the previous topic can now speak again. Keep in mind that there is a clear difference between debating and questioning. Asking questions that help members better understand a topic is allowed; debating a topic beyond the time limit is not.

When a debate appears to be over, the chair may wait a few moments to see if anyone else wants to speak. If no one does, the chair can put the question to a vote. Or, the chair may ask, "Are you ready for the question?" to assess the feelings of the majority.

Below are the commonly accepted rules of debate. Although they are the standard elements of parliamentary law, they do not supersede the bylaws of an organization. If you are setting up a new organization or revising the bylaws of an existing organization, you may wish to include some of the following guidelines.

• Rules of Debate

1. Every member is entitled to speak once on a debatable motion unless the assembly has voted to end debate.
2. The member who makes the motion is entitled to speak first. This person must speak in support of the motion.
3. The person who makes the motion may also speak on amendments and other motions that may be moved (including subsidiary, privileged, incidental, and so on) since the question is at different stages of discussion.
4. The person who seconds the motion may speak for or against it.
5. Every member may speak a second time on the same question unless other members who have not spoken wish to speak.

6. The following motions are in order when a person has been recognized by the chair but has not yet begun to speak:
   - Objection to the Consideration of a Question (see page 128)
   - Move to Reconsider, to make the motion but not to have it considered at that time.
7. No one may speak a third time on the question if anyone objects.
8. The chair may not participate in the debate unless he or she relinquishes the chair. This guideline does not hold true in small boards and committees.
9. According to the rules of parliamentary law, each speech is restricted to no more than 10 minutes. However, organizations have the right to set a shorter time limit if they wish.
10. Debating time cannot be shared; a member cannot give the unused portion of his or her time to another member. Neither can members reserve a portion of their time to use at a later date.
11. The motion to Limit or Extend Debate may be used to reduce or to increase the length of speeches allowed on a motion or specify how much time shall be allowed to debate a given question. This motion requires a second, can be amended or reconsidered, and needs a two-thirds vote to pass. In addition, the motion is not allowed in committees and generally should not be used in boards.
12. The following motions can be used to interrupt a person speaking in a debate. They should only be used if the interruption is urgent.
   - Point of Order (see page 129)
   - Point of Information (see page 132)
   - Parliamentary Inquiry (see page 131)
   - Appeal the chair's decision (see page 123)
   - Call for Orders of the Day (see page 137)
   - Request permission to withdraw or modify a motion (see page 148)
   - Call for Division of Assembly (see page 126)
   - Call for Division of Question (see page 127)
13. The debate cannot stray from the pending question.
14. People should confine themselves to the issues, not the personalities of the speakers.
15. The motion to move the Previous Question may be used to end the debate. This motion needs a second and a two-thirds vote, and it cannot be reconsidered. The motion to move the previous question is not allowed in committees and generally is not used in boards.

16. When a decision of the chair has been appealed, the chair may speak twice, once at the beginning of the debate and once at the end, without leaving the chair. Other members may speak only once on appeals.

Questions that cannot be debated Not all questions are open to debate, however. The following questions cannot be debated:

- To Fix the Time to Which Adjourn, when it is a privileged motion (see page 138)
- To Adjourn (see page 136)
- Orders of the Day and questions about the order of business (see page 180)
- An Appeal made while the Previous Question is pending (see page 123)
- Objection to the Consideration of a Question (see page 128)
- To Lay on the Table (see page 110)
- To Take from the Table (see page 112)
- The Previous Question (see page 120)
- To Reconsider a question that cannot be debated (see page 229)
- Questions about Reading Papers (see page 132)
- Questions about withdrawing motions (see page 148)
- Questions about Suspending the Rules (see page 133)
- Questions about Extending the Limits of Debate (see page 113)
- Questions about Limiting or Closing Debate (see page 113)
- Questions about granting permission to continue a speech to someone who violates debate decorum

Nonetheless, when all members agree, it is common to allow brief comments on even these undebatable topics. In the U.S. Congress, for example, it is common for a handful of members to speak on even the most undebatable topic. This is in keeping with the aims of parliamentary law to allow a full and fair expression of ideas.

Closing the Debate

Contrary to popular belief, debate is not closed when the chair rises and puts the question to a vote. Debate is not concluded until both the affirmative and negative sides have voted and the results have been tallied. Until that time, any member can take the floor and continue the debate. Here are the motions needed to close debate:

- A call for the Previous Question (see page 120). This cuts off debate and forces the group to vote on the item under discussion. This does not hold true when the motion on the floor is to Amend (see page 98), or to Commit (see page 106). In these instances, the vote applies not only to the motion to Amend or Commit but also to the question itself. When a member calls for a Previous Question on the amendment only, the debate is over and a vote is taken at once. Then a new amendment can be placed on the floor and debated.
- Limit Debate (see page 113). To limit debate means that the membership can vote to close off the amount of time devoted to a topic. In this case, the motion must be put to a debate at once.
- Close Debate. Just as the assembly can limit debate, it can close it, halting discussion of a topic. This motion works in the same way as the motion to limit debate discussed above.
- To Lay on the Table (see page 110). This motion serves to carry the question to the table. This means that the topic is set aside temporarily. A majority vote is later needed to take the item from the table.
- Objection to the Consideration of a Question (see page 128). This is used when a motion is first made. If the objection is not denied, the motion halts debate and removes the item from consideration for the current session.

Chapter 9

Nominations, Elections, and Voting

> Where there is no law, but every man does what is right in his own eyes, there is the least of real liberty.
>
> Henry M. Robert, *Robert's Rules of Order,* 1876

The Chapter at a Glance

Nominations

Definition To nominate an individual is to select that person to fill an elected position within an organization. Actually, nominations are not in order when the election is by roll call or ballot because each member is free to vote for anyone qualified to hold office, whether or not that person has been nominated. Nonetheless, nearly all organizations hold nominations before they have an election. There are a number of advantages to this process. Nominations streamline the voting process, save time, and help ensure that all qualified and interested candidates are given a fair chance at running for elected office.

Methods of nomination Six ways to nominate candidates for office are by:

1. Open nominations
2. Nominations by the chair
3. Nominations by a committee
4. Nominations by ballot
5. Nominations by petition
6. Nominations by mail

In most cases, the method of nominating a candidate for office is set forth in the bylaws of each individual organization. If this is not the case, however, nominations can be made by any of these six methods. As you will learn from the descriptions that follow, some nominating methods are better suited than others for specific types of elections and organizations. These descriptions explain how each nomination method works and when it can be used to ensure the most equitable representation within an organization.

Open Nominations

Definition Members suggest candidates from the floor; the process is also called *nominations from the floor*.

Use This method is used often in mass meetings, specifically to select a chair for the meeting. In most cases, the person who organized the mass meeting will nominate the chair from the floor. If a chair is already in place in an organization, he or she can call for open nominations during any regular or special meeting. The call for open nominations must be made at the time specified in the organization's bylaws, however.

Procedure The following example shows how to make an open nomination:

- ▶ A member says, "I move that candidates for [name of specific committee] be nominated from the floor."

  or

  The chair says, "Nominations are now in order for the office of [specific office]."

Once nominations have been opened, members can suggest candidates. Nominations for each office or committee should be made in the order in which the offices or committees are listed in the bylaws—first the president, then the vice president, and so on. The following examples show how to open and make nominations:

- ▶ A member says, "I nominate [member's name] for the office of [specific office]."

  or

  A member says, "I move that [member's name] be elected to the position of [specific office]."

  or

  A member says, "Madam Chair, I nominate [member's name]."

If a member does not wish to accept the nomination, he or she should decline at once, as this example shows:

- ▶ The nominee says, "I respectfully decline the nomination."

After each nomination, the chair should repeat the candidate's name and call for further nominations, as illustrated in the following example:

- ▶ The chair says, "[Member's name] has been nominated for [specific office/committee]. Are there any other nominations for [specific office/committee]?"

When it seems that no other candidates are going to be nominated from the floor, the chair should close nominations, as shown below:

- ▶ The chair says, "Are there any other nominations for [specific office/committee]? If there are no other nominations, the nominations are closed."

Closing Nominations—Summary

A motion to close nominations is not in order when another motion is on the floor. As an incidental motion, it requires a second and a two-thirds vote to pass. It cannot be debated or reconsidered.

Nominations can be reopened, however. To do so, a member makes a motion, as follows:

- ▶ A member says, "I move that nominations for [office/committee name] be reopened."

Reopening Nominations—Summary

A motion to reopen nominations is also an incidental motion. It is not in order when another motion is on the floor; it requires a second, can be amended, and requires a majority vote to pass. It cannot be debated and can only be reconsidered after a negative vote.

Rules The rules of open nominations are consistent with the rules of debate. Just as no member can speak a second time during a debate until everyone has had a chance to speak once, so no one can make a second nomination until everyone has had a chance to offer an initial nomination. This is true even if more than one office has to be filled at the same time. In an effort to save time, a member cannot say, "I nominate both candidate A and candidate B for the finance committee." The nominations must be separate.

Multiple offices The same member can be nominated for more than one office during the same election; the voting can even be on the same ballot. If the individual is elected to more than one office, he or she is free to serve in multiple capacities, if such an action does not violate the bylaws of the organization.

Organizations usually discourage members from holding multiple offices simultaneously. As a result, a member who is elected to more than one office is advised to select the office he or she wishes to hold and to decline the others. If the individual is not present at the time of the ballot, the membership should hold a vote to decide which office the member should hold.

Conduct The guidelines for conduct during nominations is consistent with the conduct during small and large meetings. In a small meeting, for example, members do not have to be recognized by the chair or rise to make an open nomination; in a large meeting, members should rise and make sure that their nominations are heard. If the meeting is very large, members may wish to use the microphone when making a nomination. Under any circumstances, the nominations do not require a second. Members sometimes offer a second, however, to show their support for the nomination. This is in order, although not necessary.

Nominations by the Chair

Definition The chair selects candidates for office.

Use In most cases, the chair uses this privilege only to appoint members to committees; nominating members for every office can too easily lead to charges of cronyism. It is not a good idea for the chair to use this method to select members of the nominating committee, for obvious reasons.

Procedure The chair nominates candidates for each position.

Nominations by a Committee

Definition Candidates are selected by a nominating committee.

Use By preparing a slate of candidates, a nominating committee saves meeting time and helps ensure the best possible individuals will be selected for each office. A nominating committee can also help keep frivolous nominations from the floor.

Procedure The executive board or the organization as a whole selects a nominating committee to present a slate of candidates to the entire organization. The committee usually selects only one candidate per office, but, unless expressly forbidden in the bylaws, the committee is free to present as many candidates for each office as it wishes.

Preparing the slate It is a common practice for the committee to survey members informally before preparing the slate of candidates to see which people are interested in running for office, and in what capacity. For example, the committee may have decided that Member A would be an ideal candidate for the office of treasurer, when in fact a survey reveals that Member A is far more interested in serving as secretary.

It is also a good idea for committee members to speak with all of the candidates after the slate has been prepared but before it has been distributed to members. The committee can then avoid the possibility of nominating a member who does not wish to seek office and to make sure that their decisions reflect the will of the majority. Some organizations are so strongly in favor of this practice that they include provisions for it in their bylaws.

Publicizing the slate The committee must next publicize the slate of officers to the entire organization. The timing may be mandated by the bylaws, or it may be determined by the organization's past practices. While the nominating committee must always present its report to the entire membership at a regular meeting, in many cases the committee also distributes the slate of candidates to all members in advance of the meeting. Traditionally the slate has been distributed through the mail, but today's state-of-the-art technology makes it possible to do this more quickly and easily through E-mail, fax, or modem.

Presenting the slate However the list of candidates is distributed to the membership, a suitable time for the nominating committee to present its report is at the last regular meeting before the annual meeting, when the voting usually takes place. To present the report, the chair of the nominating committee reads the list of candidates to the entire assembly. The positions are usually arranged as president, vice president, and so on, the order determined in the bylaws. The following example illustrates such a report.

▶ The chair of the nominating committee says, "Madam [or Mr.] Chair, the nominating committee would like to present the following slate of officers: For chair, Member A; for vice president, Member B; for clerk, Member C. . . ."

Other nominations Unless restrained by the bylaws, members of the committee are free to nominate themselves as candidates. To restrict members from this right not only disenfranchises them but also might dissuade suitable candidates from serving on the committee in the first place. If the entire committee cannot agree on a slate of candidates, those dissenting on the committee are free to propose others for office by preparing a minority slate.

In addition, nominations from the floor can also be accepted, when provided for in the bylaws. Nearly all organizations not only allow but also encourage nominations from the floor. To hold open nominations after a nominating committee report has been presented, the chair solicits nominations for each office one at a time, repeating the names of the nominees and asking for additional nominations. The following example illustrates this process:

▶ The chair says, "The nominating committee has nominated Member A for the office of chair. Are there any other nominations for the office of chair? Member Y has been nominated. Are there any other nominations? [pause]. If not, nominations are closed for the office of chair."
The chair continues, "Member B has been nominated for the office of vice president. Are there any other nominations for the office of vice president? [pause]. If not, nominations are closed for the office of vice president." The chair continues this process until all members have had a chance to propose additional candidates for all slots.

Open nominations can take place any time after the nominating committee report has been distributed and read, but it is suggested that nominations from the floor follow as quickly as possible after the reading of the committee report, while the names of all proposed candidates are fresh in members' minds.

To maintain impartiality, the presiding officer of the organization should not appoint the nominating committee or be a member of it, even in an ex officio capacity.

Nominations by Ballot

Definition Members nominate candidates by secret ballot.

Use Since nominating by ballot reveals the preferences of the voters, it is a useful method for assessing the will of the membership. As this method affords every qualified member a chance to be nominated, there is no reason to hold open nominations after a nomination by ballot. This method can therefore save much time and effort.

Procedure A nomination by ballot is organized in the same way as an election by ballot. The tellers distribute blank ballots to every voter, individuals write down their choices for each office, and every member who receives a vote is nominated. The tellers then announce the candidates who have been nominated.

As an added time-saver, there is no need to announce how many votes each candidate received, since even one vote is sufficient for nomination. Every candidate who received a vote is eligible to run for office, not just the two or three individuals with the most votes.

Nominations by Petition

Definition A group of members nominates an individual through a petition.

Use This method is used most often among large organizations with many smaller groups.

Procedure Members can nominate candidates of their choice, working from a list prepared by the nominating committee. Members may also choose to select a candidate who is not on the nominating list and petition for the individual's inclusion on the ballot. If it wishes, the organization can also solicit nominations by petition from its membership.

Nominations by Mail

Definition Members nominate candidates by mail.

Use This method is especially useful for organizations whose membership is worldwide, for it allows greater representation than simply polling those members who live near the meeting place.

Procedure The clerk prepares a nominating ballot and distributes it to members through the mail, or via electronic means—E-mail, fax, or modem. In place of a formal ballot, the clerk can use a blank piece of paper, which allows members greater latitude for nominations.

In either case, the ballot should contain a space for the member to write in candidates. It is also advisable that the ballot require the voter's signature, to make sure each member nominates candidates only once. The mail packet must include specific instructions for completing the ballot, including a date by which it must be returned to the clerk. As a courtesy, it is a good practice to include a stamped envelope addressed to the clerk, which helps ensure that the ballots will be returned in a timely manner.

Elections

ELECTION PROCEDURES AT A GLANCE

Election Methods

As with methods of nominations, methods of election are determined by the organization's bylaws. In the absence of specific rules, however, an organization can conduct elections by any of the following processes:

- Acclamation
- Ballot
- Cumulative vote
- Mail
- Proxy
- Rising vote
- Roll call
- Show of hands
- Unanimous consent
- Voice vote

In some organizations, the presiding officer selects the process by which an election will be conducted. The choice is usually determined by these three factors:

1. Nature of the election
2. Closeness of the expected vote
3. Size of the group

To select an election method, members can make a motion on voting, as the following examples show:

▶ A member says, "I move that the vote on this motion be taken by a show of hands."

or

A member says, "I move that the vote on this motion be taken by voice vote."

or

A member says, "I move that the vote on this motion be taken by ballot."

Motion on Voting—Summary

As a main motion, a motion on voting requires a second and is not in order when another motion is on the floor. It is debatable and amendable, and can be reconsidered. The motion requires a majority vote to pass.

Election guidelines Each election method has advantages and disadvantages; the specific process your organization selects for a particular vote should be closely matched to the nature of the election and the organization's needs. The following guidelines apply to all election methods:

- The presiding officer must always explain the process to the membership before the actual election.
- No member can be compelled to vote in any election. As a result, every member has the right to abstain or to pass in an election.
- No member should participate in any election in which that member has a financial stake and such a vote could cause embarrassment or possible charges of financial impropriety

to the organization. For example, if a motion concerns depositing money in a financial institution that a member owns, the member should abstain from voting on that motion.

- A member who owes back dues but has not been dropped from membership has the right to vote in all elections and on all motions.

The following sections explain how each election method works and when it can be used to ensure the most equitable representation within an organization. Analyze these methods and select the ones appropriate for your organization's needs. This information should be included in the bylaws.

Unless expressly forbidden by the bylaws, members can vote for any person who is eligible to hold office, no matter what election method is used and whether or not the person has been nominated for office. These election processes can also be used for decisions where the issue does not pertain to the selection of officers, such as the purchase or sale of land, the distribution of stock, or the qualifications of prospective members.

Acclamation

Definition This method describes an election by unanimous consent.

Use When only one candidate is running for office, the chair can declare that the candidate is elected rather than taking a voice vote.

Procedure No formal vote is taken; instead, the presiding officer declares that the candidate is elected.

Ballot

Definition A ballot is a piece of paper on which members write their choice of candidate. There are two different ways to use a ballot. In the first, nominations for all offices are completed and members vote on all candidates at once, with one ballot. In the second method, nominations for each office are completed and members vote on each office in turn.

Use The ballot method is much used by all organizations because it affords the least opportunity for a miscount and is the most effective way to maintain secrecy, when so desired. It is used most often to elect officers and to decide on prospective members.

Each of the two methods of balloting defined above has advantages and disadvantages. The first method—closing all nominations and voting on all candidates at once—can save a great deal of time because the entire election is conducted at once. Unfortunately it does not allow for as much choice, since members are presented with an entire slate at once.

The second method—drawing up a ballot on each office in turn—allows members a wider choice, as they are voting for specific candidates rather than a complete slate. This method also has the advantage of allowing members to see who has been elected for each office before turning to the next. On the other hand, it takes more time to ballot this way. It is practical only when the membership is small enough to count the ballots quickly between each election.

In either case, the balloting should be conducted early in the meeting to make sure there is enough time to hold another election if no candidate receives enough votes to be elected or if neither side of an issue gathers enough votes to pass.

Procedure If the membership has planned a vote ahead of time, the clerk, tellers, or members of the elections committee can prepare ballots before the meeting; if not, they can prepare a simple ballot during the meeting. It is recommended that only the clerk, tellers, or members of the elections committee be allowed to prepare the ballots. It is not an advisable practice to have members cut up their own pieces of paper to make ballots. Doing so makes it difficult to keep track of legal and illegal ballots, which may compromise the legality of the election. As a result, legal ballots should be used in all organizations for all elections. Below are two sample ballots:

Sample Ballots

Mark an X on the line before your choice of candidate for the office of chair. Vote for only one candidate.

__________ Stephen Kravbitz
__________ Janice Race
__________ Gary Smithers

_________ Pauline Larocca
_________ Other

or

Show your vote with an X
Shall the [name of organization] hold its annual meeting at Captain Andy's Restaurant, 114 Conklin Street?
Yes _________ No _________

Selecting tellers To conduct an election through the ballot method, the chair should appoint at least two members to distribute, collect, and tally the ballots. These members are called *tellers* and should be well-respected individuals. Often tellers are selected who represent both sides of the issue, to protect the interests of each side. As members of the organization, tellers—as well as chairs—are allowed to vote in the election. The number of tellers selected to manage the vote depends on the size of the meeting and the number of voters.

Tellers should collect the ballots, making sure that each member voted only once. Then the chair closes the polls, as shown in the following example.

▶ The chair says, "Have all members voted? If no one else wants to vote, the polls are now officially closed."

Closing and Reopening the Polls—Summary

The chair usually closes the polls, but the membership can also close the polls by a two-thirds vote. If members arrive after the polls have been closed, they can be reopened by a majority vote.

Tallying the ballots The tellers can tally the ballots in another room or in front of the membership. This can be decided by a bylaws provision or according to common practice within the organization. In tallying the vote, incorrectly written names should be counted as long as the intention of the writer is clear. Two or more completed ballots folded together are considered illegal, and neither one should be counted in the tally; however, if one of the two is blank, the filled-out ballot is valid. If a member did not vote for enough candidates, the ones who did receive votes are counted. Blank ballots are not counted.

Abstention—Summary

An abstention is not considered a vote. As a result, it is not counted in any final tally. Members should invoke their right to abstain on an issue that might present a potential conflict, such as any issue in which they have a personal interest.

Reporting the tally In large meetings, one teller is selected as chair to report the tally to the group. The teller should stand, address the chair, read the tally, and hand the document to the chair—without announcing the result. The chair, not the teller, always announces the result. Below are two sample teller's reports. The first shows the results of an election for office; the second, a ballot on a motion:

Sample Teller's Report: Election

Number of votes cast	100
Number of votes necessary for election	51
Stephen Kravbitz received	60
Janice Race	20
Gary Smithers	9
Pauline Larocca	8
Other	2
Illegal votes	1

Sample Teller's Report: Motion

Number of votes cast	60
Number of votes necessary for adoption	31
Votes in favor of the motion	43
Votes against the motion	15
Illegal votes	2

In reading the second sample teller's report, the chair would say, "The total number of votes cast was 60, and the number necessary for passage of the motion is 31. There were 43 votes for the motion, 15 against, and 2 illegal votes. Having received the required number of votes, the motion is approved."

When there is only one candidate for office and the organization's bylaws require an election by ballot, the clerk can be authorized to cast the assembly's vote in favor of the candidate. If any member objects, however, ballots must be distributed and a complete vote taken.

Other guidelines When using the ballot method whereby each candidate is elected in turn, the procedure is repeated with new ballots for each office. All nominations can be completed at once, or nominations can be made for each candidate in turn.

With this method, however, there is a chance that none of the candidates will poll a sufficient number of votes to win. In such instances, the chair must have the teller repeat the election procedure with new ballots until a candidate receives a sufficient number of votes to be elected. The ballots contain the names of all candidates; candidates' names are not removed from the ballots and no candidates are forced to withdraw, no matter how few votes they may have received.

This affords members the widest possible choice of candidates, for it may emerge that the candidate with a low number of initial votes proves to be the most acceptable to the greatest number of people. In the same way, the chair must order a new election to break a tie if two candidates receive an equal number of votes.

Voting machines If an organization uses voting machines in place of distributing and tallying ballots by hand, it is important to make sure that the machines are delivered well ahead of the election. This allows the election committee or the tellers to check the machines to make sure that they are all working properly. It is also important to make sure that all members are familiar with the operation of these machines. The election committee may wish to demonstrate how to use the machines to members ahead of the election.

Cumulative Vote

Definition Every member casts one vote for each office to be filled. As with proxy votes (page 246), cumulative votes can be transferred.

Use Since a voter can use all of his or her votes for one candidate, a minority faction may be able to slant the election in favor of their candidate. As a result, this method is not in keeping with the overall principles of parliamentary law and its spirit of majority rule.

Procedure Each member is allowed to cast one vote for each office and the votes can be massed. For instance, if there are four offices to be filled, the member can allocate all four votes to the same candidate.

Mail

Definition Members elect candidates or vote on an issue by mail.

Use Election by mail is used most often for absentee ballots. Some organizations with widely scattered memberships use this method when they want a more representative vote than can be obtained at a meeting. It clearly affords greater representation than simply polling those members who live near the meeting place. If this method is used, it is crucial that the organization's mailing list correspond exactly to its membership rolls. While this method has a number of advantages, it tends to be expensive, time-consuming, and difficult to tally.

Procedure The clerk prepares ballots and distributes them to members through the mail. Increasingly, ballots are being distributed through electronic means: E-mail, fax, or modem. For nominations, a blank piece of paper can be used; but for an election, formal ballots must be prepared. The ballot lists the names of the nominated individuals, and it should also include a space for members to write in candidates. The voter must sign the ballot, to make sure each member has voted only once.

The ballot packet must include specific instructions for completing the ballot, including a date by which it must be returned to the clerk. It is also a good practice to include a stamped envelope addressed to the clerk. This helps make sure that the ballots will be returned quickly and to the correct address.

Proxy

Definition Proxy voting is giving another member the power to cast a member's vote. This is most often accomplished by giving power of attorney.

Use Proxy voting is used most commonly in stockholding companies, where membership is transferrable, rather than in deliberative assemblies, where it is not. In fact, it is not permitted in ordinary deliberative assemblies unless provided for in the organization's bylaws or unless the laws of the state in which the organization is incorporated require it. Proxy voting violates the spirit of parliamentary law, which guarantees one vote per member.

Procedure Since stockholders are often widely scattered, proxy voting is usually done by mail. The proxy form is prepared by the clerk or staff and mailed to all eligible members. A detailed instruction sheet and self-addressed stamped envelope are included.

Rising Vote

Definition With this election process, members vote by rising, or standing up, and being counted. In the simplest rising vote, the members are not actually counted but rather measured to judge the outcome of the election.

Use A rising vote is one of the most effective methods for verifying an inconclusive voice vote. In addition, it is a fair and effective way to save time when the meeting agenda is very full. It is also a good method to use when a close vote is anticipated, or in elections requiring a two-thirds vote. A rising vote is not an effective method, however, when members may wish to keep their votes secret. In these cases, a ballot is a better method.

Procedure The doors to the meeting room are closed to prevent other people from entering. Then the chair calls for a rising vote in the following manner:

- ▶ The chair says, "Those in favor of [motion or election] will stand [or rise]. Please be seated. Those opposed will now stand [or rise]. Please be seated."

Affirmative votes are always counted first, then negative ones. On occasions when the results of a standing vote are not conclusive, the members can be individually counted. In small meetings, the chair can count members who are standing for either call; in large meetings, the chair can appoint tellers to make the count. The following example shows how this is done:

▶ The chair says, "The question is whether [the motion/election issue]. Those members in favor of the motion [or election of a specific candidate] will rise and remain standing until counted [pause]. You may be seated now. Those opposed to the motion [or election of a specific candidate] will rise and remain standing until counted [pause]. You may be seated now."

As with other election methods, the chair, not the clerk or the tellers, announces the result of a rising vote. Below is an example of the chair's announcement:

▶ The chair says, "The affirmative vote has it and the motion is carried."

or

The chair says, "The negative vote has it and the motion is defeated."

Roll Call

Definition To state their preference on an issue, members respond with aye or no when their names are called from the official membership roll. Without a specific bylaw provision to the contrary, a roll-call vote can be taken only when a motion is made and approved by majority vote.

Use A roll call clearly shows how each member voted on the specific issue before the assembly. This method is especially useful when the outcome of the election might be very close and it is important that the votes are recorded precisely. The process is used often in large conventions, when the chair of a delegation announces the votes of his or her delegation. When the issue is delicate, such as an election, and members may wish to keep their votes secret, a roll-call vote should not be used. In such cases a ballot is preferable.

Procedure The chair puts the question to the assembly to take a roll-call vote. The clerk calls the list of members in alphabetical order. The chair's name is called last, and only when his or her vote will affect the outcome of the election. Members who have not decided how to vote can pass when their names are called; their names will then be called last, affording them additional time to make a decision. The clerk repeats each member's name and vote. The following example shows one way for the chair to take a roll call:

▶ The chair says, "All those in favor of the motion will say aye when their names are called. Those opposed will say no. Those members who wish to abstain will say abstain or present. The clerk will now call the roll."

Each organization must establish the minimum number of members necessary to order a roll-call vote. Without this provision, a majority is required.

Show of Hands

Definition Members vote by raising their right hands.

Use A show of hands is often used in place of a rising vote in meetings with relatively few members. Among small organizations, it is common to use a show of hands in place of a rising vote. The method does not work well in large organizations, however, for it is often difficult to get an accurate count of the number of hands that have been raised. Regardless of the size of an assembly, some members may prefer to keep their votes secret, in which case a ballot is used.

Procedure The following example illustrates how this election method is used:

▶ The chair says, "You have heard the motion. Those in favor of its adoption please raise their right hands [pause for the hands to be counted]. Those opposed please raise their right hands."

The chair announces the result of the vote, placing the affirmative count first, regardless of the outcome. Below is a possible way the chair can make the announcement:

▶ The chair says, "There are 32 affirmative votes and 5 negative ones. The affirmative has it and the motion is carried."

or

The chair says, "There are 14 affirmative votes and 35 negative ones. The negative has it and the motion is defeated."

Unanimous Consent

Definition Election by unanimous consent does not imply that all members agree on an issue; rather, it suggests that the opposition has decided that the issue is not important enough to force through the assembly.

Use Unanimous consent can be used for major decisions such as electing officers and committee members as well as for such minor decisions as approving the minutes. It is a useful way to save time because it allows the assembly to take action without having to go through the process of a regular vote. Since the method is both fair and expeditious, it can be a valuable time-saver and should be used whenever there is general agreement among the majority of members, as the following example illustrates:

▶ The chair says, "If there are no objections, the minutes stand approved as read."

Procedure If one or more members objects to electing by unanimous consent, however, the issue has to be put to a vote. Keep in mind that a member who objects to using unanimous consent may be focusing not so much on the specific issue as on the need to bring the matter to a vote that can be counted, such as by ballot or show of hands. Regardless of motive, though, the rights of the minority must be protected; a quantitative election method must be used when there is an objection to using unanimous consent.

Changing a Vote—Summary

No matter which election method is used, all members have the right to change their votes up to the time when the results are announced. After that point in the process, a vote can only be changed by a majority vote of the assembly.

Voice Vote

Definition Members vote by saying aye or no when asked for their votes. This method can also be called *viva voce*.

Use This is the easiest and most widely used method of voting on an issue. It is used most often in mass meetings, in elections where the candidate is running unopposed, or in instances when the election is not controversial or emotional. Since the method gives a strong advantage to those candidates whose names are called earlier in the election, it is not a suitable method for contested elections. Many organizations do not use it for elections at all. In addition, it should not be used when the bylaws require a vote by ballot.

Although it is a popular election method, a voice vote should not be used when it is anticipated that the vote will be very close or when the issue is highly emotional and members may wish to keep their votes a secret. In the first instance, a ballot, rising vote, or show of hands is preferable; in the second case, a ballot is the preferred method.

Procedure The presiding officer stands before the group and explains what the aye and no votes mean, as well as the result of each. Then the chair calls first for the affirmative vote and next for the negative vote. During an election of more than two candidates, the candidates are voted on in the order in which they were nominated. Finally, the chair announces the result of the vote, and states whether the motion has been passed or defeated. The election is over as soon as one of the candidates has a majority vote for a specific office. No other candidates can be voted on for that office, and the chair moves on to filling the next office in line. Below are some examples of this election method:

▶ The chair says, "As many as are in favor of [the motion/the candidate] say aye [pause]. As many as are opposed say no."

or

The chair says, "It has been moved and seconded that [the motion]. Those in favor of the motion say aye [pause]. Those opposed say no."

After the vote, the chair announces the result. Below is a format for the announcement:

▶ The chair says, "The ayes have it and the motion is adopted."

or

The chair says, "The ayes have it and [candidate's name] is elected to [specific office]."

or

The chair says, "The no votes have it and the motion is defeated."

or

The chair says, "The no votes have it and [candidate's name] is not elected to [specific office]."

Retaking a Vote

Parliamentary procedure allows for retaking a vote when the outcome is unclear or in dispute. Whenever a member doubts the result of a voice vote, a rising vote, or a show of hands, the member can call for a *division,* thereby requiring that the vote be taken again by rising. A vote should never be retaken by the same method as the original vote. The following examples illustrate how a vote is retaken:

▶ A member says, "I call for a division."

or

A member says, "Division!"

The chair then says, "A division has been called. Those in favor of the division will rise." The chair then counts the number of members standing and announces the number.

Next, the chair says, "Those opposed will rise." The chair counts the number of members standing and announces the number.

The chair says, "The motion is carried."

or

The chair says, "The motion is lost."

In a small meeting where everyone present can clearly see everyone else, an inconclusive vote may be retaken by just requesting a show of hands. In most cases the chair will take the count, inviting the person who called for the recount to also count.

Voting

Voting Methods at a Glance

Parliamentary law, as with any democracy, is predicated on the foundation of fair and equitable representation. Unless otherwise stated in the bylaws of an organization, the rule of "one person, one vote" is the guideline. In most instances, all actions taken by a representative assembly are based on a *majority vote*. According to parliamentary law, a majority vote means *more than half* the individuals voting.

Types of votes Parliamentary law specifies three main types of votes: the majority vote, the two-thirds vote, and the plurality vote. The type of vote taken in each election depends on the nature of the issue being decided as well as the composition of the organization and the provisions of its bylaws and constitution. Usually only one type of vote is allowed; in a few instances, however, more than one type can be taken. The following sections describe the three main types of votes. The reference chart on page 255 explains when each type of vote is used.

Majority Vote

Definition A majority is more than half the votes actually cast in an election by people who are entitled to vote.

Use Majority votes are used most often when assemblies are dealing with motions and elections. For a majority vote to be considered valid, the following four conditions must be met:

1. Abstention votes are not counted.
2. Blank ballots are not counted.
3. A quorum is present.
4. The meeting is properly called.

Procedure The following list shows the tally for a majority vote:

Number of Votes Cast	*Number Needed for a Majority*
29 votes	15 votes
30 votes	16 votes

31 votes	16 votes
32 votes	17 votes

Two-thirds Vote

Definition At least two-thirds of the members entitled to vote must cast ballots in the election.

Use A two-thirds vote is used for specific motions to:

- Prevent a question from being brought to the floor
- Close nominations
- Close debate
- Extend debate
- Limit debate
- Suspend the rules
- Change the rules
- Revoke membership
- Remove an officer
- Grant additional rights

For a two-thirds vote to be considered valid, the following four conditions must be met:

1. Abstention votes are not counted.
2. Blank ballots are not counted.
3. A quorum is present.
4. The meeting is properly called.

Procedure Since a two-thirds vote is often used in situations that affect members' rights, it is wise for the chair to use a rising vote to make sure that the count is valid. In very small meetings, a show of hands can be used in place of a rising vote.

The following list describes the tally for a two-thirds vote:

Number of Votes Cast	*Number Needed for a Two-Thirds Vote*
60 votes	40 votes
61 votes	41 votes
62 votes	42 votes
63 votes	42 votes

Plurality Vote

Definition A plurality vote is the largest number of votes given to any candidate in an election of three or more choices. A candidate with the greatest number of votes is said to have the *plurality*.

Use A plurality vote is commonly used to elect government officials. Election by plurality is only possible, however, when authorized by the organization's bylaws. A plurality that is not a majority of the membership is never sufficient to elect a candidate to office or to pass a proposition, unless specifically allowed in the bylaws. Allowing a plurality is not advisable, for it effectively denies the rights of the majority. It is rarely used in parliamentary assemblies.

Procedure The following illustrates the outcome of a plurality vote.

Number of Votes Cast
Candidate A—120 votes
Candidate B—130 votes
Candidate C—140 votes
Candidate D—150 votes

Candidate D has the plurality.

Motions and Required Types of Votes

The following reference chart summarizes when to use each type of vote.

Motion	Type of Vote
Adjourn	Majority
Adjourn to a future time	Majority
Adopt a constitution	Majority
Adopt a report	Majority
Adopt bylaws to form an organization	Majority
Adopt special rules of order	Two-thirds and previous notice, or majority of entire membership
Adopt standing rules	Majority
Adopt convention rules	Two-thirds

Adopt convention agenda	Majority
Amend a pending motion	Majority
Amend an amendment	Majority
Amend a previously adopted motion	Two-thirds, or majority with notice, or majority of membership
Amend adopted convention agenda	Two-thirds, or majority of registered voting members
Amend constitution or bylaws	Two-thirds and previous notice, or majority of entire membership, or according to rules in existing bylaws
Amend special rules of order	Two-thirds and previous notice, or majority of all members
Annul	Two thirds, or majority with notice, or majority of all members
Appeal	Majority, to reverse chair's ruling
Approve a main motion	Majority
Ballot (to order a vote)	Majority
Blanks (filling in)	Majority
Closing the polls when voting	Two-thirds
Commit a pending question	Majority
Committee (refer to)	Majority
Confirm	Majority
Consider informally	Majority
Consider by paragraph	Majority
Continue speaking (after discipline)	Majority
Discharge a committee	Two thirds, or majority with notice, or majority of all members
Division of the assembly	Single member call
Division of a question	Majority
Excused from duty	Majority
Extend debate	Two-thirds

Extend time for considering a pending question	Two-thirds
Lay on the table	Majority
Limit debate	Two-thirds
Make a special order	Two-thirds
Main motion	Majority
Minutes (approval of)	Majority
Minutes (correction of)	Majority
Minutes (dispense with reading of)	Majority
Modify a motion	Majority
Nominations (to make)	Majority
Nominations (to close)	Two-thirds
Nominations (to reopen)	Majority
Objection to the consideration of a question	Two-thirds
Orders of the day	One member, unless set aside by two-thirds vote
Parliamentary inquiry	Not voted on; chair responds
Point of information	Not voted on
Point of order	Not voted on; chair rules
Postpone indefinitely	Majority
Postpone to a certain time	Majority
Postpone a scheduled event	Two-thirds, or majority with notice, or majority of entire membership
Previous question	Two-thirds
Question of privilege (main motion in order)	Majority
Question of privilege	Not voted on; chair rules
Ratify	Majority
Read papers	Majority
Recess	Majority
Recommit a pending question	Majority
Reconsider	Majority
Reconsider in committee	Two thirds, or majority if every member who voted on winning side was notified or is present

Refer a pending question	Majority
Repeal	Two thirds, or majority with notice, or majority of all members
Rescind	Two thirds, or majority with notice, or majority of all members
Special order	Two-thirds
Suspend the rules	Two thirds, depending on bylaws
Suspend standing rules	Majority
Take from the table	Majority
Voting motions	Majority
Withdraw a motion	Majority

Voting guideline No matter what type of vote is being taken, follow this basic guideline: When determining the outcome of the vote, be concerned only with the number of votes cast, not the number of people present—since no one is required to vote. The only exception would be when the organization has adopted a rule to the contrary, in which case the rule must appear in the organization's bylaws or in any special or standing rules.

Changing Voting Methods

Any assembly has the right to change the way a vote is taken. When making such a decision, the organization should consider how many members must agree for the vote to be valid and to whom the percentage applies. Unless otherwise stated, the percentage is always the number of members present at the meeting when the voting takes place.

It is generally not a good idea to change voting requirements based on the number of people present at a meeting, because an abstention would be counted in the same way as a negative vote. As a result, the organization would in effect be denying members the right to remain neutral on an issue. Also, members who do not vote on an issue because they do not feel strongly about it or believe they lack sufficient knowledge to cast a responsible vote can have a decided negative effect on the outcome of the election.

If a change in voting rules is adopted, however, it is important to carefully count the number of people present, to make sure that the vote is valid. Previous notice must always be given if an organization does decide to change voting methods. Usually, members are notified by mail before the meeting or at the meeting before the election.

Officers' Voting Rights

All officers of an organization generally have the same voting privileges as other members. However, presiding officers should vote only when the vote is by secret ballot or when their votes will affect the outcome of the election; this will help protect a chair's impartiality. Such instances include breaking a tie (which will pass a motion), creating a tie (which will defeat a motion), and deciding the outcome of a two-thirds vote. Although such votes are desirable, they are not mandatory.

An effective chair casts the deciding vote only when doing so would be in the best interests of the organization. Under no circumstances can the chair vote more than once. The following examples illustrate the outcome of a chair's vote:

► The chair says, "There are 44 votes in the affirmative and 44 in the negative. The chair votes in the affirmative, so that the affirmative has it and the motion is carried."

or

The chair says, "There are 44 votes in the affirmative and 44 in the negative. The chair votes in the negative, so that the negative has it and the motion is defeated."

Chapter 10

Discipline

The Chapter at a Glance

Maintaining Decorum

Members are expected to behave during all meetings with dignity and decorum, and in the vast majority of instances they do uphold these standards. However, there are instances when emotions run high and tempers flare. On such occasions, even the most considerate individuals may insult other members, disrupt the meeting, or say things that they later regret. In almost all such situations, it is better to handle the outbursts on an informal basis; formal disciplinary action is a strong step that should be taken only as a last resort.

Barring Nonmembers

Although an organization is allowed under parliamentary law to decide who can attend its meetings, all *members* are allowed to be present at a meeting unless they have been specifically barred from attending. Members can be barred from attending a meeting only when they are under disciplinary action or have not paid their dues.

However, an organization can bar any or all *nonmembers* from its meetings or remove them at any time during the meeting. People who are not members of an organization have no rights in an assembly. They can be ejected at the chair's will, and they have no recourse to appeal. The same rule holds true for attendees at a mass meeting; anyone disrupting the meeting can be treated as a nonmember and ejected.

If the chair orders a nonmember to leave and he or she refuses, the chair has the power to have the sergeant-at-arms or other security people remove the offender, using force if necessary. In addition, the chair has the authority to call the police to assist in the removal. While these actions are well within the authority of parliamentary law, they should be taken only as a last resort, since the offender may retaliate with a lawsuit.

Keeping Order at a Meeting

The following sections provide a series of guidelines to help both chairs and members defuse potentially explosive situations and avoid serious disciplinary procedures. These suggestions rely on the good faith of members and the effective leadership of officers. Each of the guidelines uses the elements of parliamentary procedure to help ensure that the rights of both the majority and the minority will be fully protected.

Having clear rules Potential problems with maintaining order during a meeting may be eliminated or smoothed out by having a set of clearly defined rules of procedure that govern the rights and the conduct of members and guests. Because of the increasing number of citizens who are involved in matters of government and the noted breakdown in the traditional boundaries of decorum, there is a greater need for such written guidelines. Depending on the nature of the organization, possible topics could include the following: who is entitled to attend meetings, who can participate in debate, and who can have items placed on the agenda.

Organizations that anticipate fractious meetings may wish to post the guidelines in a prominent place in the meeting hall or to read them aloud after the opening ceremonies. Members and guests should also have copies.

Establishing a disciplinary committee Many organizations establish a disciplinary committee to deal with the behavior of members and guests during meetings. The committee is charged with studying ways to use parliamentary law to guide members and meetings. To this end, the committee should also study its organization's bylaws thoroughly. Matters of discipline can then be referred to committee for further study and recommendation for action.

The committee may be charged with holding trials in cases of extreme discipline problems, but it is rarely empowered to impose punishments. If the committee is powerful and well-respected, just the threat of the matter being referred to the committee may serve as a sufficient deterrent for impulsive or ill-behaved members. In any event, the committee can save the organization a great deal of time, embarrassment, and even scandal by handling matters quietly.

Speaking to the issue When members debate, they should confine their remarks to the topic at hand. It is important to keep the focus on the issue, not on the individual speakers. To help keep personalities out of the discussion, members should avoid referring to speakers by name and instead use some impersonal but polite designation, as the following examples show:

▶ Do not say, "As Mr. Wilson said in his remarks, . . ."
Instead, say, "As the member who spoke last said, . . ."

In addition, officers of the assembly should always be referred to by their titles.

▶ Do not say, "As Ms. Malhotra remarked, . . ."
Instead, say, "As the chair remarked, . . ."
or
Do not say, "As Sean Kelly argued, . . ."
Instead, say, "As the vice president argued, . . ."

This does not mean that members cannot speak strongly on issues. All members may speak out as vigorously as they like, but they must make sure that they praise or condemn the issue, not the speaker. As a rule of thumb, speakers should always refer to the motion on the floor, not to the member speaking.

Deferring to the chair To help maintain decorum, members must always defer to the chair. For example, if the chair rises to state a point of order or to make an announcement, members should stop speaking, take their seats, and let the chair have the floor. If a member is called to order, the member must sit down, stop speaking, and remain silent until the question of order is resolved. If speakers are indeed judged to be out of order, they cannot resume speaking if anyone else objects unless they get the permission of the assembly by a majority vote. The question cannot be debated.

Further, members should avoid side comments and conversations, humorous remarks, or other actions that could distract the speakers and disrupt the meeting. Members should also remain seated unless debating, as standing up or walking around the room is distracting and discourteous to everyone.

If a member commits a minor breach of decorum, such as speaking to side issues or addressing another member rather than the chair in a debate, the chair can simply tap lightly with the gavel and point out the situation to the offending individual. The debate continues, and the member is free to speak again. More serious outbursts, however, are handled differently.

Extending courtesy The chair can remind members and guests that the best guarantee they have to speak and be listened to in return is to accord the same courtesy to others. In dealing with any breach of decorum in a meeting, the chair should always be calm and courteous. Nonetheless, the chair can use a firm tone in maintaining order. The chair should never respond to any member or guest rudely, or attempt to use the gavel to drown out a disorderly speaker. By maintaining a professional tone, the chair sets the tone for the meeting. A chair's firm leadership can often prevent small breaches in decorum from snowballing into major problems.

Granting the floor Sometimes a disruptive member can be controlled by inviting him or her to speak, with the clear understanding that he or she must then allow the next member to speak without interruption. The following example illustrates one way that this can be accomplished:

► The chair says, "Mr. Kitter, under the bylaws of this organization, you are allotted five minutes to speak to the motion. You may speak to the motion at this time, but when the five-minute time limit is up, you must give the floor to the next speaker. You may not speak again until everyone has had a chance to speak to the issue."

Amending the agenda If a large crowd turns out for a meeting and demands to be heard on a topic that is not on the agenda, there is nothing to prevent members from amending the agenda to include that topic, if the officers and members feel that the request is valid and not likely to disrupt the meeting. Alternatively, the topic can be scheduled for the next regular meeting or for a special meeting, which will allow the current meeting to follow its regular agenda.

Dealing with Disruptive Behavior

Increasing security If a chair anticipates some very serious behavior problems, he or she might wish to post security personnel both inside and outside the meeting room. The sergeant-at-arms, if there is one, would be placed in charge of recruiting and organizing the security personnel. For this method to be most effective, the security people must be highly visible. They should be placed at doorways, in the aisles, and near the podium, for example, and they can wear nametags, similar colored clothing, or other designations to make them more obvious.

Using the "silent treatment" The chair can refuse to recognize a member who is disruptive until the meeting has formally come to order and the members have settled down. Most people do not like the "silent treatment" and will quickly give their attention to the chair to end it. This method is often most effective with small to medium-sized meetings.

Cutting off the microphone The chair should be familiar with the way a microphone and public-address system work. That way, when a microphone is used, the chair can shut it off quickly and easily if the member becomes abusive.

Taking a recess When a meeting appears to be getting out of hand, consider taking one or more recesses. Giving members a chance to compose themselves can help temper the situation and prevent more serious outbursts. A recess will also afford the chair an opportunity to consult with fellow officers and colleagues to decide what other steps should be taken to defuse the tension and prevent further problems.

Going into executive session When tempers start to flare, it can also be helpful to go into *executive session,* the portion of a meeting at which the proceedings are secret. In addition to affording members an opportunity to compose themselves, going into executive session also allows officers a chance to confer quietly among themselves. The term originally was used for "executive business," such as presidential nominations to appointed offices. Today the term is used for any matters relating to discipline or other business that should not be shared with the general meeting public. The following guidelines apply to this procedure:

- The motion to go into executive session is a question of privilege and therefore adopted by a majority vote.
- In general, only those officers named in the bylaws are allowed to attend an executive session. However, some organizations also invite certain guests and other members, as the necessity arises.
- The proceedings of an executive session cannot be shared with the general membership. As a result, the minutes of an executive session can be read only in another executive session.
- Any member who violates the secrecy of an executive session can be officially disciplined.

Adjourning the meeting If the meeting has become chaotic and uncontrollable, it is best to move for an adjournment. When members want to end a meeting, they have to wait either for the speaker to yield the floor or for the speaker's time limit to end. Recall that under parliamentary law each speaker is accorded 10 minutes to speak to an issue, unless the time has been changed by the organization's rules.

As soon as the floor has been yielded, a member can make an immediate motion for adjournment. If there is a second, the chair can put the motion to a vote at once, since no amendment or debate is allowed. If the motion for adjournment is passed, the chair can follow this procedure:

► The chair says, "The motion is carried. This meeting stands adjourned."

or

If no other meeting is scheduled, the chair says, "The motion is carried. This meeting stands adjourned sine die [without day]."

Handling More Serious Outbursts

If a member speaks in an unseemly, insulting, or indecorous fashion, the comments should be recorded by the secretary or by the person who objects to the comments. If the individual then denies having spoken these words, the assembly will have to vote on the issue. The vote must pass by a majority of members. If the speaker's petition is defeated, then he or she will then have to apologize for the indecorous comments. If the member refuses to acknowledge the comments, apologize, or justify his or her behavior, the assembly is forced to take action. The manner in which the outburst is handled depends on the nature of the comments and the organization's bylaws.

If the insulting words are personal and directed at one or more members, the person who made the comment and the target of the invective should leave the room. This is in keeping with the general rule that members should not be present when they are the object of discussion or debate. Then the members talk about the situation and decide what action would be appropriate.

Calling a member to order To deal with slightly more serious breaches of decorum, such as bringing side issues into a debate or impugning the motives of other members, the chair can *call the member to order*. In these instances, the chair can simply tap lightly with the gavel and point out the offense, as the following example illustrates:

▶ The chair says, "The member is out of order."

In addition, any member can call another to order, if the situation merits it, as shown in this example:

▶ The member says, "Mr. Chair, I call the member to order."

If the chair agrees with the point of order, he or she states the offense and then decides what action to take. If the offense is minor, the member can continue speaking after having been called to order.

In cases where the breach of conduct is more serious, however, the chair can decide whether the member should be allowed to continue speaking. The chair would then bring the matter before the entire assembly, as the following example shows:

▶ The chair says, "Shall the member be allowed to continue addressing the assembly?"

The issue cannot be debated; the assembly immediately takes a vote, and the chair announces the results.

Naming a Member

If none of the previous methods is sufficient to prevent a member from behaving in an inappropriate manner, the chair can *name* the member. This is a serious action that should not be taken lightly. Here are the steps for naming a member:

1. The chair directs the secretary to write down what the member has said that is objectionable.
2. The chair explains the offense to the member, addressing him or her by name, as the following illustration shows:

▶ The chair says, "Mr. Solovey! The chair has asked you twice to refrain from insulting other members by using offensive personal remarks. Despite these warnings, you have continued in your inappropriate actions."

3. If the member ceases his or her offensive behavior, the matter is over, if the assembly so decides. The member should apologize to the assembly or to the individual members who have been offended.
4. If the person continues to display inappropriate behavior, however, any member can request punishment. Possible penalties include having the member make an apology, censuring the member, asking the member to leave the meeting, suspending the member, or even expelling the individual from the organization. The chair lacks the authority to impose any punishment or to eject the member from the meeting; that power rests with the assembly. As a result, the chair asks the assembly what punishment to impose, as the following example shows:

▶ The chair says, "What penalty does the assembly wish to impose on this member?"

5. The member is then allowed to present a defense. If necessary, the secretary can read back the transcript of the offending comments. There is no reason to hold a trial and call witnesses, since everyone present has heard the evidence and will decide the punishment. If there is any disagreement about whether the accused did indeed make the remarks, the matter can be settled with a vote. The penalty is decided by either a ballot or voice vote. A two-thirds vote is necessary to expel a member from the organization.
6. If the member refuses to abide by the punishment, the chair can take the necessary measures to enforce the punishment. This can include having the sergeant-at-arms or the police escort the member from the meeting. Refusing to comply with an order to leave the meeting can result in even stronger punishment, however.

Holding a Formal Trial

A trial is the strongest and potentially most disruptive way of dealing with misconduct or dereliction of duty. It is strongly recommended that members be allowed the opportunity to resign from the organization before a trial is begun. If the individual chooses not to resign, however, there are specific steps to follow when holding a formal trial, as described below.

Give notice The members must instruct the accused member to appear before the members at a meeting, where he or she can hear and respond to the charges. The secretary is charged with informing the member of the meeting and giving him or her a copy of the charges. At this time, the member should be given a chance to show cause why he or she should not be expelled from the organization.

Investigate the matter A committee of members whose character is above reproach should be formed to look into the matter. Use the following format for the resolution to form the committee and describe its duties:

▶ "*Resolved,* That a committee of [number of people] be formed to investigate the [specific charges] levied against [name of member] and be instructed to report its findings and resolutions."

Notice that the resolution is vaguely worded. This is intentional, to protect the rights of the accused and the reputation of the organization as much as possible. A resolution should never be passed that suggests that rumors of malfeasance or other misdeeds are true. If possible, the committee's investigation should be kept confidential. Under all circumstances, however, the findings must be kept secret.

Keep in mind that the committee does not have the power to compel anyone to give testimony, especially the accused. Nonetheless, a sense of fair play demands the committee meet with the accused to get his or her side of the story. At this point, if the charges appear to be true, it is not inappropriate to suggest that the individual correct the situation or resign from the organization.

Place "under arrest" After having been charged formally, the member is considered to be "under arrest." Until the case is resolved, the individual does not have any rights in the organization. In some cases, this requirement is waived, depending on the nature of the accusation and the feelings of the members.

Report on the matter If the committee finds that the member is not guilty of any breach of conduct, it should report as such and the matter is dropped. But if the committee finds that there is a basis for the accusation, it should prepare a written report and have every member of the committee sign it.

Below is a possible sample format to use for the report. The *charge* explains the offense; the *specifications* give specific examples of what the accused is said to have done. For example, the charge might be conduct unbecoming a member of the society; the specifications might be stealing money from the organization's treasury or physically assaulting another member.

Sample Trial Committee Report

Resolved, That [member's name] is cited to appear on July 15, 1994, at 11:00 a.m. for a trial to show cause why [he or she] should not be expelled from the [name of the organization] on the following charge:

Charge Conduct unbecoming to a member of this organization.

Specification 1: [specific complaint against the member]

Specification 2: [specific complaint against the member]

Resolved, That a trial committee consisting of [names of committee members] will hear the case.

Hold the trial In most instances, the trial is held at a later date, not at the same meeting when the member was charged or at a regular meeting. The trial may be held in front of the entire assembly, but if the situation is embarrassing, it is recommended that a special committee be appointed to conduct the trial. This protects both the accused and the organization from scandal. Usually the individual is given at least 30 days to respond to the charges and to prepare for the trial.

The accused member must also be given official notice that he or she is going to be tried. The notice should be sent out by the secretary, and it should be worded as the following sample shows:

Sample Trial Notice

Dear [name of the accused member]:

The [name of organization] adopted the following resolution at its April 25th meeting: [text of resolution]

You are hereby cited to appear for a trial at the time indicated above to show cause why you should not be expelled from this organization.

Sincerely,

[name of secretary]

Evidence Evidence is presented at the trial. In most instances, the report of the disciplinary committee is sufficient. The chair of the committee should read the report and give any additional information required. The accused member should then be allowed to present his or her side of the case and call witnesses, if desired. As with a conventional trial, both sides are allowed to examine all witnesses and present rebuttals. If the accused does not attend, the trial is held anyway. The purpose of the trial is to uncover the truth, not to prosecute the accused.

Defense The accused person has the right to be represented by an attorney, but the attorney must be a member of the organization. This requirement can be overturned by a vote, however, and an outside individual or attorney can represent the accused. Any attorney or representative who transcends the bounds of acceptable behavior is also open for censure, according to the bylaws of the organization. The accused also has the right to call witnesses in his or her own defense. These people may or may not be members.

Trial events The following list describes the order of events at a trial:

1. Chair calls the meeting to order and points out that the meeting is an executive session. It is recommended that the chair stress the need for secrecy.
2. Chair asks the secretary to read the charges.
3. Chair verifies that the accused has a copy of the charges and has read and understood them.
4. Chair asks the accused whether he or she pleads guilty or not guilty to each of the specifications and then to the charge.
5. If the accused pleads guilty, the trial is not held. Instead, the penalty is decided.
6. If the accused pleads not guilty, the trial is held in this order:
   - Both sides present opening statements.
   - Witnesses testify.
   - Rebuttal witnesses testify.
   - Both sides present closing arguments.

Deliberation When all the evidence has been produced, the members should deliberate the issue without the accused person present.

Voting When the deliberations are completed, the group should take a vote on the issue. The question is called as follows:

► The chair says, "The question before the committee [or assembly] is: Is [member's name] guilty of the charge and specification?"

The charges and specifications are read one at a time and voted on separately. No one should be expelled without at least a two-thirds vote in favor of the action. A quorum must be present for the voting.

Penalty If the person is found guilty, the chair asks those assembled for an appropriate punishment. A motion on the punishment is made and seconded. The motion can be debated and amended. The vote on the punishment must be conducted by ballot. After the vote, the accused is called back and informed of the decision.

Fortunately, parliamentary law provides many different ways to maintain order and decorum that enable members to more often than not avoid the disruption of official censure and trial.

The Role of the Chair

The greatest burden for assuring the orderly and expeditious transaction of an organization's business rests with the presiding officer, the chair. To be an effective leader, this person must:

- Have a sense of fair play.
- Use good manners.
- Maintain decorum, even under the most tense situations.
- Act quickly to restore order and attention at the first sign of disturbance.
- Maintain the parliamentary principles of equal right to speak.
- Preserve each speaker's right to protection from interruption.
- Adhere to the question on the floor and no other.
- Refuse to allow members to resort to name-calling, especially when situations get tense and emotional.
- Disallow attacks upon members or their motives.
- Insist that all remarks be addressed to the chair.
- Exercise self-control and not be drawn into verbal battles.
- Avoid trying to drown out opposition by shouting or banging the gavel.
- Maintain dignity and composure, however great the provocation.

Coping with an Arbitrary Chair

METHODS AT A GLANCE

The chapter to this point has focused on ways to deal with fractious members and hostile meetings. However, what can members do when the chair is arbitrary and the cause of problems within the organization? What actions characterize a tyrannical chair? A dictatorial chair is one who:

- Refuses to recognize members.
- Ignores points of order.
- Ignores appeals.
- Will not put legitimate motions to a vote.
- Rejects proper amendments.
- Interrupts members during debate.
- Seizes the floor.
- Violates the bylaws.
- Refuses to follow the will of the majority.
- Will not protect the rights of the minority.
- Is arrogant or abusive to members and guests.
- Imposes his or her will on the group.
- Ignores the agenda, deviating from it at will.
- Adjourns meetings against the will of the members.

If the behavior of the chair of an organization fits five or more of these characteristics, it is likely that members are dealing with an arbitrary, dictatorial presiding officer. What can individual members and other officers do to deal with this situation? Try some of the measures described in the following sections.

Using Parliamentary Law

Members dealing with an unreasonable or despotic chair should first try to remedy the situation through the provisions of parliamentary law. To this end, points of order and appeals are especially useful tools.

Point of order A member whose motion is ignored can use a Point of Order to draw the chair's attention to the situation. If the chair decides to ignore the point of order, the member can make the motion again. If the chair still refuses to grant the member the floor, the member can put the motion to a vote. The member does not have to assume the chair to do so. The motion must be a serious one, however, for the chair is justified in ignoring any trivial motion.

Appeal In the same way, a member who is dissatisfied with a chair's ruling can ask for an Appeal. Members should not be reluctant to appeal a chair's ruling; the process is no different from appealing the decision of any other member (see also page 123).

Appeal—Summary

As an incidental motion, an appeal is in order when another motion has the floor, but the appeal must be made right after the ruling. The motion can be debated and reconsidered, but it is not amendable. It requires a second and a majority vote.

Holding a Discussion

If parliamentary law does not remedy the situation, members can try holding an amicable, nonthreatening discussion with the chair. This is best done in private, so as not to embarrass the individual. To avoid seeming to gang up on the chair, don't start with a large number of dissatisfied members. Instead, have two or three members speak to the chair quietly. The presence of a small group of people indicates that this is not an isolated incident or a grudge levied by an individual. Having more than one person also helps shield an individual from reprisals, if the chair is vindictive. This method is also useful with other officers who may not be handling their duties properly or responsibly.

Voting No Confidence

If the abuse of power continues unabated or intensifies, a member may vote *no confidence* in the chair. The motion requires a second, is debatable and amendable, and needs a majority vote for approval. This motion is not as strong a condemnation as a vote of censure.

Censuring a Chair

If these methods do not work and the chair's behavior continues to interfere with the orderly conduct of business, a motion can be made to *censure* the chair. Censure is an expression of indignation, a reprimand aimed at preventing further offending actions. This is a very serious charge against a chair (or against any other officer, for that matter) and should only be brought after extensive reflection. To censure a chair, the following steps must be taken in this order:

Make the motion A member makes a motion for censure. The motion needs a second, can be debated and amended, and requires a majority vote to pass.

Vote on the motion Since the motion cannot be put to a vote by the president, it is put to a vote by the vice president. If the vice president is not willing, the task falls to the secretary. If neither is present or willing to entertain the motion, it is put to a vote by the maker of the motion.

Debate the motion The chair is free to participate in the debate of the motion. This is in sharp contrast to the usual procedure, when a chair cannot participate in the debate.

Removing a Chair or Other Officer

In extreme cases, if the problem becomes unbearable, steps may be taken to remove the chair or other officer from his or her office. It is the strongest action that can be brought against an officer. As a result, it is best not to resort to this extreme measure unless the situation truly calls for it and the organization cannot wait until the next regularly scheduled election to vote the person out of office. If the members do decide to remove the chair from office, it must be done by strictly following the bylaws of the organization. Here are the steps to follow:

Rescind the election If the bylaws read: "The chair may serve for ________ year(s) or until his/her successor is elected," the election of the chair can be rescinded by a two-thirds vote and a successor elected for the remainder of the term.

Amend the bylaws If the bylaws are specific as to the length of the term of office or if they state: "The chair shall serve for ________ years *and* until a successor is elected," then the presiding officer can be deposed only by amending the bylaws to shorten the term of office or by holding a formal trial after charges have been brought.

Hold a trial This procedure is described in full on page 270. It should be undertaken only as a last resort, as it causes great disruption to an organization and its members.

Glossary

The following terms are used most often in meetings run according to the laws of parliamentary procedure. For further description of each term, see also the various sections of this book.

Abstain	To decide not to vote on an issue. To abstain, the member answers "present" or "abstain" in a roll-call vote.
Accept	To pass a motion; *adopt* is the preferred term.
Accepting a report	Adopting a report, not just receiving it.
Adjourn	To end a meeting officially. Adjournment is accomplished either by direct vote or by unanimous consent. It is not a debatable motion and requires a second.
Adjourn sine die	To adjourn *without day*. The term usually refers to the close of a session of several meetings.
Adopt	To pass a motion; the preferred term to use, instead of *accept* or *agree to*.

Agenda A list of items of business that the people attending a meeting consider. An agenda has a specific arrangement and content.

Agree to To pass a motion; *adopt* is the preferred term.

Amend To change a resolution or a motion by adding, striking out, or substituting a word or phrase. The motion requires a second, is debatable, can be amended, requires a majority vote, and can be reconsidered.

Amend the amendment A motion pertaining to the amendment to which it is attached; it must be disposed of before another amendment can be added. No more than two amendments can be considered by the assembly at the same time. The motion requires a second, is debatable, can be amended, requires a majority vote, and can be reconsidered.

Amend the main motion A motion that must be voted on before a vote is taken on the original motion. The amendment must pertain to the motion to which it is attached. Passing an amendment does not pass the original motion. The motion requires a second, is debatable, can be amended, requires a majority vote, and can be reconsidered.

Appeal A question by a member of the assembly or a convention delegate about a decision by the chair. It is used when the member believes that an error in parliamentary procedure has occurred. An appeal must have a second, is debatable, requires a majority vote, can be reconsidered, and can interrupt. The decision of the chair is sustained by a majority vote or a tie vote.

Assembly An organized group of people meeting to conduct business.

Assembly rules Rules that an assembly establishes. Assemblies operate more fairly and smoothly if certain rules are always included and if some rules are easier to set aside than others. The four main types of rules are *corporate charter, bylaws or constitution, rules of order,* and *standing rules.*

Ballot A written vote that assures the secrecy of an individual's election decision.

Board An administrative, managerial, or quasi-judicial body of officials who are elected or appointed and given specific authority to set policy for an organization. A board, unlike a committee, is considered to be a form of assembly; there is no minimum size and its function is determined by the powers delegated by the organization. Boards are often much smaller than deliberative assemblies. In order for an executive board to function smoothly, the bylaws of the organization must specify its composition, duties, and meeting schedule.

Bylaws A set of rules by which an organization conducts business; an organization's laws. The bylaws may not be suspended, but they can be amended. The term comes from the Danish laws set up for the *bye* or town.

Call for orders of the day A motion that brings to the chair's attention the fact that a specific item of business was due to come up in the meeting at a specific time. The motion can interrupt, and the chair decides the outcome.

Candidate Person seeking elected office. The term comes from the white toga worn by candidates in ancient Rome.

Chair Presiding officer of an organization, usually the same as the president. The chair may also be called the *chairman, chairwoman, president,* or *presiding officer,* depending on the will of the majority of people in an organization. The term comes from the honored place for the king or his deputy to sit when there is only one seat available. To reflect the use of gender-free language, the nonsexist form of address such as *chair* rather than *chairman* is gaining in popularity. Each particular organization decides which terms of address will be used.

Commit *See* Refer.

Committee A group of members elected or appointed by an organization to consider or take action on a specific subject. Unlike a board, a committee is not considered to be a form of assembly.

Committee of the whole A committee of the entire assembly, under a provision of parliamentary law that enables the assembly to operate by committee rules, which are less stringent. Alternate forms are the *quasi committee of the whole* and *informal consideration of a question.*

Consensus The term used to denote general agreement or unanimity of feeling within a group. The concept plays an important part in meetings held by Quakers and Native Americans who seek to reach decisions by finding positions that all members can accept.

Consent A provision in the election process that allows for consent without having a formal vote. Also called *unanimous consent* or *general consent.*

Constitution The rules that apply to a particular organization. The terms *bylaws* and *constitution* are often used interchangeably, although the term *bylaws* is used more commonly.

Convention An assembly of delegates selected specifically to represent a larger group of people in an assembly at one session. In most cases, a local organization will select delegates to attend a national or international meeting of the group. Only those delegates who have the proper credentials are allowed to vote at a convention; at the end of the convention, the assembly is disbanded.

Convention rules Rules determined by the delegates to a convention. Convention rules provide an orderly procedure to accomplish business most efficiently within a convention period. A two-thirds vote is required for adoption of convention rules, and for any later change after the rules have been adopted. The motion must have a second, is debatable, and can be reconsidered.

Corporate charter A legal document that includes the information necessary to incorporate the organization under state or federal law.

Debate The act of discussing the merits of a specific question.

Decorum Rules of behavior in a debate. This includes refraining from attacking someone's motives, addressing all remarks through the chair, avoiding the use of members' names, speaking only for your own motion, and refraining from disturbing the assembly.

Deliberative assembly A number of people gathered to discuss an issue of importance to the entire group. The group operates on its own to reach a consensus. All members have the right to speak and to reach their own decisions on the issues. The term also describes a gathering in which parliamentary law can be applied. The term was first defined by Edmund Burke at Bristol in 1774.

Divide a motion A motion to consider a long or complex main motion, such as a series of resolutions, in individual sections rather than as one whole motion. It can help members understand the issues under discussion and make more informed decisions and rulings. The motion requires a second, can be amended, and needs a majority vote to pass.

Division A demand that a vote be retaken. Division can be ordered by the chair of a meeting or by individual delegates. It can interrupt debate or discussion.

Division of the question Separating the parts of a motion to be considered and voted on as if they were separate motions. The issue arose in 1640 during debate over the election of two knights. The issue was codified in 1888, when voters were required to leave the room.

Ex officio People who are members of a board or committee by virtue of holding an office in the organization. Depending on the organization's bylaws, the ex officio member may have all the rights of a regular member (such as making motions and voting) but none of the obligations.

Extend debate To officially extend the amount of time that members have to debate an issue. The motion needs a second, can be amended, requires a two-thirds vote, and can be reconsidered.

Floor The right of a person to speak to people at a meeting and have their undivided attention. A member or a delegate recognized by the chair is regarded as "having the floor."

Gavel A small mallet that represents the authority of the presiding officer. Many chairs open and close a meeting by rapping once or twice with the gavel.

Incidental motions Motions that relate to the pending business or to the business on the floor.

Informal consideration of a question A variation of a committee of the whole, suitable for small organizations.

Lay on the table *See* Table.

Legislative body A group of people elected for a specific term of office to make laws. Congress and a state legislature are examples of legislative bodies.

Limit debate To officially restrict the amount of time that members may talk about an issue. The motion needs a second, can be amended, requires a two-thirds vote, and can be reconsidered.

Main motion A method of introducing new business to an assembly. Only one main motion can be under consideration at a time. The motion requires a second, can be debated and amended, requires a majority vote to pass, and can be reconsidered.

Majority More than half of the members present and voting on an issue. The people who do not vote are not counted in the final tally.

Mass meeting A gathering of an unorganized group which has been called to address a particular problem and is open to anyone who has an interest in the issues being discussed. Despite its name, a mass meeting does not have to be a large gathering; on the contrary, there may be relatively few people in attendance.

Meeting Members assembled to transact business.

Minutes The record of the proceedings of a deliberative assembly. The term comes from the journal of proceedings of Parliament, given legal status in the courts under Queen Elizabeth I in 1580.

Motion A proposal for action by the group. Motions are introduced with the words, "I move that ________," with the specific motion filling in the blank. Each motion requires a second, can be debated and amended, requires a majority vote to pass, and can be reconsidered.

Motion on voting A motion that proposes that a vote be taken in a specific way. A motion on voting needs a second, can be debated and amended, requires a majority vote to pass, and can be reconsidered.

New business Items that do not correctly belong under other classes of business introduced to the membership for the first time.

Objection A term used when a member is strongly opposed to the main motion. A member can then rise and call out, "Mr. [or Madam] Chair, I object to the consideration of that question," immediately after it has been stated by the chair. Do not confuse this action with the phrase "I object"; the only time that should be used is when the chair attempts to pass a motion by unanimous consent and someone objects to doing so.

Order of business The order in which the items on the agenda are discussed at the meeting. The order of business helps ensure that all items are dealt with in a fair and timely manner.

Order of the day A privileged motion by which a member can demand that the meeting follow its agenda.

Organized society A gathering of people who belong to an organization that meets on a regular basis. The members of an organized society may undertake civic, charitable, or political projects, for example.

Parliament
An important meeting held for the purpose of a discussion. The first official record of a parliament occurred in England in 1258. At that time, a parliament was used for the king's business and for handling the state of the realm. The term comes from the French word *parler,* to speak.

Parliamentary inquiry
A request for an immediate answer to a question concerning parliamentary law. It is directed at the chair, who may turn to the parliamentarian (if the organization has a person in that role) for assistance. The motion can interrupt and the chair decides the outcome. It cannot be appealed because it is an opinion, not a ruling.

Pending business
Business that is before the assembly for its consideration.

Plurality
The largest number of votes given any candidate when there are three or more choices. A plurality does not have to be a majority of votes received by any one of the candidates.

Point of information
A request for an immediate answer to a question concerning the background or content of a motion or resolution. It is directed at the chair. The information requested pertains to the business on the floor, not parliamentary procedure (covered under Parliamentary inquiry). A point of information can interrupt debate or discussion, and the chair decides the outcome.

Point of order A motion raised against any proceeding or motion that the member decides is in violation of the rules. A point of order can interrupt debate or discussion, but it must be raised at the time of the alleged infraction. The chair rules on the validity of the order. This ruling can be appealed.

Postpone indefinitely A motion to reject the main motion in a decorous manner. If this motion is passed, the main motion cannot be brought up again in its original form at that particular session. The motion requires a second, can be debated, needs a majority vote to pass, and can be reconsidered.

Postpone to a certain time A motion to defer consideration of a main motion and all attached motions until a future date. At that time, the matter will be brought up again under the heading Unfinished Business. The motion requires a second, can be debated and amended, needs a majority vote to pass, and can be reconsidered. To make sure that the motion gets priority consideration, it should be made a *special order,* in which case it requires a two-thirds vote to pass.

Precedence of motion The claim of a motion to "the right of way" over another motion.

Previous question A motion to close debate and vote immediately on a motion. Moving the previous question requires a second, is not debatable, and needs a two-thirds vote for adoption. This requires two separate votes: one to call the question, and one to deal with the original motion.

Previous question in its entirety A motion to close debate on a main motion (a resolution and all pending questions). It needs a second and a two-thirds vote for adoption, and it can be reconsidered.

Privileged motions Motions that have to do with pressing matters of importance. As such, these motions can interrupt any business on the floor. There are five privileged motions, and they fit into an order of precedence.

Program The agenda for a specific meeting, including time for speakers, meals, and other social matters.

Pro tem A term meaning *temporary*.

Proxy The practice of authorizing one person to act as the deputy or substitute for another, or the written authorization empowering another person to vote or act for the signer.

Quasi committee of the whole A variation of a *committee of the whole*. It enables the assembly to function under committee rules, which are less stringent than assembly rules. A quasi committee of the whole is suitable for organizations with memberships of approximately 50–100 members.

Question of personal privilege A request for the immediate consideration of a matter that affects the comfort, safety, or orderliness of a member.

Quorum The number of members needed to conduct business. A quorum is established by the bylaws of an organization.

Rank of motion *See* Precedence of motion.

Recess A short break or intermission in a meeting. Most commonly, a recess is used when the meeting has lasted for a long time and people need a break, but it is also used when the board needs time to conduct some business, such as counting votes. The motion to take a recess needs a second, may be amended, and is passed by majority vote.

Reconsider A motion to review a previous decision and to vote on it again. It must be made by a person who voted on the prevailing (winning) side, and it may not be moved more than once on the same motion. The motion needs a second, can be debated, and requires a majority vote.

Refer to committee A motion to have the chair create a committee to do research and report its findings back to the group. The chair may also refer the matter to an existing committee rather than create a new committee. The motion needs a second, can be debated and amended, requires a majority vote, and can be reconsidered.

Regular meeting The scheduled meeting of an organization.

Rescind A motion to nullify a vote taken at a previous meeting. It can be made by any member, but only if no action has been taken on the motion. The motion must be seconded, can be debated, amended, and reconsidered, and requires a two-thirds vote for adoption without previous notice.

Roll call To call the names of the members of an organization. Also, a method of voting.

Rules of order The parliamentary rules that an organization follows. The rules of order pertain to parliamentary law in general; the bylaws refer to the specific workings of the organization. As such, the rules of order can pertain to nearly all organizations; the bylaws are specific to one. Most organizations adopt rules of order by specifying which book of parliamentary law to use.

Second An indication that a member wants a motion discussed by the membership.

The member says, "I second the motion" or "second."

Session
A meeting or a group of meetings devoted to a single order of business, in which each meeting continues the work of the one before it.

Special committees
Committees appointed for a particular purpose, which cease to exist once that purpose has been served. They are also called *select* or *ad hoc* committees.

Special meetings
Meetings called to discuss a specific topic or topics. Only those items indicated in the meeting notice may be discussed.

Standing committees
Committees that have a continued existence.

Standing rules
Additional rules adopted by an organization to cover the day-to-day workings of the group.

Subsidiary motions
Motions that help dispose of main motions.

Table
A motion to place a main motion and all pending amendments aside temporarily (to Lay on the Table), with the intention of bringing them back at a later time for action. The motion requires a second, is not debatable, cannot be amended, and requires a majority vote. Tabling a motion cannot

be used to defeat a main motion by disposing of it permanently.

Take a recess — *See* Recess.

Take from the table — A motion to bring a previously tabled motion back before the assembly. It requires a second, is not debatable, cannot be amended, and requires a majority vote.

Tellers — Members selected to tally votes.

Time and place at which to adjourn — A motion that provides for the time and place of the next meeting (Fix the Time at which to Adjourn). It is usually imposed only when a temporary organization does not have a regular meeting schedule. Passing this motion does not serve to adjourn the meeting. The motion requires a second and a majority vote to pass.

Treasurer's report — The financial report of an organization.

Two-thirds vote — A method of voting in which twice as many people vote yes as those who vote no. For instance, assume there are 100 people in a meeting and only 15 vote. If 10 vote yes and 5 vote no, the motion will be passed by a two-thirds vote.

Unanimous consent — A situation when no one objects to a motion. Unanimous consent can also be called *general consent*.

Unfinished business Any matter that may have been pending at the time that the previous meeting was adjourned. It also includes any questions that may have been postponed to the present meeting.

Withdraw a motion A situation when a person who makes a motion decides to take it back. A person may withdraw a motion by merely requesting to do so up until the time it is stated by the chair. After the chair has stated the motion, the person who made it can withdraw it only by the consent of the members. The motion must have a second, and a majority vote to pass; it can interrupt and be reconsidered.

Index

D